Aberrant

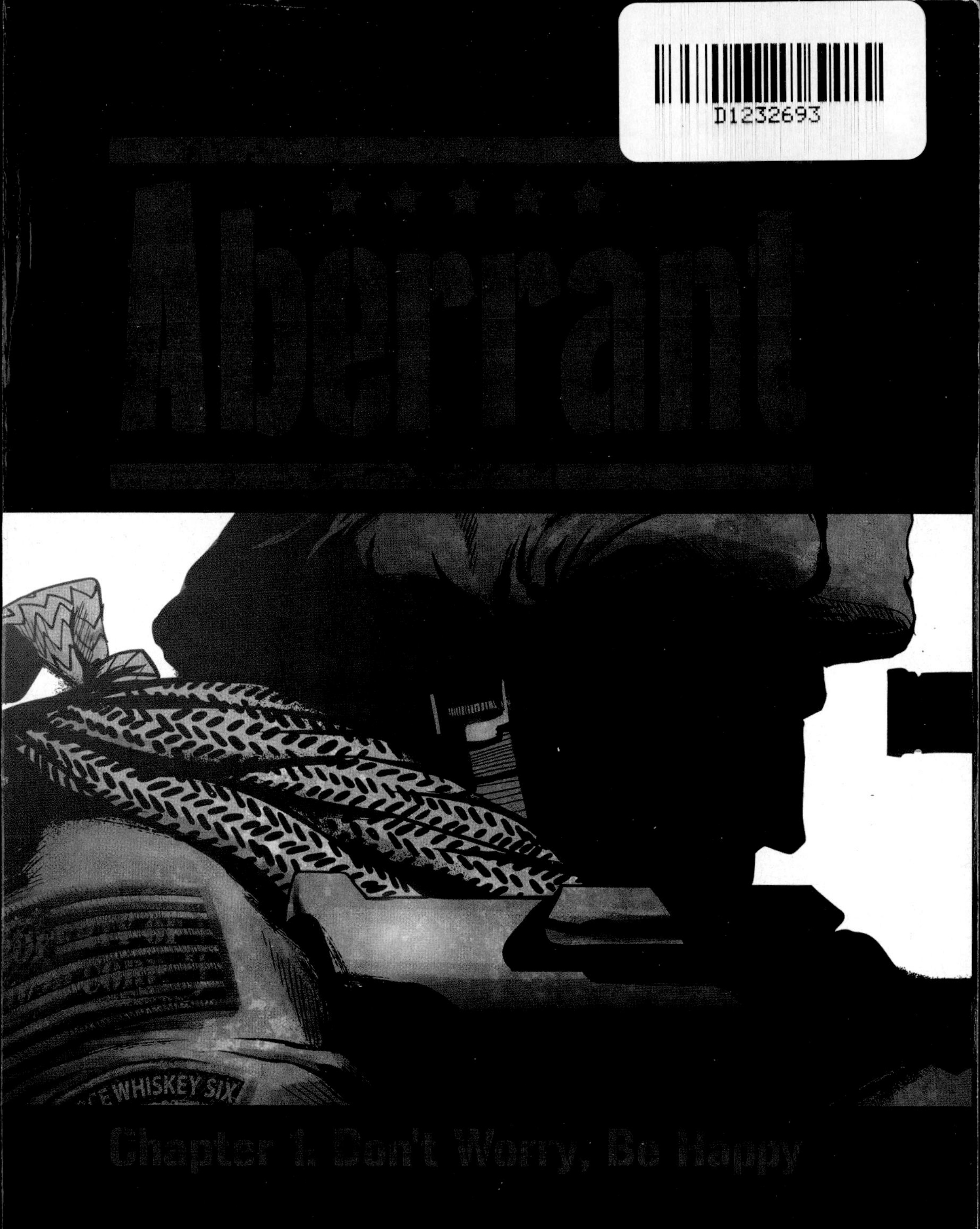
WHISKEY SIX

Chapter 1: Don't Worry, Be Happy

Rylend Grant

Writer/Director
@rylendgrant

Zsombor Huszka

Artist
@zsomborhuska

Ivan Jaka Triyono

Colorist

HdE

Letterer

RJ Hendricks

Executive Producer

RISING SPIRIT
ENTERTAINMENT

Executive Producer: Ryan Colucci
Graphic Designer: Jessie Weinberg @jeweinbe

Jason Martin: Publisher • Shawn Gabborin: Editor in Chief • Nicole D'Andria: Marketing Director/Editor
Danielle Davison: Executive Administrator • Bryan Seaton: CEO • Shawn Pryor: President of Creator Relations

Special thanks to Karl Nappi, Jeff Leeds, Steven Prince, Karol Wisniewski, Jim Higgins
and everyone at Meltdown Comics

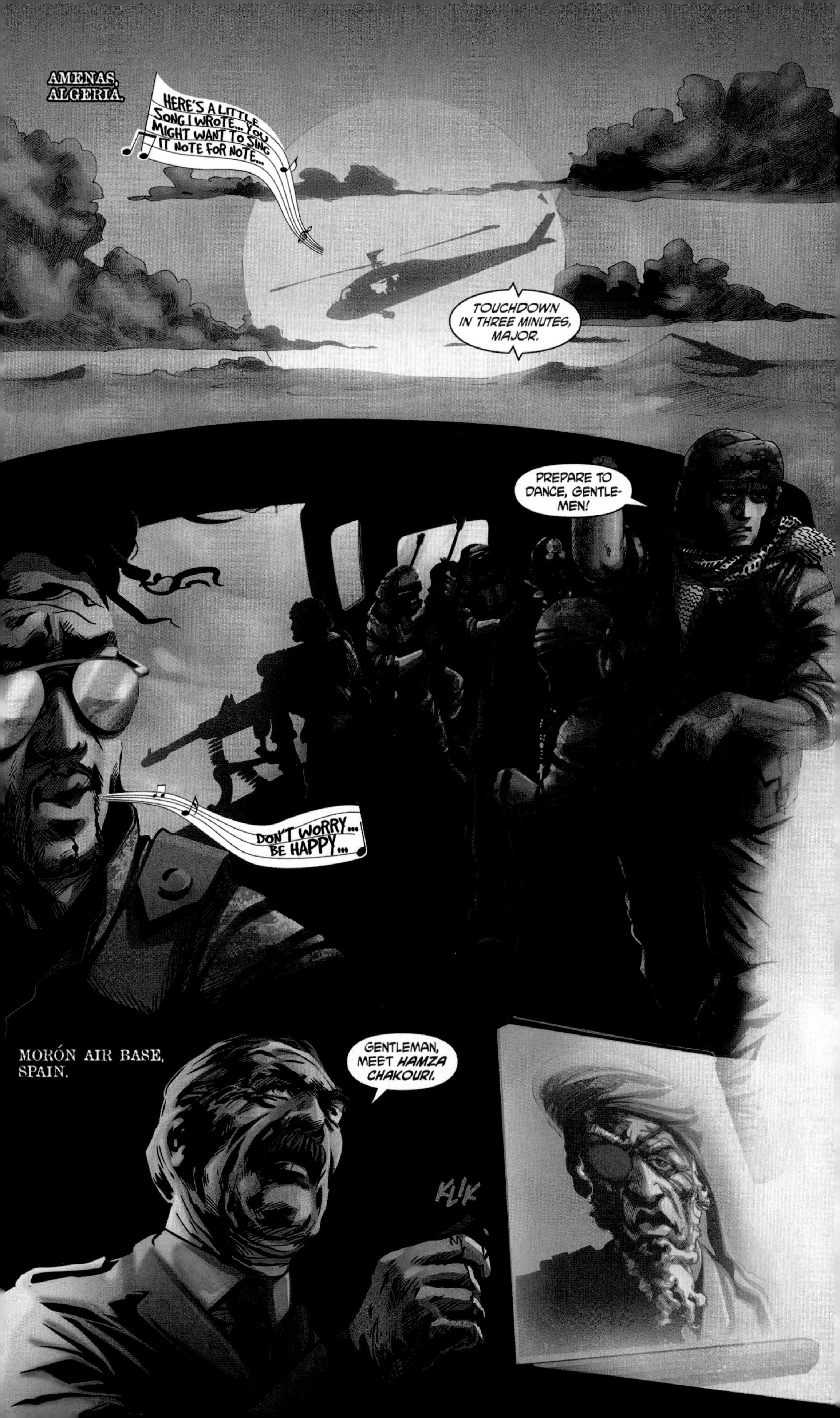
AMENAS, ALGERIA.
HERE'S A LITTLE SONG I WROTE... YOU MIGHT WANT TO SING IT NOTE FOR NOTE...
TOUCHDOWN IN THREE MINUTES, MAJOR.
PREPARE TO DANCE, GENTLE-MEN!
DON'T WORRY... BE HAPPY...
MORÓN AIR BASE, SPAIN.
GENTLEMAN, MEET HAMZA CHAKOURI.
KLIK

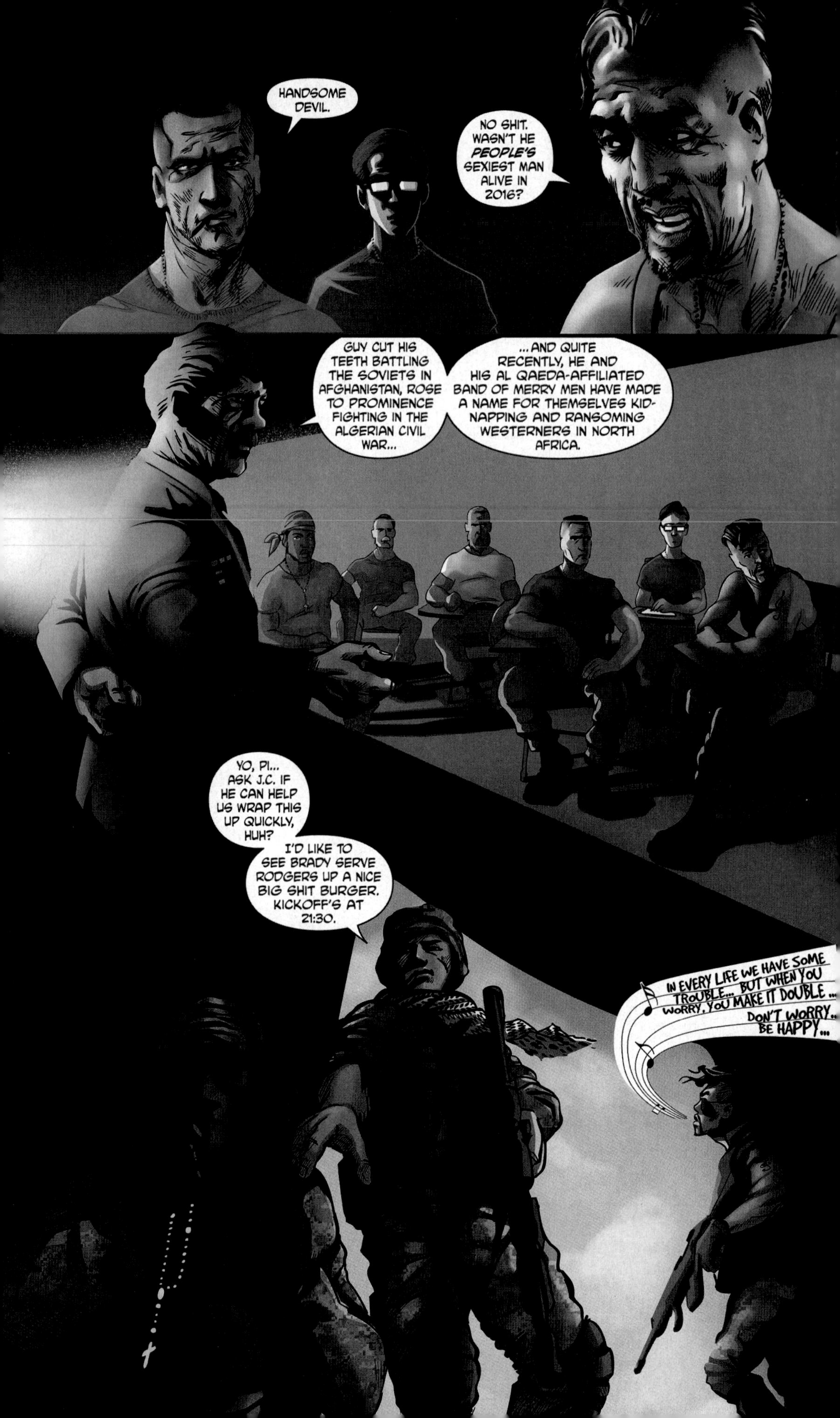
HANDSOME DEVIL.
NO SHIT. WASN'T HE *PEOPLE'S* SEXIEST MAN ALIVE IN 2016?
GUY CUT HIS TEETH BATTLING THE SOVIETS IN AFGHANISTAN, ROSE TO PROMINENCE FIGHTING IN THE ALGERIAN CIVIL WAR...
...AND QUITE RECENTLY, HE AND HIS AL QAEDA-AFFILIATED BAND OF MERRY MEN HAVE MADE A NAME FOR THEMSELVES KID-NAPPING AND RANSOMING WESTERNERS IN NORTH AFRICA.
YO, PI... ASK J.C. IF HE CAN HELP US WRAP THIS UP QUICKLY, HUH?
I'D LIKE TO SEE BRADY SERVE RODGERS UP A NICE BIG SHIT BURGER. KICKOFF'S AT 21:30.
IN EVERY LIFE WE HAVE SOME TROUBLE... BUT WHEN YOU WORRY, YOU MAKE IT DOUBLE...
DON'T WORRY... BE HAPPY...

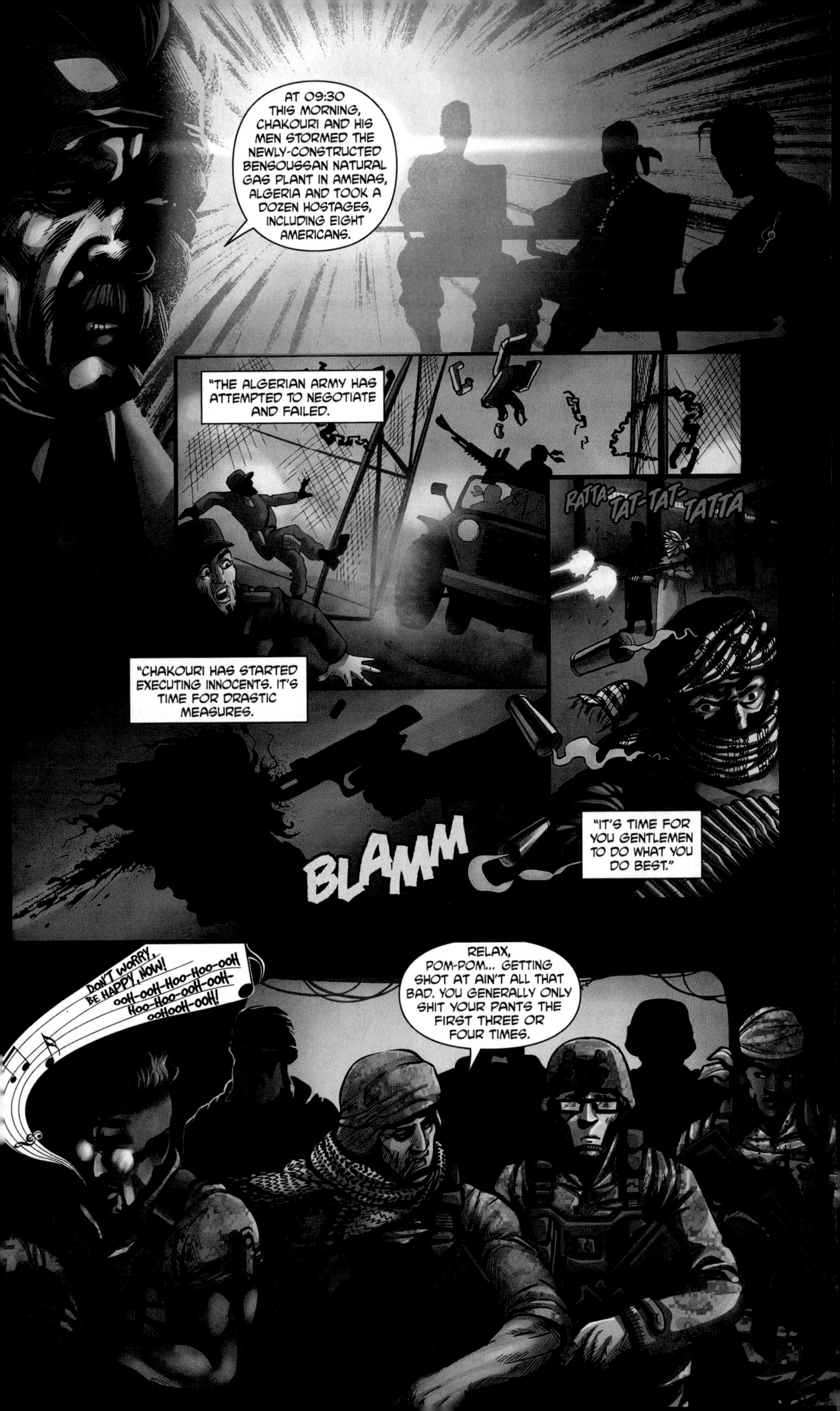
AT 09:30 THIS MORNING, CHAKOURI AND HIS MEN STORMED THE NEWLY-CONSTRUCTED BENSOUSSAN NATURAL GAS PLANT IN AMENAS, ALGERIA AND TOOK A DOZEN HOSTAGES, INCLUDING EIGHT AMERICANS.
"THE ALGERIAN ARMY HAS ATTEMPTED TO NEGOTIATE AND FAILED.
RATTA-TAT-TAT-TATTA
"CHAKOURI HAS STARTED EXECUTING INNOCENTS. IT'S TIME FOR DRASTIC MEASURES.
BLAMM
"IT'S TIME FOR YOU GENTLEMEN TO DO WHAT YOU DO BEST."
DON'T WORRY, BE HAPPY, NOW! OOH-OOH-HOO-HOO-OOH HOO-HOO-OOH-OOH-OOHOOH-OOH!
RELAX, POM-POM... GETTING SHOT AT AIN'T ALL THAT BAD. YOU GENERALLY ONLY SHIT YOUR PANTS THE FIRST THREE OR FOUR TIMES.

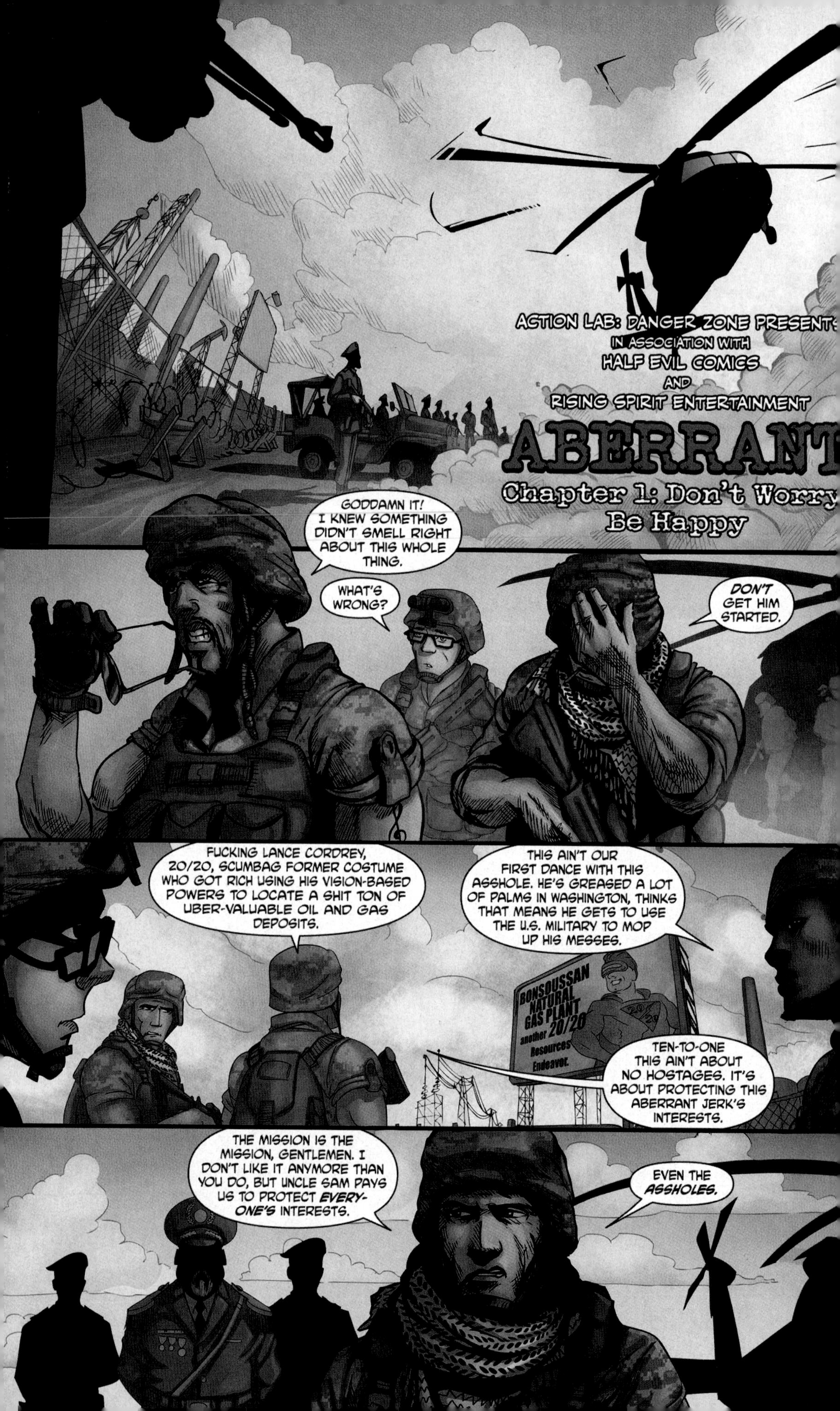
ACTION LAB: DANGER ZONE PRESENTS
IN ASSOCIATION WITH
HALF EVIL COMICS
AND
RISING SPIRIT ENTERTAINMENT
ABERRANT
Chapter 1: Don't Worry Be Happy
GODDAMN IT! I KNEW SOMETHING DIDN'T SMELL RIGHT ABOUT THIS WHOLE THING.
WHAT'S WRONG?
DON'T GET HIM STARTED.
FUCKING LANCE CORDREY, 20/20, SCUMBAG FORMER COSTUME WHO GOT RICH USING HIS VISION-BASED POWERS TO LOCATE A SHIT TON OF UBER-VALUABLE OIL AND GAS DEPOSITS.
THIS AIN'T OUR FIRST DANCE WITH THIS ASSHOLE. HE'S GREASED A LOT OF PALMS IN WASHINGTON, THINKS THAT MEANS HE GETS TO USE THE U.S. MILITARY TO MOP UP HIS MESSES.
BONSOUSSAN NATURAL GAS PLANT
another 20/20 Resources Endeavor.
TEN-TO-ONE THIS AIN'T ABOUT NO HOSTAGES. IT'S ABOUT PROTECTING THIS ABERRANT JERK'S INTERESTS.
THE MISSION IS THE MISSION, GENTLEMEN. I DON'T LIKE IT ANYMORE THAN YOU DO, BUT UNCLE SAM PAYS US TO PROTECT EVERY-ONE'S INTERESTS.
EVEN THE ASSHOLES.

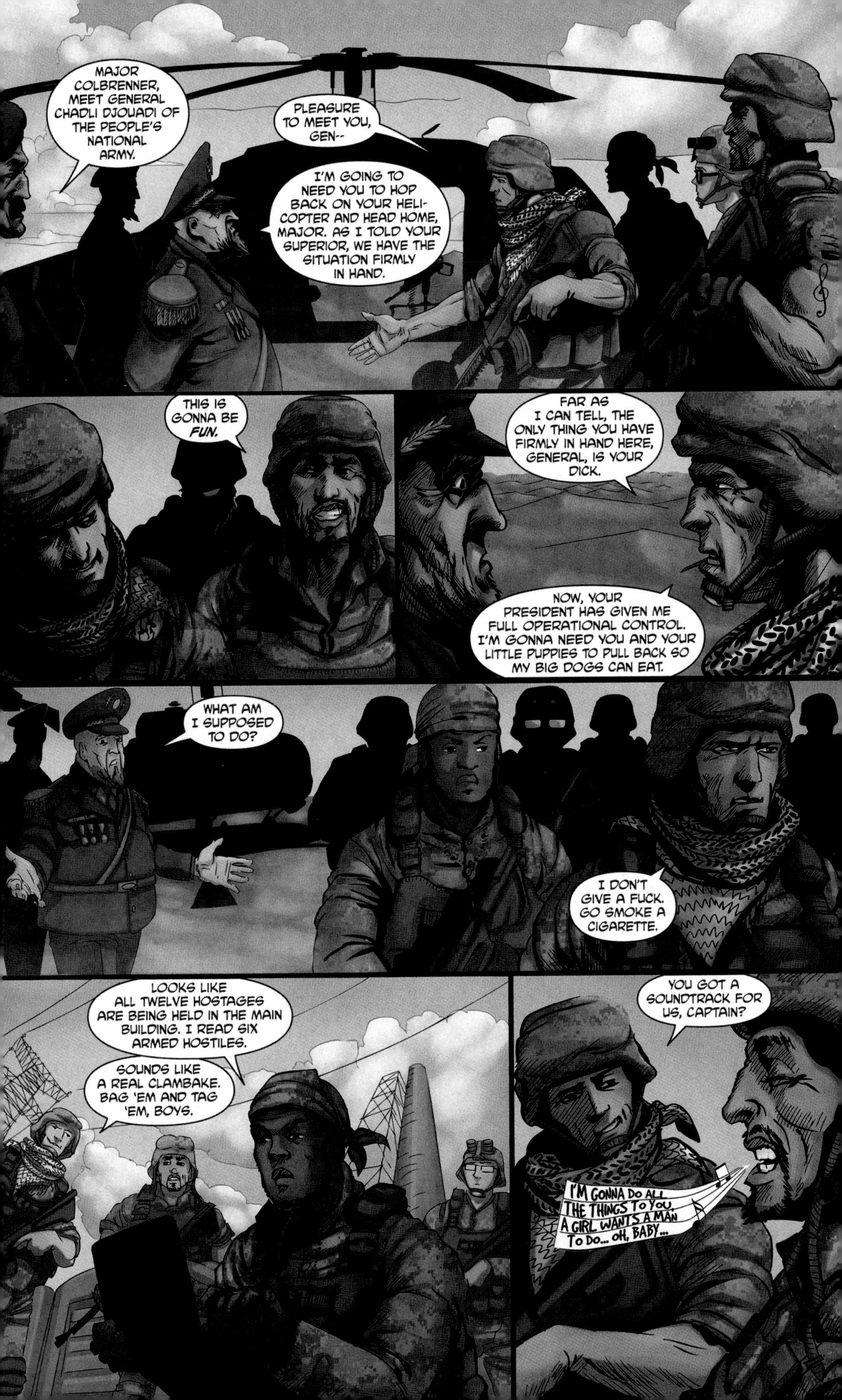
MAJOR COLBRENNER, MEET GENERAL CHADLI DJOUADI OF THE PEOPLE'S NATIONAL ARMY.
PLEASURE TO MEET YOU, GEN--
I'M GOING TO NEED YOU TO HOP BACK ON YOUR HELI-COPTER AND HEAD HOME, MAJOR. AS I TOLD YOUR SUPERIOR, WE HAVE THE SITUATION FIRMLY IN HAND.
THIS IS GONNA BE FUN.
FAR AS I CAN TELL, THE ONLY THING YOU HAVE FIRMLY IN HAND HERE, GENERAL, IS YOUR DICK.
NOW, YOUR PRESIDENT HAS GIVEN ME FULL OPERATIONAL CONTROL. I'M GONNA NEED YOU AND YOUR LITTLE PUPPIES TO PULL BACK SO MY BIG DOGS CAN EAT.
WHAT AM I SUPPOSED TO DO?
I DON'T GIVE A FUCK. GO SMOKE A CIGARETTE.
LOOKS LIKE ALL TWELVE HOSTAGES ARE BEING HELD IN THE MAIN BUILDING. I READ SIX ARMED HOSTILES.
SOUNDS LIKE A REAL CLAMBAKE. BAG 'EM AND TAG 'EM, BOYS.
YOU GOT A SOUNDTRACK FOR US, CAPTAIN?
I'M GONNA DO ALL THE THINGS TO YOU A GIRL WANTS A MAN TO DO... OH, BABY...

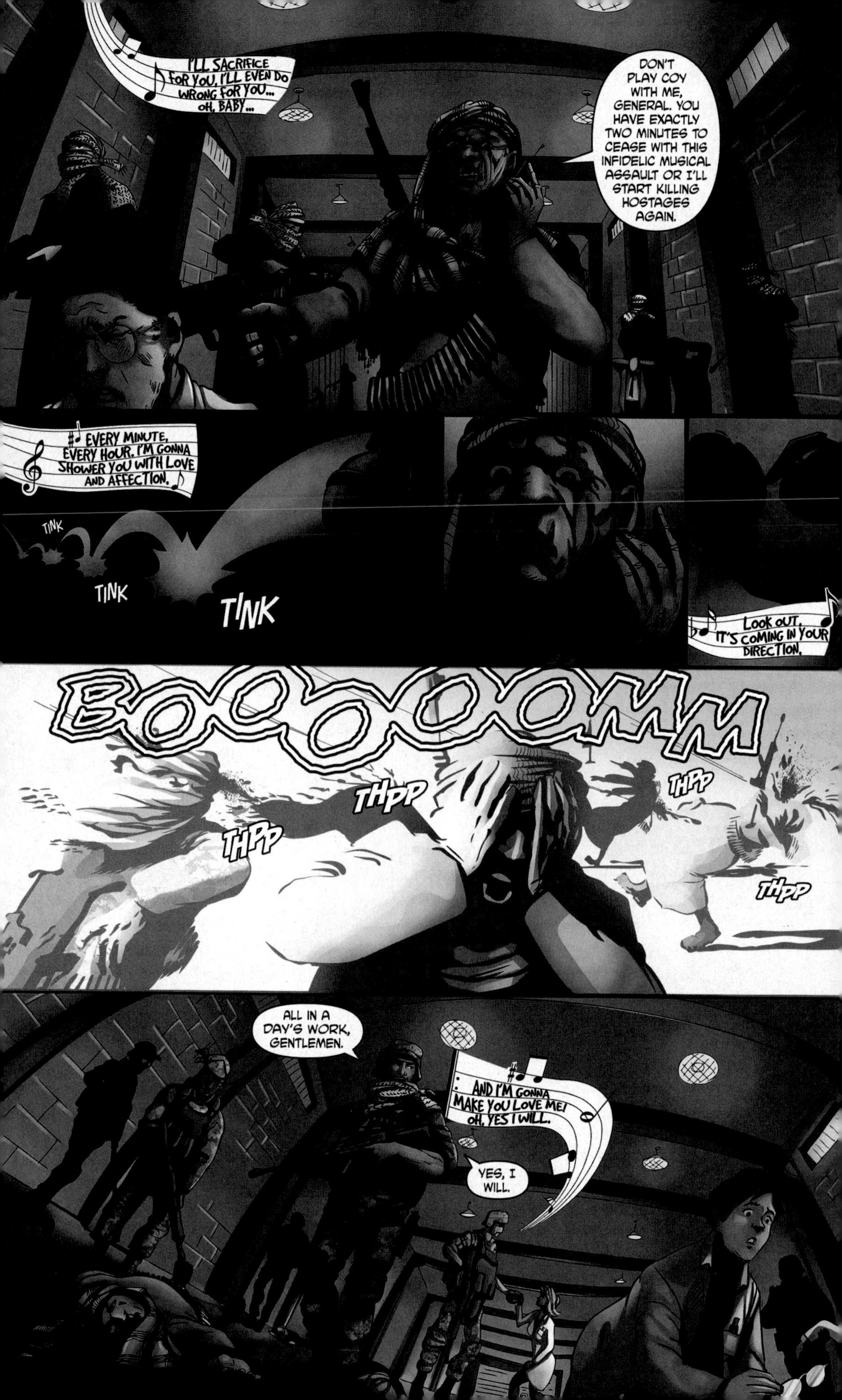
I'LL SACRIFICE FOR YOU, I'LL EVEN DO WRONG FOR YOU... OH, BABY...
DON'T PLAY COY WITH ME, GENERAL. YOU HAVE EXACTLY TWO MINUTES TO CEASE WITH THIS INFIDELIC MUSICAL ASSAULT OR I'LL START KILLING HOSTAGES AGAIN.
EVERY MINUTE, EVERY HOUR, I'M GONNA SHOWER YOU WITH LOVE AND AFFECTION.
TINK
TINK
TINK
LOOK OUT, IT'S COMING IN YOUR DIRECTION.
BOOOOOMM
THPP
THPP
THPP
THPP
ALL IN A DAY'S WORK, GENTLEMEN.
AND I'M GONNA MAKE YOU LOVE ME! OH, YES I WILL.
YES, I WILL.

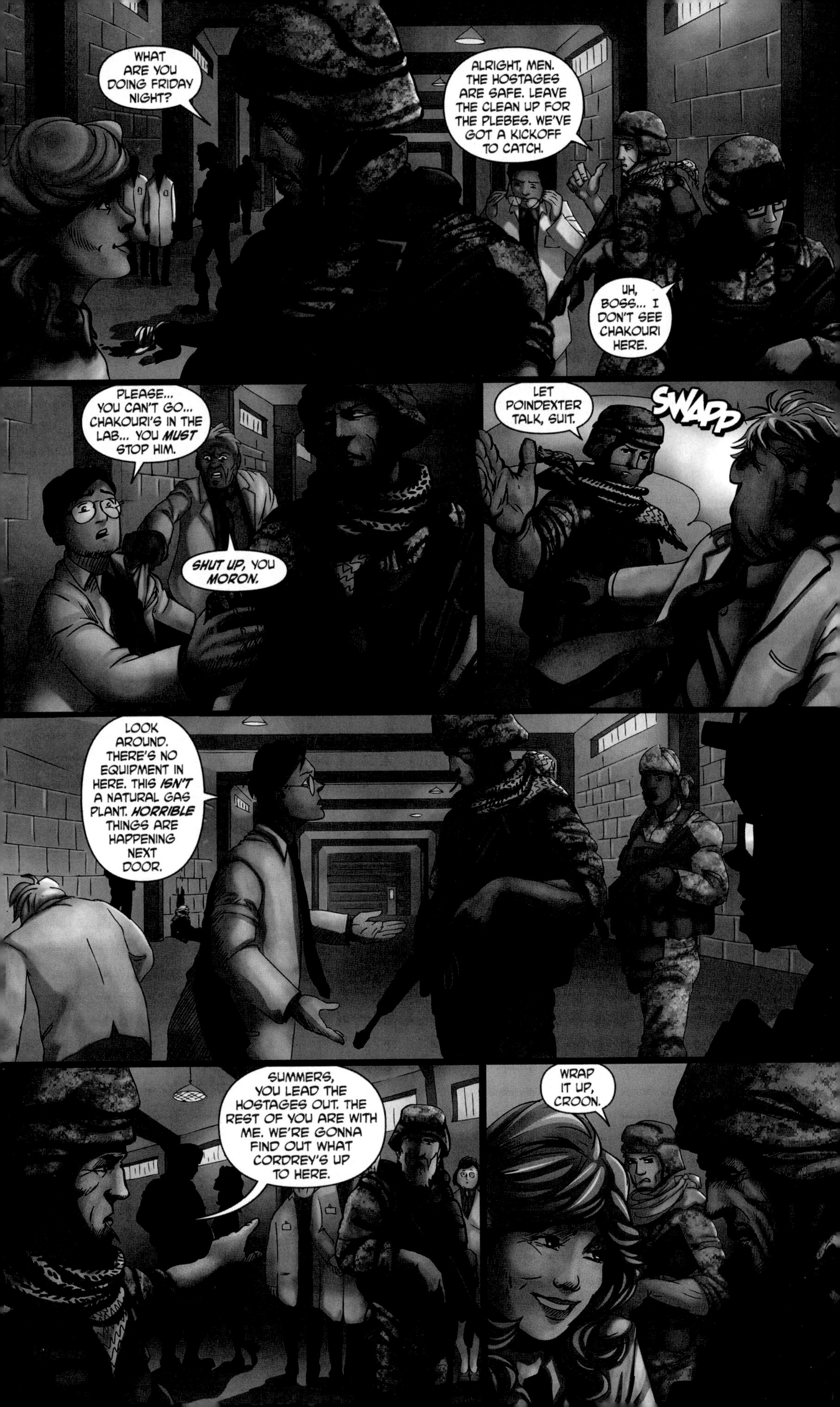

WHAT ARE YOU DOING FRIDAY NIGHT?
ALRIGHT, MEN. THE HOSTAGES ARE SAFE. LEAVE THE CLEAN UP FOR THE PLEBES. WE'VE GOT A KICKOFF TO CATCH.
UH, BOSS... I DON'T SEE CHAKOURI HERE.
PLEASE... YOU CAN'T GO... CHAKOURI'S IN THE LAB... YOU MUST STOP HIM.
SHUT UP, YOU MORON.
LET POINDEXTER TALK, SUIT.
SWAPP
LOOK AROUND. THERE'S NO EQUIPMENT IN HERE. THIS ISN'T A NATURAL GAS PLANT. HORRIBLE THINGS ARE HAPPENING NEXT DOOR.
SUMMERS, YOU LEAD THE HOSTAGES OUT. THE REST OF YOU ARE WITH ME. WE'RE GONNA FIND OUT WHAT CORDREY'S UP TO HERE.
WRAP IT UP, CROON.

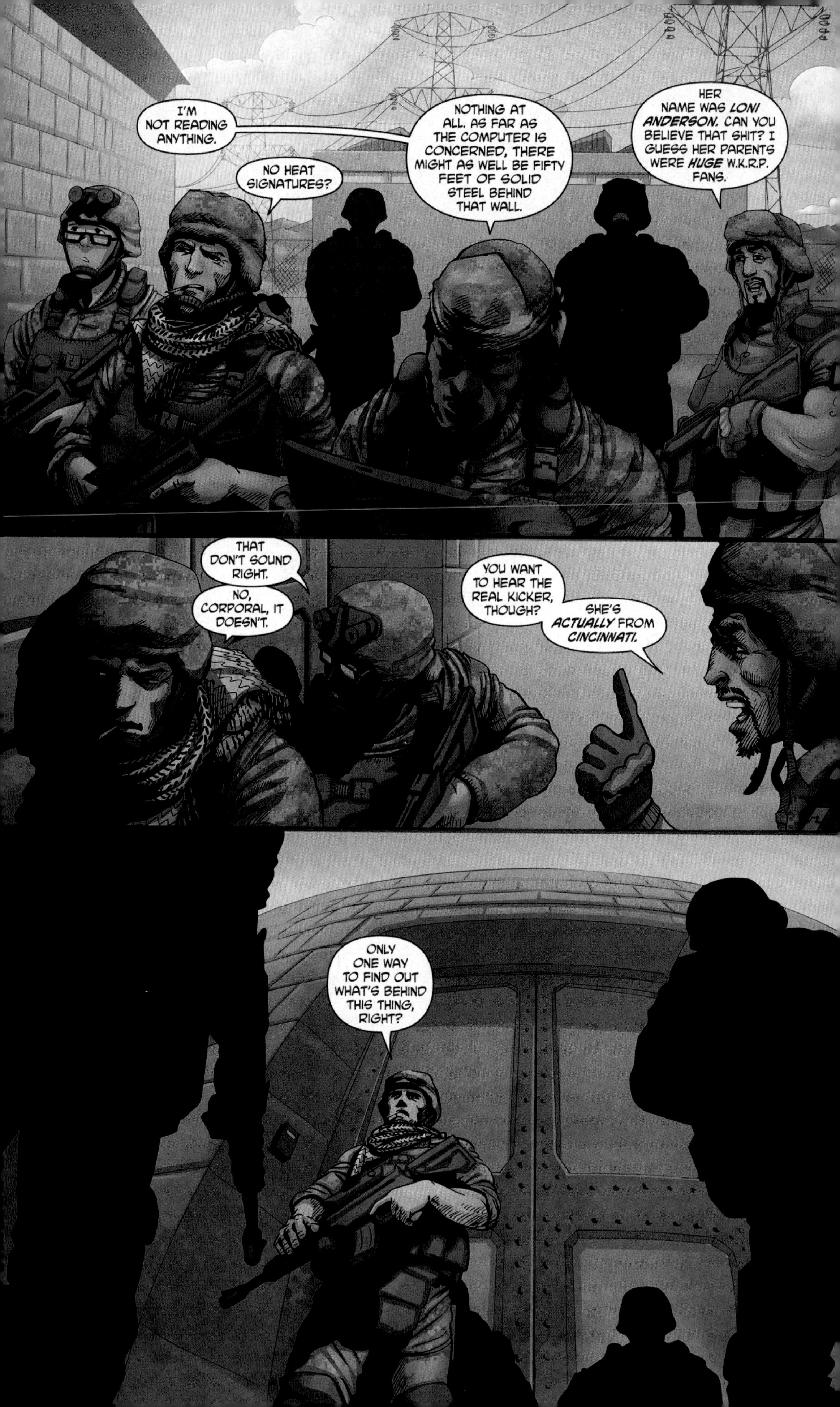

I'M NOT READING ANYTHING.
NO HEAT SIGNATURES?
NOTHING AT ALL. AS FAR AS THE COMPUTER IS CONCERNED, THERE MIGHT AS WELL BE FIFTY FEET OF SOLID STEEL BEHIND THAT WALL.
HER NAME WAS LONI ANDERSON. CAN YOU BELIEVE THAT SHIT? I GUESS HER PARENTS WERE HUGE W.K.R.P. FANS.
THAT DON'T SOUND RIGHT.
NO, CORPORAL, IT DOESN'T.
YOU WANT TO HEAR THE REAL KICKER, THOUGH?
SHE'S ACTUALLY FROM CINCINNATI.
ONLY ONE WAY TO FIND OUT WHAT'S BEHIND THIS THING, RIGHT?

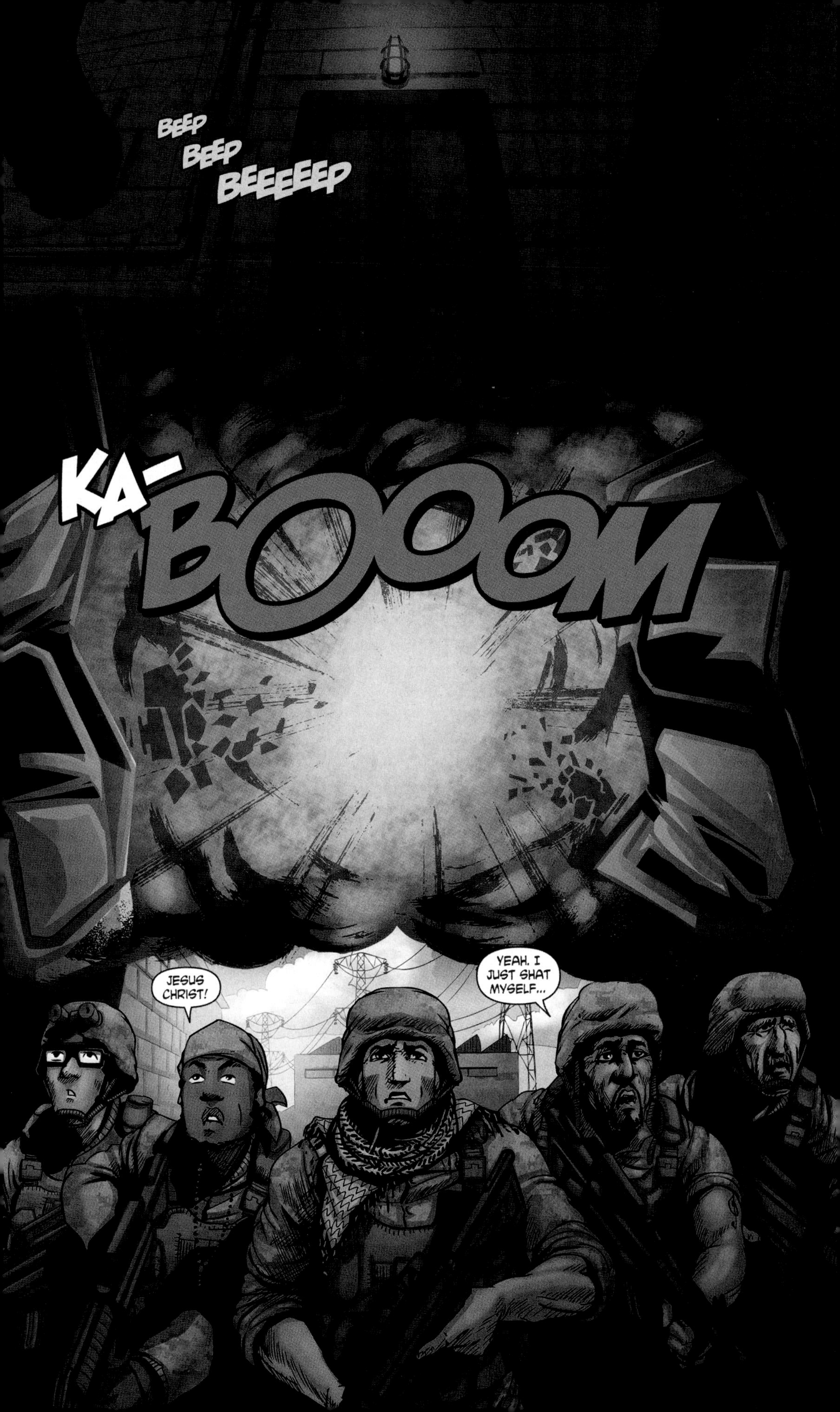
BEEP
BEEP
BEEEEEP
KA-BOOOM
JESUS CHRIST!
YEAH. I JUST SHAT MYSELF...

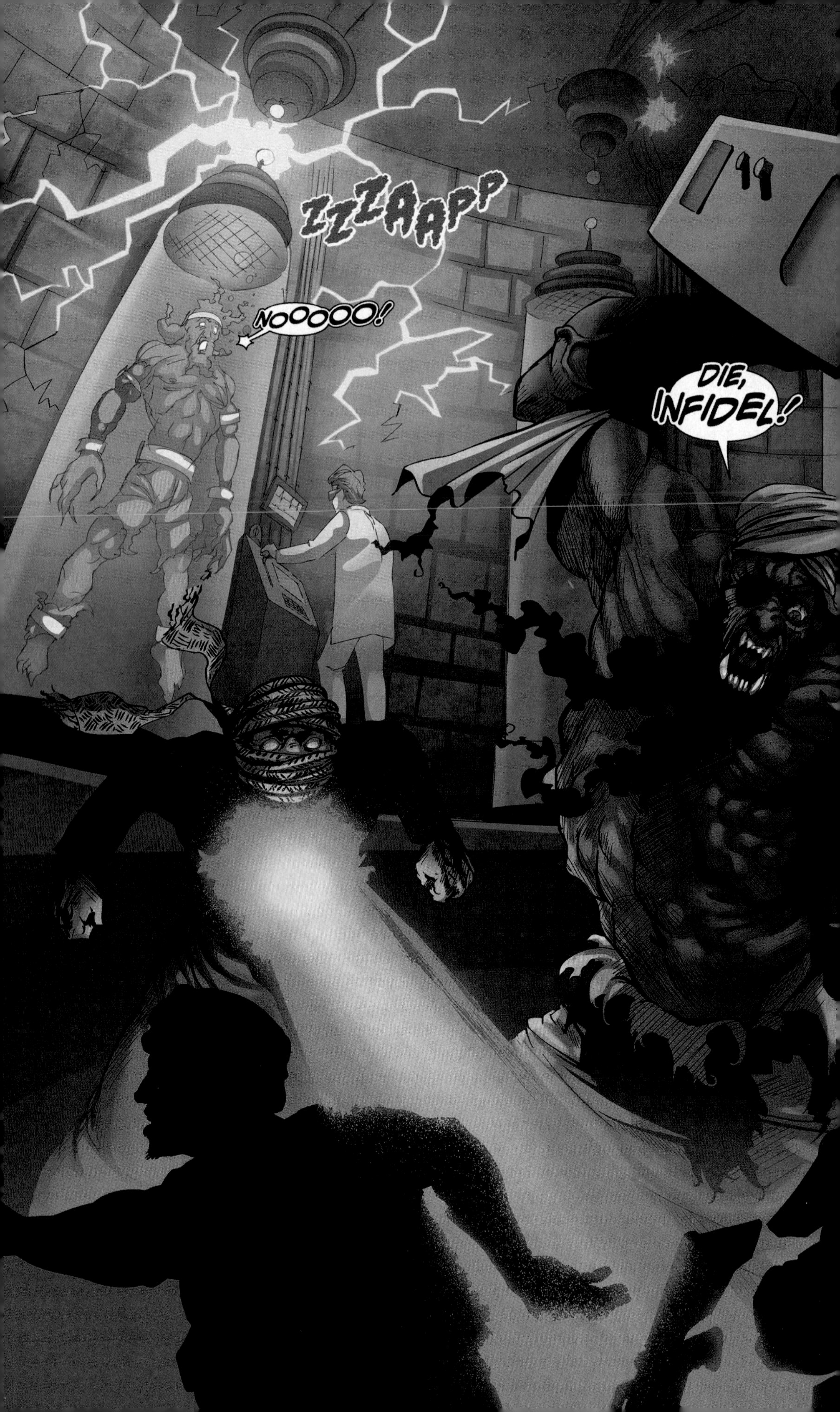
ZZZAAPP
NOOOOO!
DIE, INFIDEL!

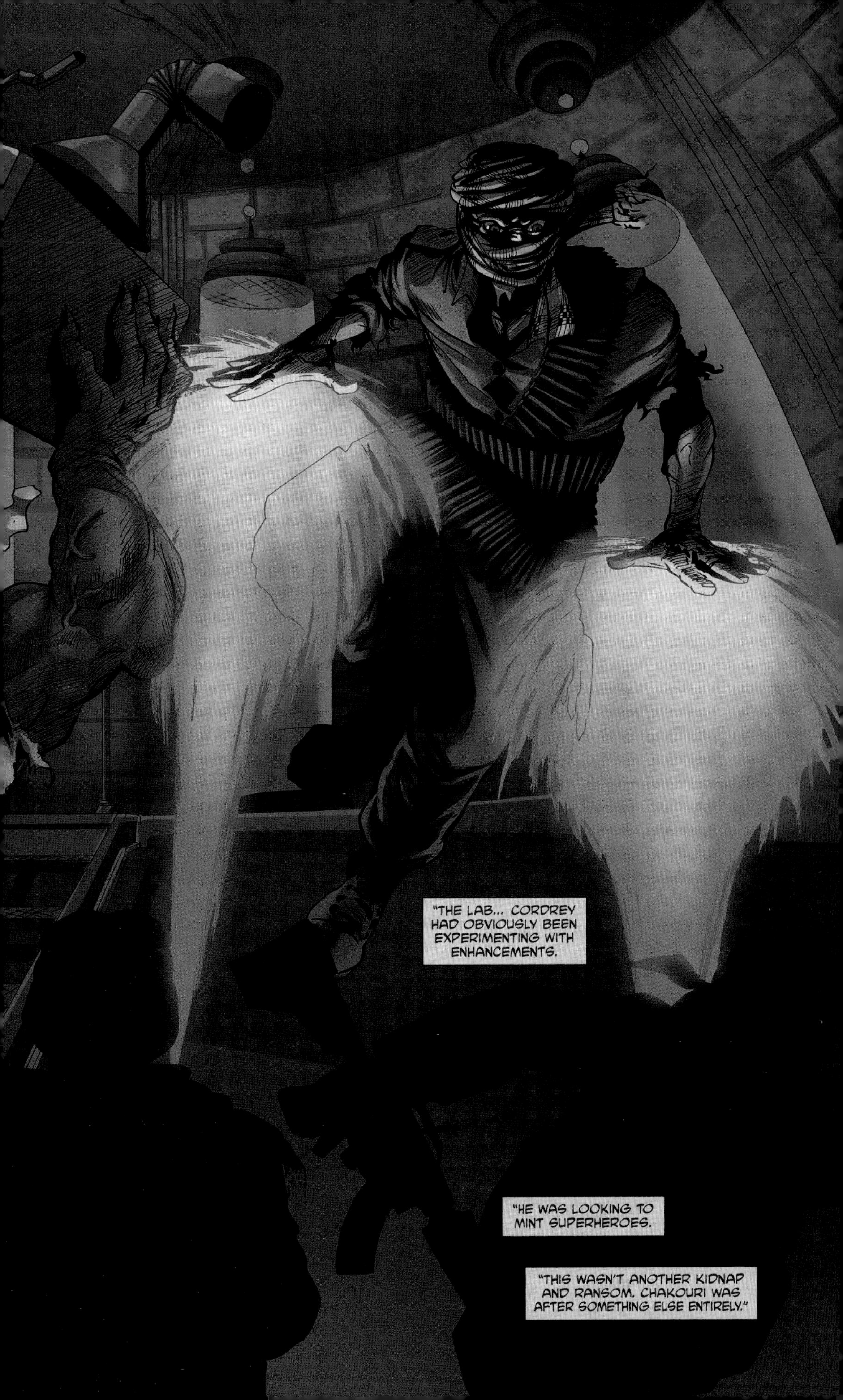
"THE LAB... CORDREY HAD OBVIOUSLY BEEN EXPERIMENTING WITH ENHANCEMENTS.
"HE WAS LOOKING TO MINT SUPERHEROES.
"THIS WASN'T ANOTHER KIDNAP AND RANSOM. CHAKOURI WAS AFTER SOMETHING ELSE ENTIRELY."

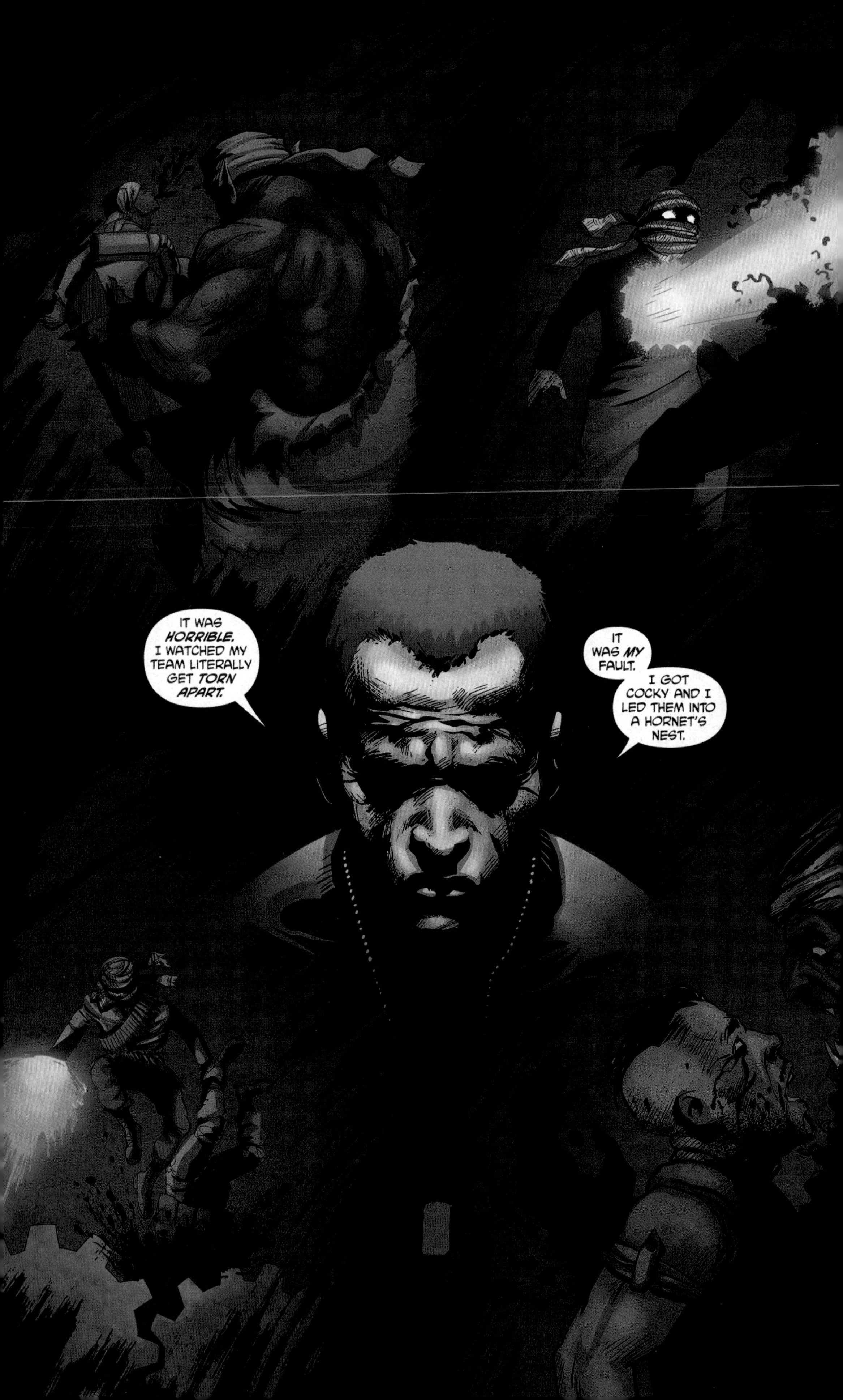
IT WAS *HORRIBLE.* I WATCHED MY TEAM LITERALLY GET *TORN APART.*
IT WAS *MY* FAULT.
I GOT COCKY AND I LED THEM INTO A HORNET'S NEST.

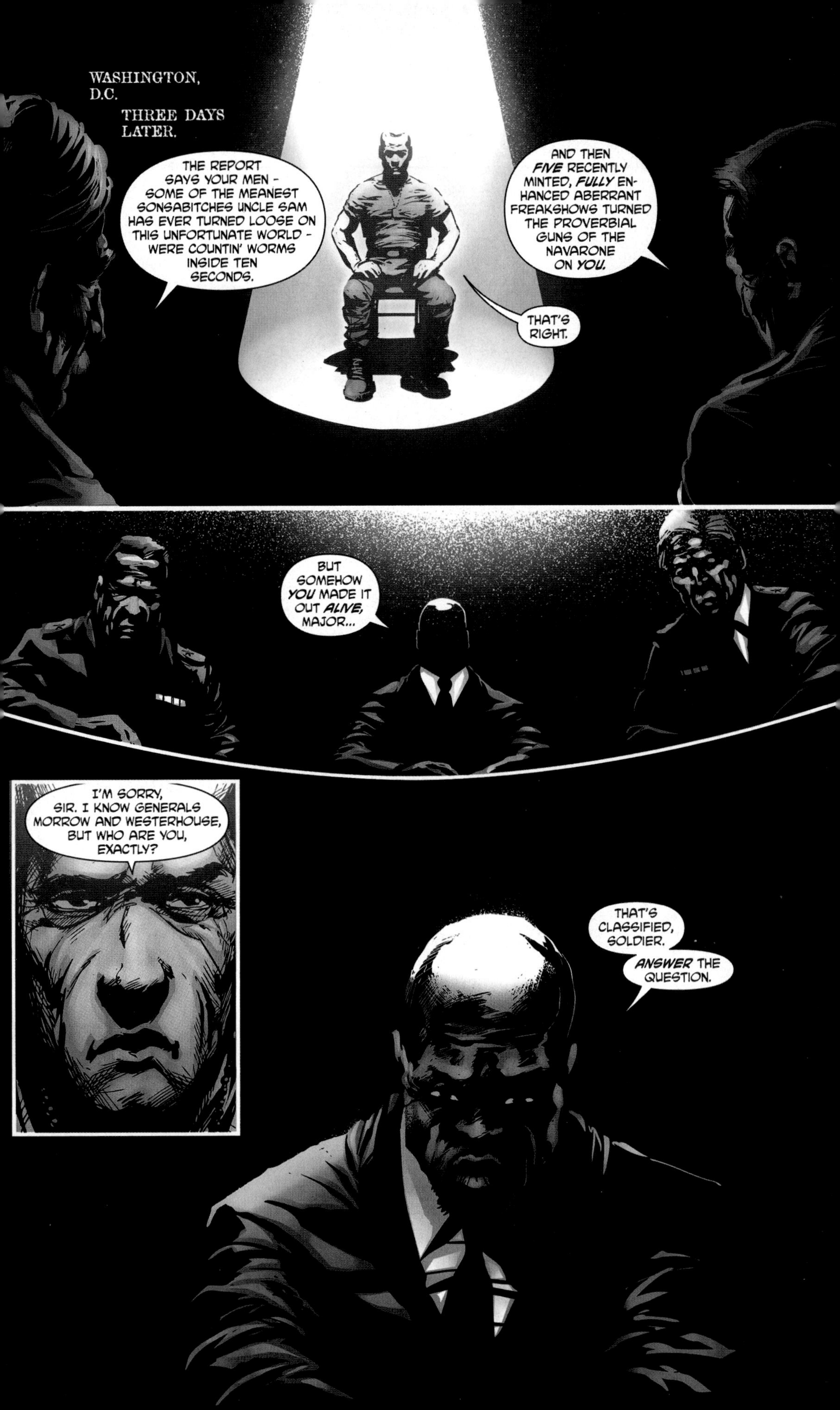
WASHINGTON, D.C.
THREE DAYS LATER.
THE REPORT SAYS YOUR MEN - SOME OF THE MEANEST SONSABITCHES UNCLE SAM HAS EVER TURNED LOOSE ON THIS UNFORTUNATE WORLD - WERE COUNTIN' WORMS INSIDE TEN SECONDS.
AND THEN FIVE RECENTLY MINTED, FULLY ENHANCED ABERRANT FREAKSHOWS TURNED THE PROVERBIAL GUNS OF THE NAVARONE ON YOU.
THAT'S RIGHT.
BUT SOMEHOW YOU MADE IT OUT ALIVE, MAJOR...
I'M SORRY, SIR. I KNOW GENERALS MORROW AND WESTERHOUSE, BUT WHO ARE YOU, EXACTLY?
THAT'S CLASSIFIED, SOLDIER.
ANSWER THE QUESTION.

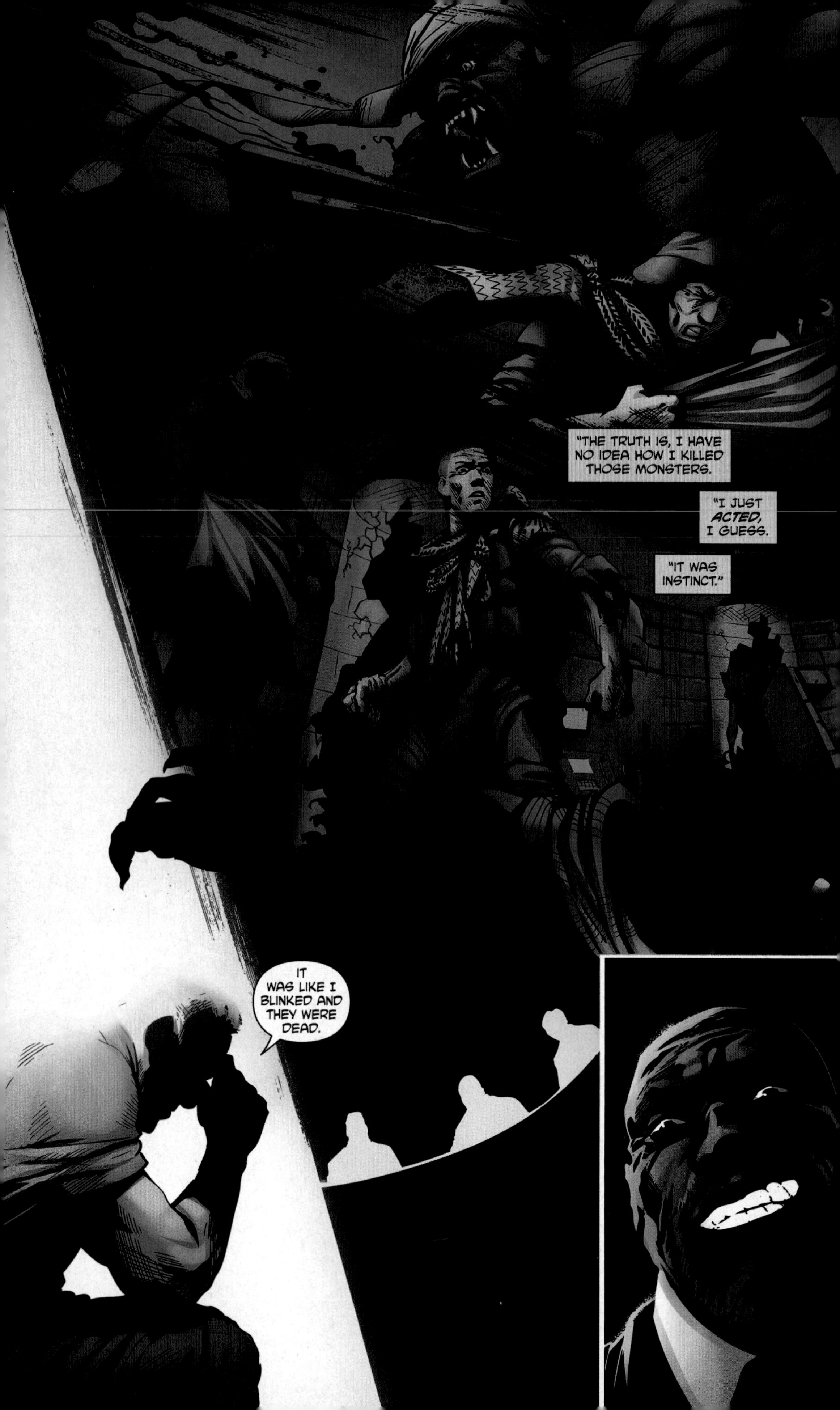
"THE TRUTH IS, I HAVE NO IDEA HOW I KILLED THOSE MONSTERS.
"I JUST *ACTED,* I GUESS.
"IT WAS INSTINCT."
IT WAS LIKE I BLINKED AND THEY WERE DEAD.

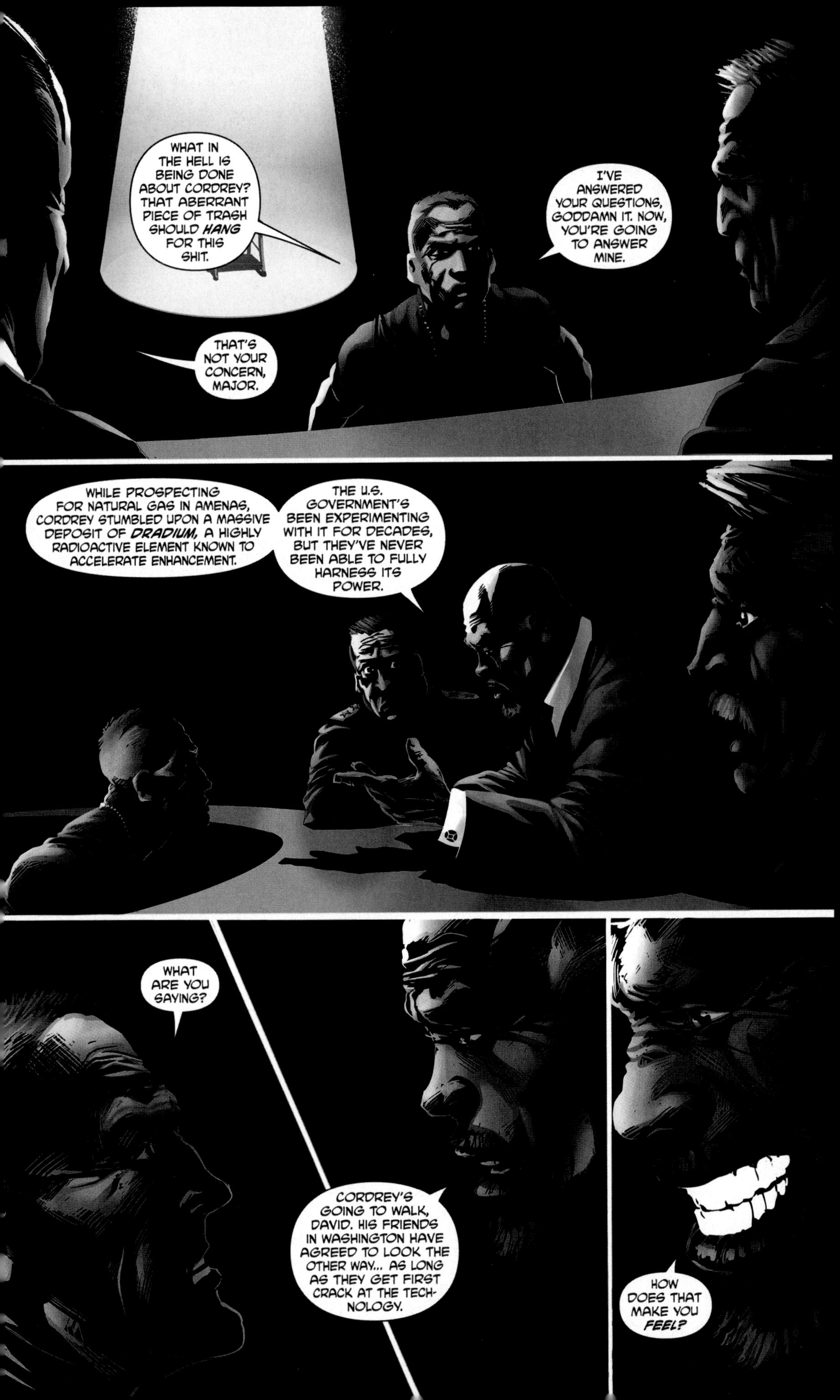
WHAT IN THE HELL IS BEING DONE ABOUT CORDREY? THAT ABERRANT PIECE OF TRASH SHOULD *HANG* FOR THIS SHIT.
THAT'S NOT YOUR CONCERN, MAJOR.
I'VE ANSWERED YOUR QUESTIONS, GODDAMN IT. NOW, YOU'RE GOING TO ANSWER MINE.
WHILE PROSPECTING FOR NATURAL GAS IN AMENAS, CORDREY STUMBLED UPON A MASSIVE DEPOSIT OF *DRADIUM,* A HIGHLY RADIOACTIVE ELEMENT KNOWN TO ACCELERATE ENHANCEMENT.
THE U.S. GOVERNMENT'S BEEN EXPERIMENTING WITH IT FOR DECADES, BUT THEY'VE NEVER BEEN ABLE TO FULLY HARNESS ITS POWER.
WHAT ARE YOU SAYING?
CORDREY'S GOING TO WALK, DAVID. HIS FRIENDS IN WASHINGTON HAVE AGREED TO LOOK THE OTHER WAY... AS LONG AS THEY GET FIRST CRACK AT THE TECH-NOLOGY.
HOW DOES THAT MAKE YOU *FEEL?*

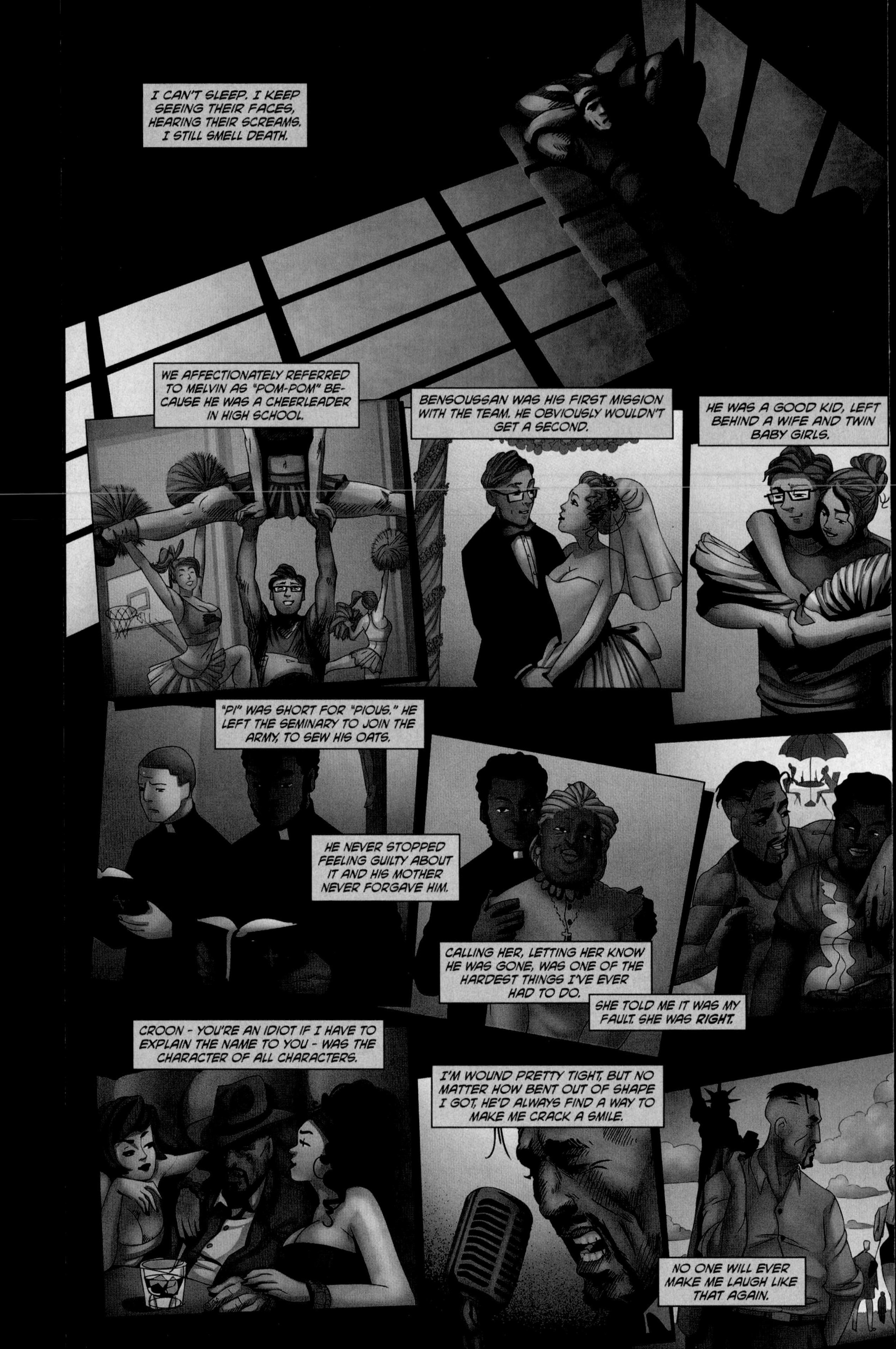
I CAN'T SLEEP. I KEEP SEEING THEIR FACES, HEARING THEIR SCREAMS. I STILL SMELL DEATH.
WE AFFECTIONATELY REFERRED TO MELVIN AS "POM-POM" BECAUSE HE WAS A CHEERLEADER IN HIGH SCHOOL.
BENSOUSSAN WAS HIS FIRST MISSION WITH THE TEAM. HE OBVIOUSLY WOULDN'T GET A SECOND.
HE WAS A GOOD KID, LEFT BEHIND A WIFE AND TWIN BABY GIRLS.
"PI" WAS SHORT FOR "PIOUS." HE LEFT THE SEMINARY TO JOIN THE ARMY, TO SEW HIS OATS.
HE NEVER STOPPED FEELING GUILTY ABOUT IT AND HIS MOTHER NEVER FORGAVE HIM.
CALLING HER, LETTING HER KNOW HE WAS GONE, WAS ONE OF THE HARDEST THINGS I'VE EVER HAD TO DO.
SHE TOLD ME IT WAS MY FAULT. SHE WAS RIGHT.
CROON - YOU'RE AN IDIOT IF I HAVE TO EXPLAIN THE NAME TO YOU - WAS THE CHARACTER OF ALL CHARACTERS.
I'M WOUND PRETTY TIGHT, BUT NO MATTER HOW BENT OUT OF SHAPE I GOT, HE'D ALWAYS FIND A WAY TO MAKE ME CRACK A SMILE.
NO ONE WILL EVER MAKE ME LAUGH LIKE THAT AGAIN.

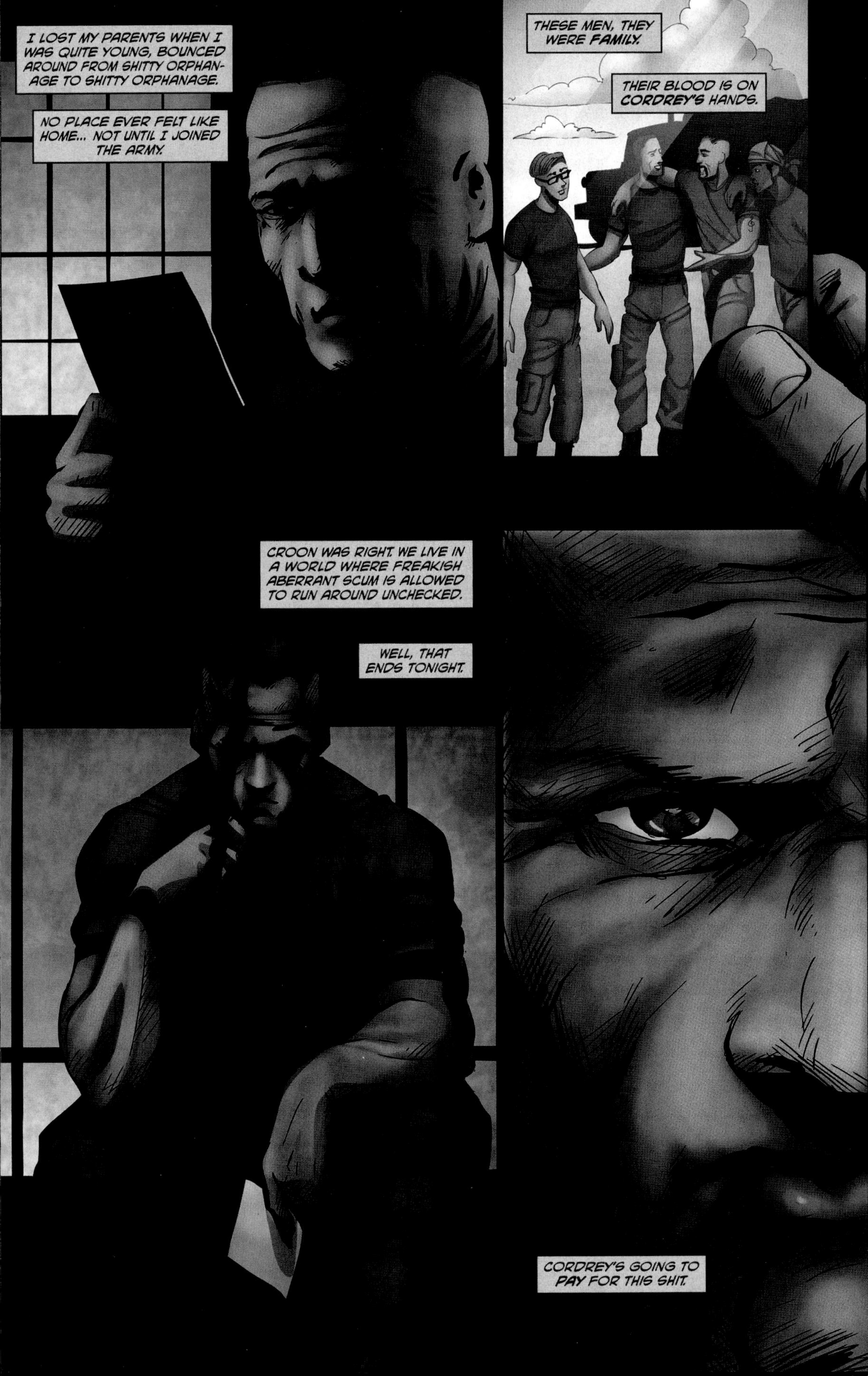
I LOST MY PARENTS WHEN I WAS QUITE YOUNG, BOUNCED AROUND FROM SHITTY ORPHANAGE TO SHITTY ORPHANAGE.
NO PLACE EVER FELT LIKE HOME... NOT UNTIL I JOINED THE ARMY.
THESE MEN, THEY WERE FAMILY.
THEIR BLOOD IS ON CORDREY'S HANDS.
CROON WAS RIGHT. WE LIVE IN A WORLD WHERE FREAKISH ABERRANT SCUM IS ALLOWED TO RUN AROUND UNCHECKED.
WELL, THAT ENDS TONIGHT.
CORDREY'S GOING TO PAY FOR THIS SHIT.

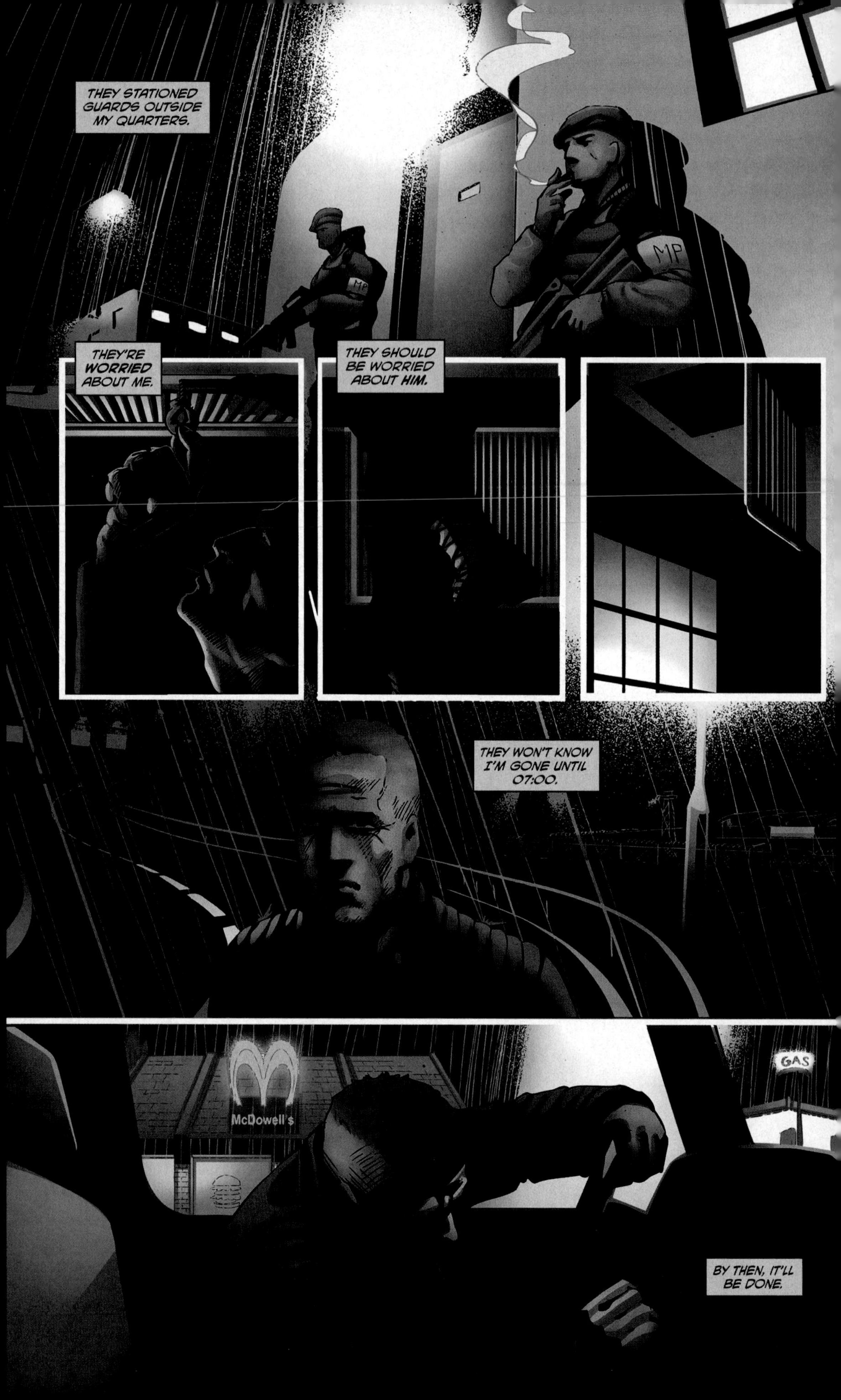
THEY STATIONED GUARDS OUTSIDE MY QUARTERS.
MP
MP
THEY'RE WORRIED ABOUT ME.
THEY SHOULD BE WORRIED ABOUT HIM.
THEY WON'T KNOW I'M GONE UNTIL 07:00.
McDowell's
GAS
BY THEN, IT'LL BE DONE.

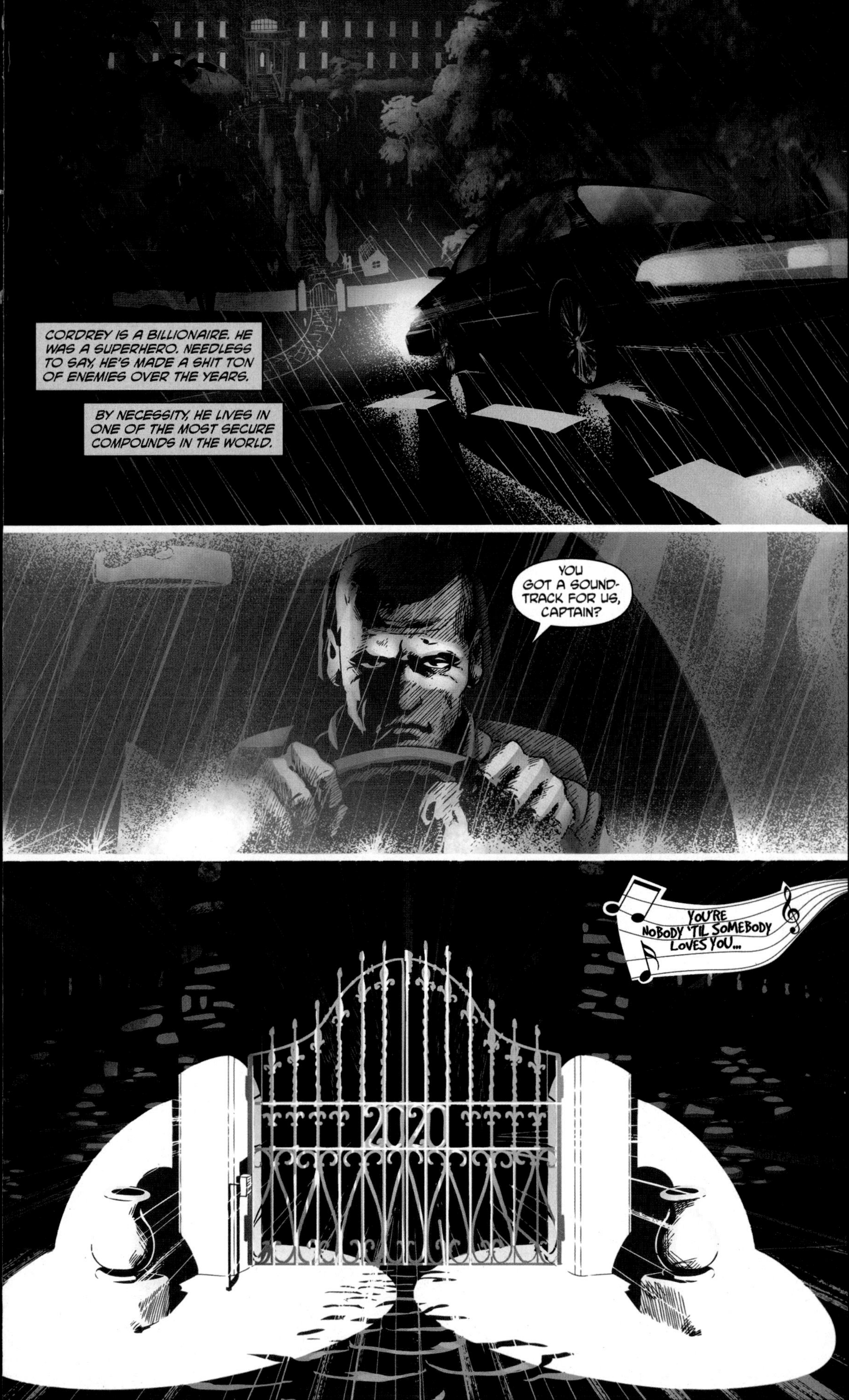
CORDREY IS A BILLIONAIRE. HE WAS A SUPERHERO. NEEDLESS TO SAY, HE'S MADE A SHIT TON OF ENEMIES OVER THE YEARS.
BY NECESSITY, HE LIVES IN ONE OF THE MOST SECURE COMPOUNDS IN THE WORLD.
YOU GOT A SOUND-TRACK FOR US, CAPTAIN?
YOU'RE NOBODY 'TIL SOMEBODY LOVES YOU...
2020

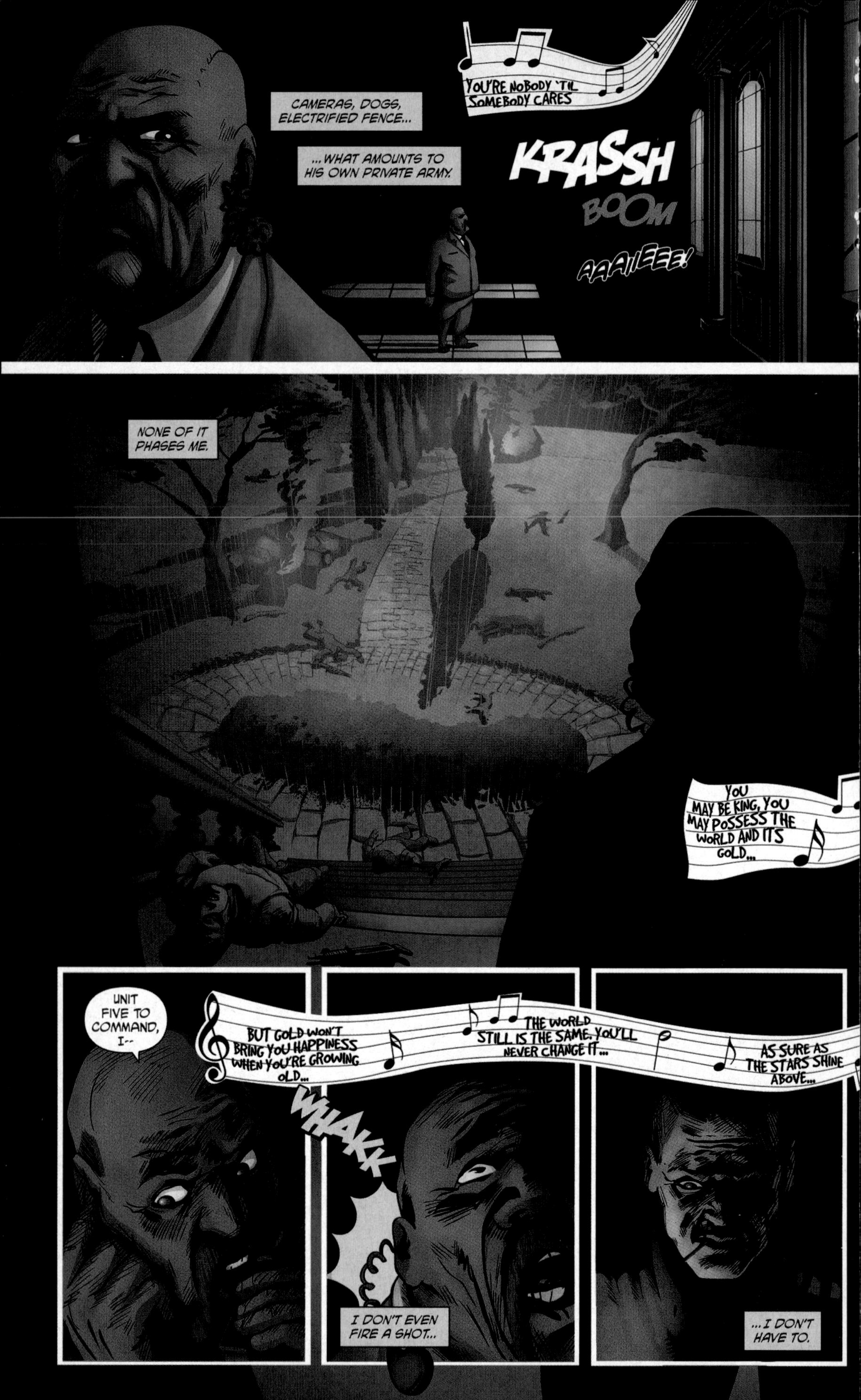
CAMERAS, DOGS, ELECTRIFIED FENCE...
...WHAT AMOUNTS TO HIS OWN PRIVATE ARMY.
YOU'RE NOBODY 'TIL SOMEBODY CARES
KRASSH
BOOM
AAAIIEEE!
NONE OF IT PHASES ME.
YOU MAY BE KING, YOU MAY POSSESS THE WORLD AND ITS GOLD...
UNIT FIVE TO COMMAND, I--
BUT GOLD WON'T BRING YOU HAPPINESS WHEN YOU'RE GROWING OLD...
THE WORLD STILL IS THE SAME, YOU'LL NEVER CHANGE IT...
AS SURE AS THE STARS SHINE ABOVE...
WHAKK
I DON'T EVEN FIRE A SHOT...
...I DON'T HAVE TO.

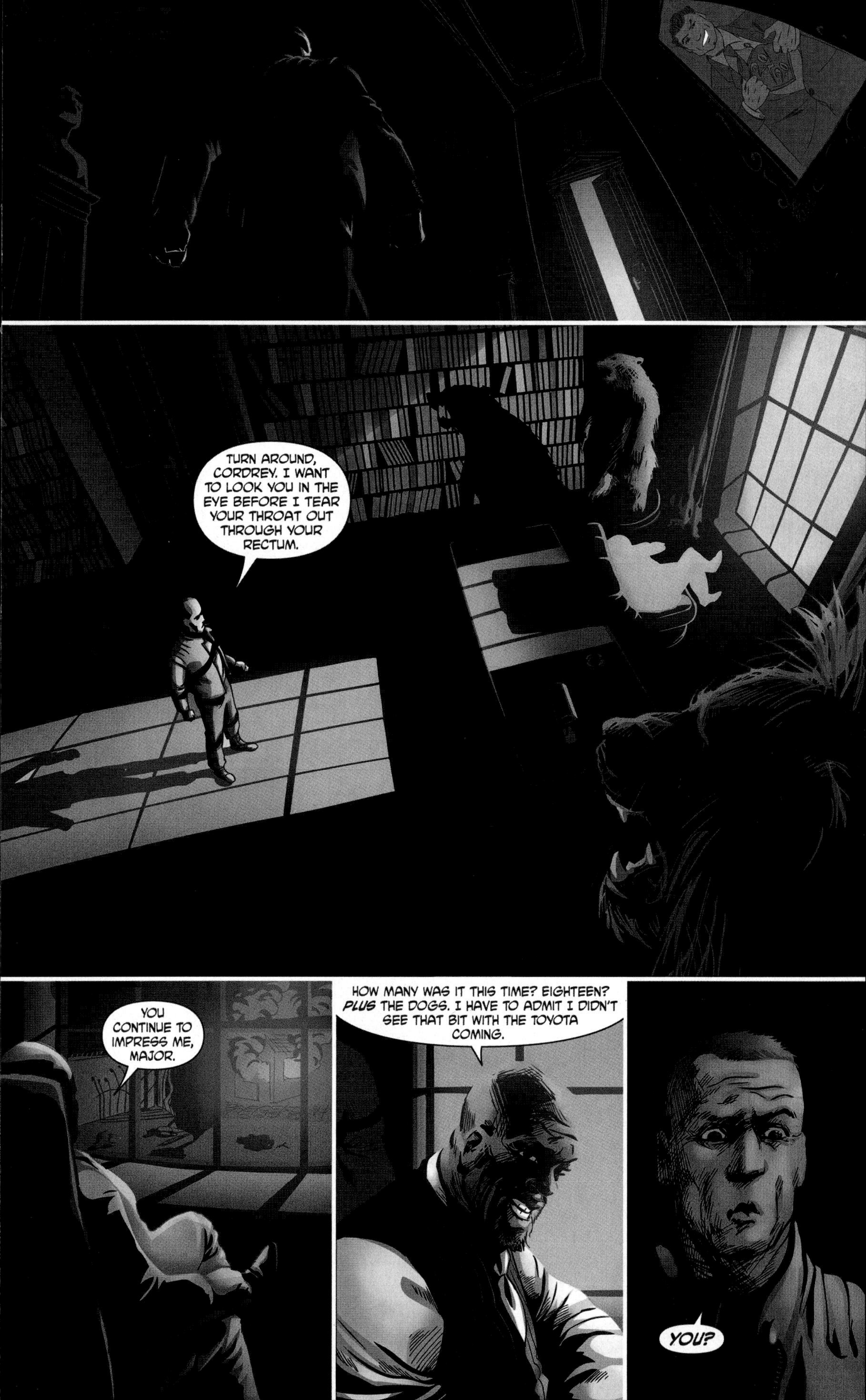
TURN AROUND, CORDREY. I WANT TO LOOK YOU IN THE EYE BEFORE I TEAR YOUR THROAT OUT THROUGH YOUR RECTUM.
YOU CONTINUE TO IMPRESS ME, MAJOR.
HOW MANY WAS IT THIS TIME? EIGHTEEN? *PLUS* THE DOGS. I HAVE TO ADMIT I DIDN'T SEE THAT BIT WITH THE TOYOTA COMING.
YOU?

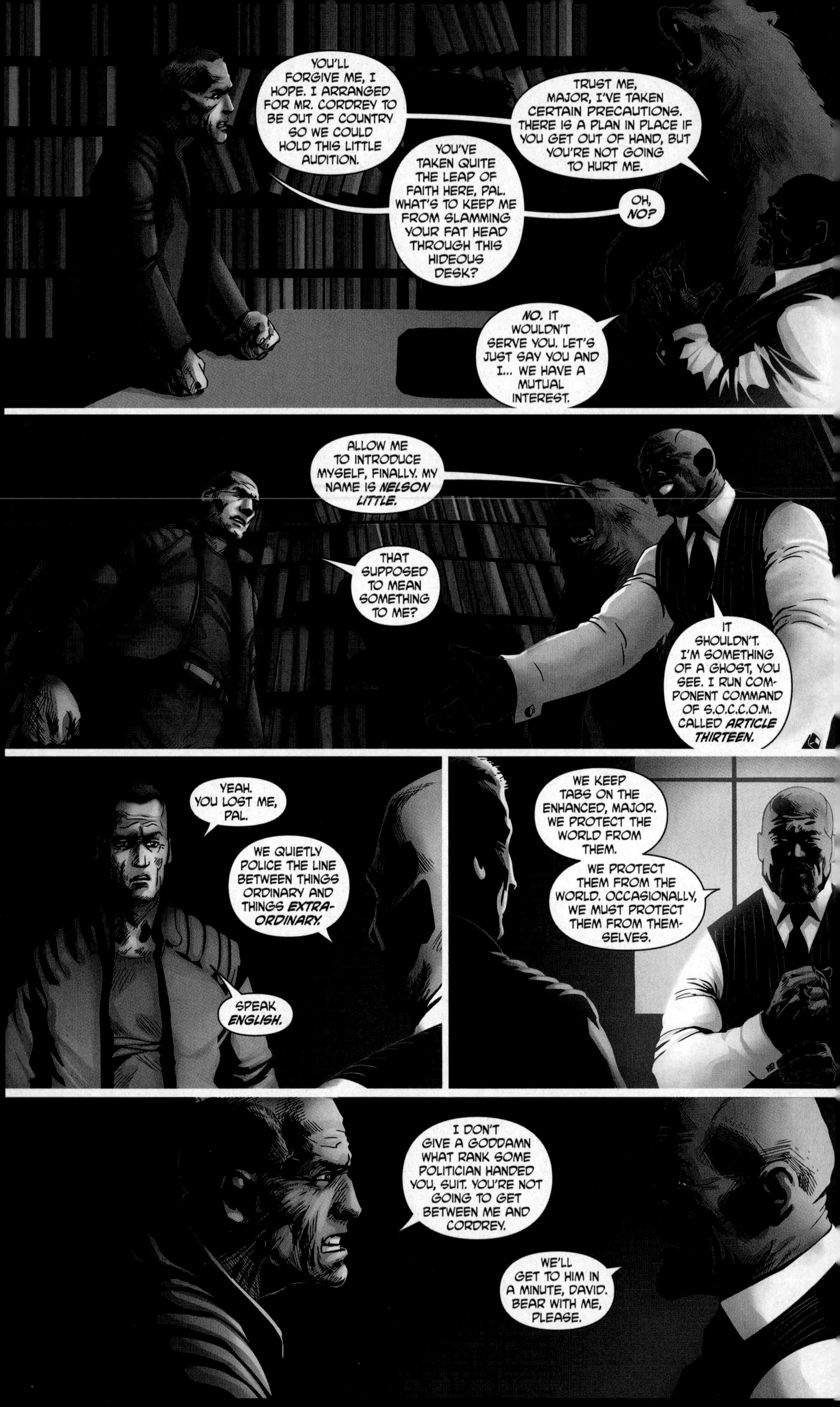

YOU'LL FORGIVE ME, I HOPE. I ARRANGED FOR MR. CORDREY TO BE OUT OF COUNTRY SO WE COULD HOLD THIS LITTLE AUDITION.
YOU'VE TAKEN QUITE THE LEAP OF FAITH HERE, PAL. WHAT'S TO KEEP ME FROM SLAMMING YOUR FAT HEAD THROUGH THIS HIDEOUS DESK?
TRUST ME, MAJOR, I'VE TAKEN CERTAIN PRECAUTIONS. THERE IS A PLAN IN PLACE IF YOU GET OUT OF HAND, BUT YOU'RE NOT GOING TO HURT ME.
OH, *NO?*
NO. IT WOULDN'T SERVE YOU. LET'S JUST SAY YOU AND I... WE HAVE A MUTUAL INTEREST.
ALLOW ME TO INTRODUCE MYSELF, FINALLY. MY NAME IS ***NELSON LITTLE.***
THAT SUPPOSED TO MEAN SOMETHING TO ME?
IT SHOULDN'T. I'M SOMETHING OF A GHOST, YOU SEE. I RUN COMPONENT COMMAND OF S.O.C.C.O.M. CALLED ***ARTICLE THIRTEEN.***
YEAH. YOU LOST ME, PAL.
WE QUIETLY POLICE THE LINE BETWEEN THINGS ORDINARY AND THINGS ***EXTRAORDINARY.***
SPEAK ***ENGLISH.***
WE KEEP TABS ON THE ENHANCED, MAJOR. WE PROTECT THE WORLD FROM THEM.
WE PROTECT THEM FROM THE WORLD. OCCASIONALLY, WE MUST PROTECT THEM FROM THEMSELVES.
I DON'T GIVE A GODDAMN WHAT RANK SOME POLITICIAN HANDED YOU, SUIT. YOU'RE NOT GOING TO GET BETWEEN ME AND CORDREY.
WE'LL GET TO HIM IN A MINUTE, DAVID. BEAR WITH ME, PLEASE.

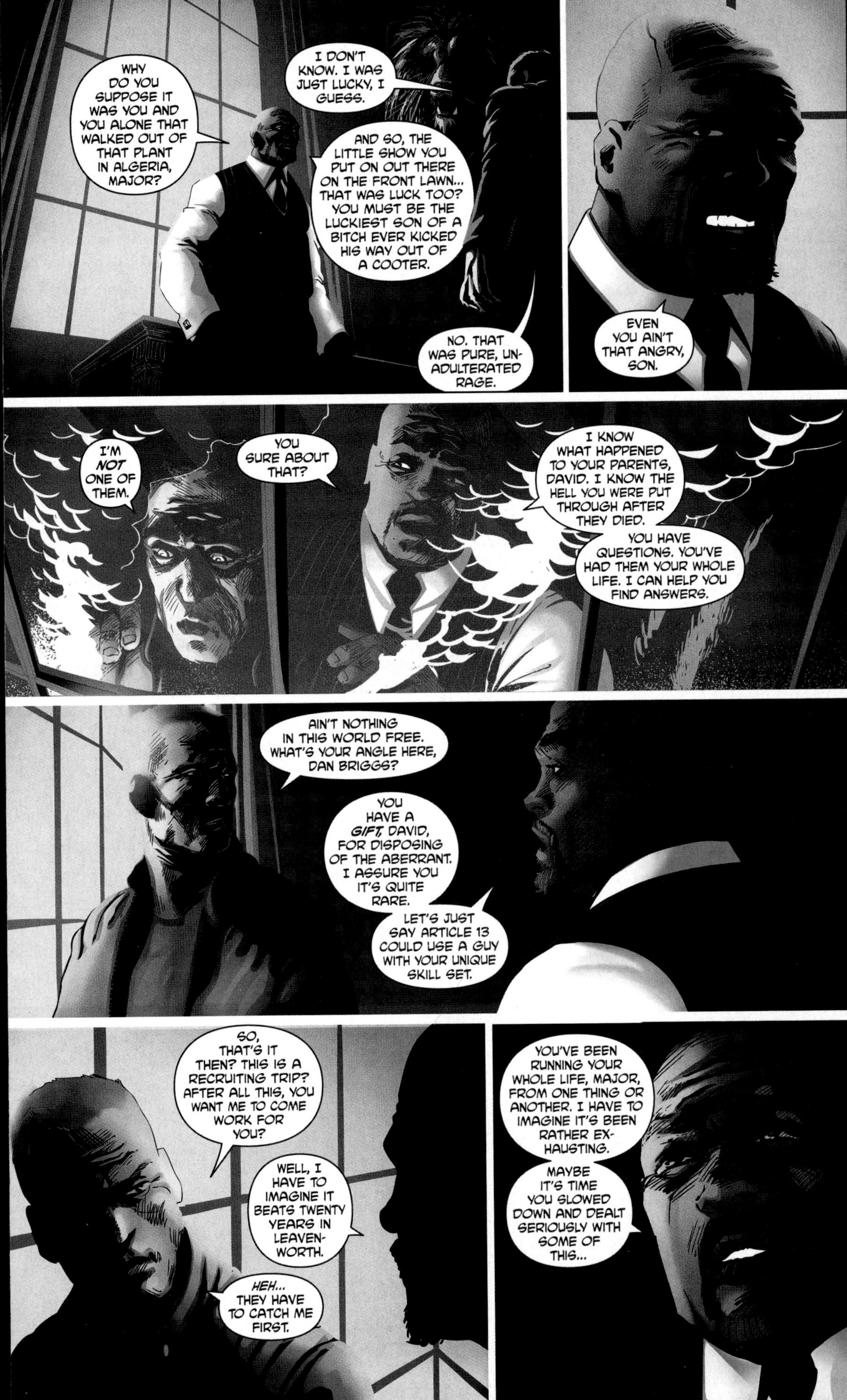
WHY DO YOU SUPPOSE IT WAS YOU AND YOU ALONE THAT WALKED OUT OF THAT PLANT IN ALGERIA, MAJOR?
I DON'T KNOW. I WAS JUST LUCKY, I GUESS.
AND SO, THE LITTLE SHOW YOU PUT ON OUT THERE ON THE FRONT LAWN... THAT WAS LUCK TOO? YOU MUST BE THE LUCKIEST SON OF A BITCH EVER KICKED HIS WAY OUT OF A COOTER.
NO. THAT WAS PURE, UN-ADULTERATED RAGE.
EVEN YOU AIN'T THAT ANGRY, SON.
I'M *NOT* ONE OF THEM.
YOU SURE ABOUT THAT?
I KNOW WHAT HAPPENED TO YOUR PARENTS, DAVID. I KNOW THE HELL YOU WERE PUT THROUGH AFTER THEY DIED.
YOU HAVE QUESTIONS. YOU'VE HAD THEM YOUR WHOLE LIFE. I CAN HELP YOU FIND ANSWERS.
AIN'T NOTHING IN THIS WORLD FREE. WHAT'S YOUR ANGLE HERE, DAN BRIGGS?
YOU HAVE A *GIFT,* DAVID, FOR DISPOSING OF THE ABERRANT. I ASSURE YOU IT'S QUITE RARE.
LET'S JUST SAY ARTICLE 13 COULD USE A GUY WITH YOUR UNIQUE SKILL SET.
SO, THAT'S IT THEN? THIS IS A RECRUITING TRIP? AFTER ALL THIS, YOU WANT ME TO COME WORK FOR YOU?
WELL, I HAVE TO IMAGINE IT BEATS TWENTY YEARS IN LEAVEN-WORTH.
HEH... THEY HAVE TO CATCH ME FIRST.
YOU'VE BEEN RUNNING YOUR WHOLE LIFE, MAJOR, FROM ONE THING OR ANOTHER. I HAVE TO IMAGINE IT'S BEEN RATHER EX-HAUSTING.
MAYBE IT'S TIME YOU SLOWED DOWN AND DEALT SERIOUSLY WITH SOME OF THIS...

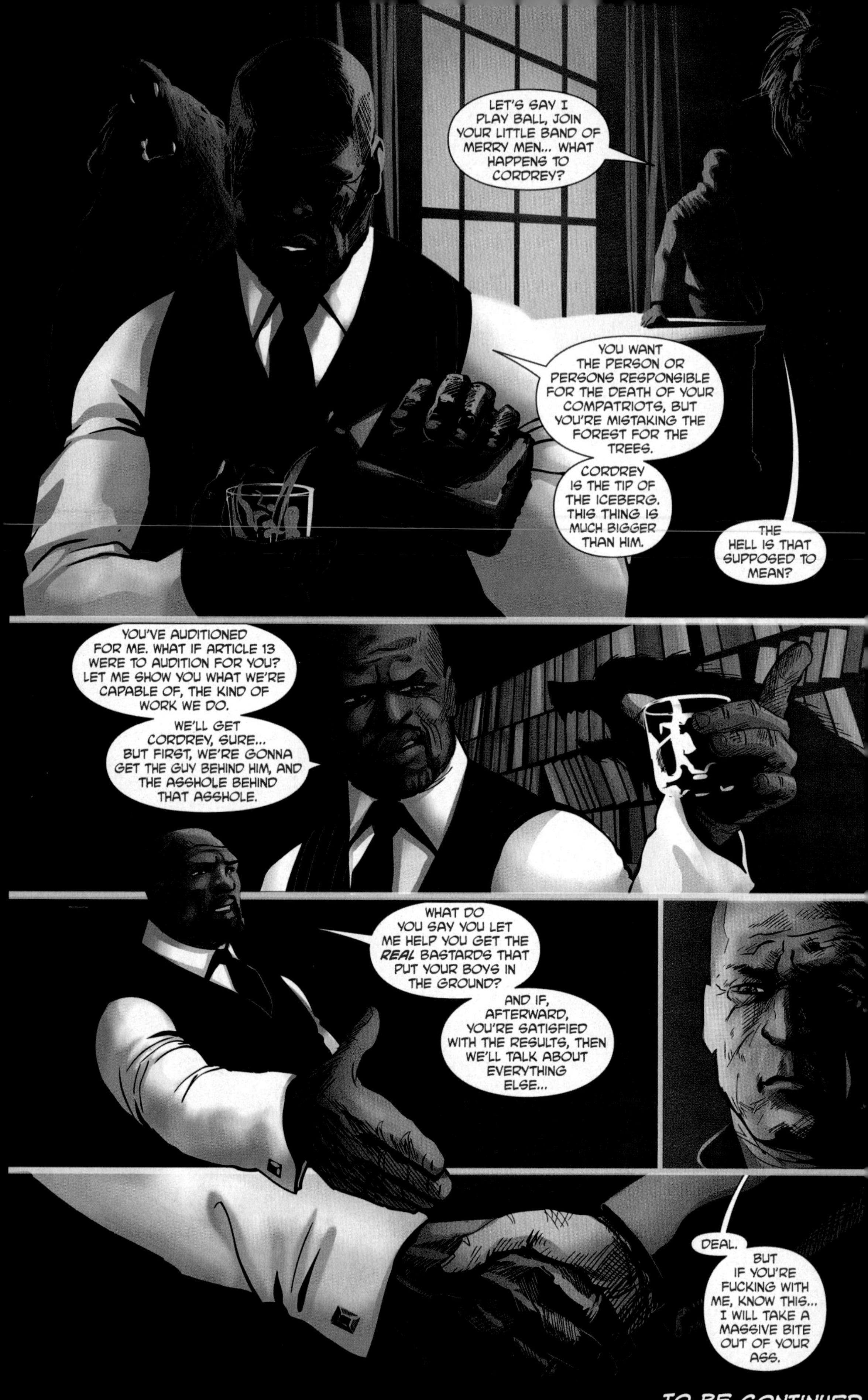

LET'S SAY I PLAY BALL, JOIN YOUR LITTLE BAND OF MERRY MEN... WHAT HAPPENS TO CORDREY?
YOU WANT THE PERSON OR PERSONS RESPONSIBLE FOR THE DEATH OF YOUR COMPATRIOTS, BUT YOU'RE MISTAKING THE FOREST FOR THE TREES.
CORDREY IS THE TIP OF THE ICEBERG. THIS THING IS MUCH BIGGER THAN HIM.
THE HELL IS THAT SUPPOSED TO MEAN?
YOU'VE AUDITIONED FOR ME. WHAT IF ARTICLE 13 WERE TO AUDITION FOR YOU? LET ME SHOW YOU WHAT WE'RE CAPABLE OF, THE KIND OF WORK WE DO.
WE'LL GET CORDREY, SURE... BUT FIRST, WE'RE GONNA GET THE GUY BEHIND HIM, AND THE ASSHOLE BEHIND THAT ASSHOLE.
WHAT DO YOU SAY YOU LET ME HELP YOU GET THE *REAL* BASTARDS THAT PUT YOUR BOYS IN THE GROUND?
AND IF, AFTERWARD, YOU'RE SATISFIED WITH THE RESULTS, THEN WE'LL TALK ABOUT EVERYTHING ELSE...
DEAL.
BUT IF YOU'RE FUCKING WITH ME, KNOW THIS... I WILL TAKE A MASSIVE BITE OUT OF YOUR ASS.

TO BE CONTINUED.

Aberrant

GOT ABERRANT-RELATED RANTS, RAVES, FULMINATIONS, VOCIFERATIONS, INVECTIVES, OR OBLOQUIES? GOT FAN ART? THOUGHTS ON O.J'S PAROLE? A GREAT RECIPE FOR LOBSTER BISQUE?

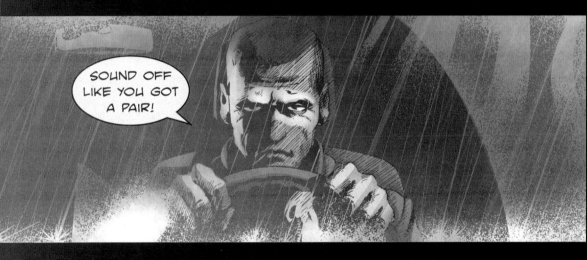

SOUND OFF LIKE YOU GOT A PAIR!

SEND ALL BUSINESS FIT TO PRINT TO: HALFEVILCOMICS@GMAIL.COM

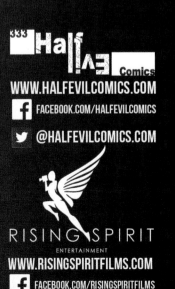

333 Half Evil Comics
WWW.HALFEVILCOMICS.COM
FACEBOOK.COM/HALFEVILCOMICS
@HALFEVILCOMICS.COM

RISING SPIRIT ENTERTAINMENT
WWW.RISINGSPIRITFILMS.COM
FACEBOOK.COM/RISINGSPIRITFILMS

This Month's Music:

Don't Worry, Be Happy
Words and Music by Bobby McFerrin

You're Nobody 'Til Somebody Loves You
Words and Music by Russ Morgan, Larry Stock
and James Cavanaugh

I'm Gonna Make You Love Me
Words and Music by Kenneth Gamble, Jerry Ross and
Leon Huff

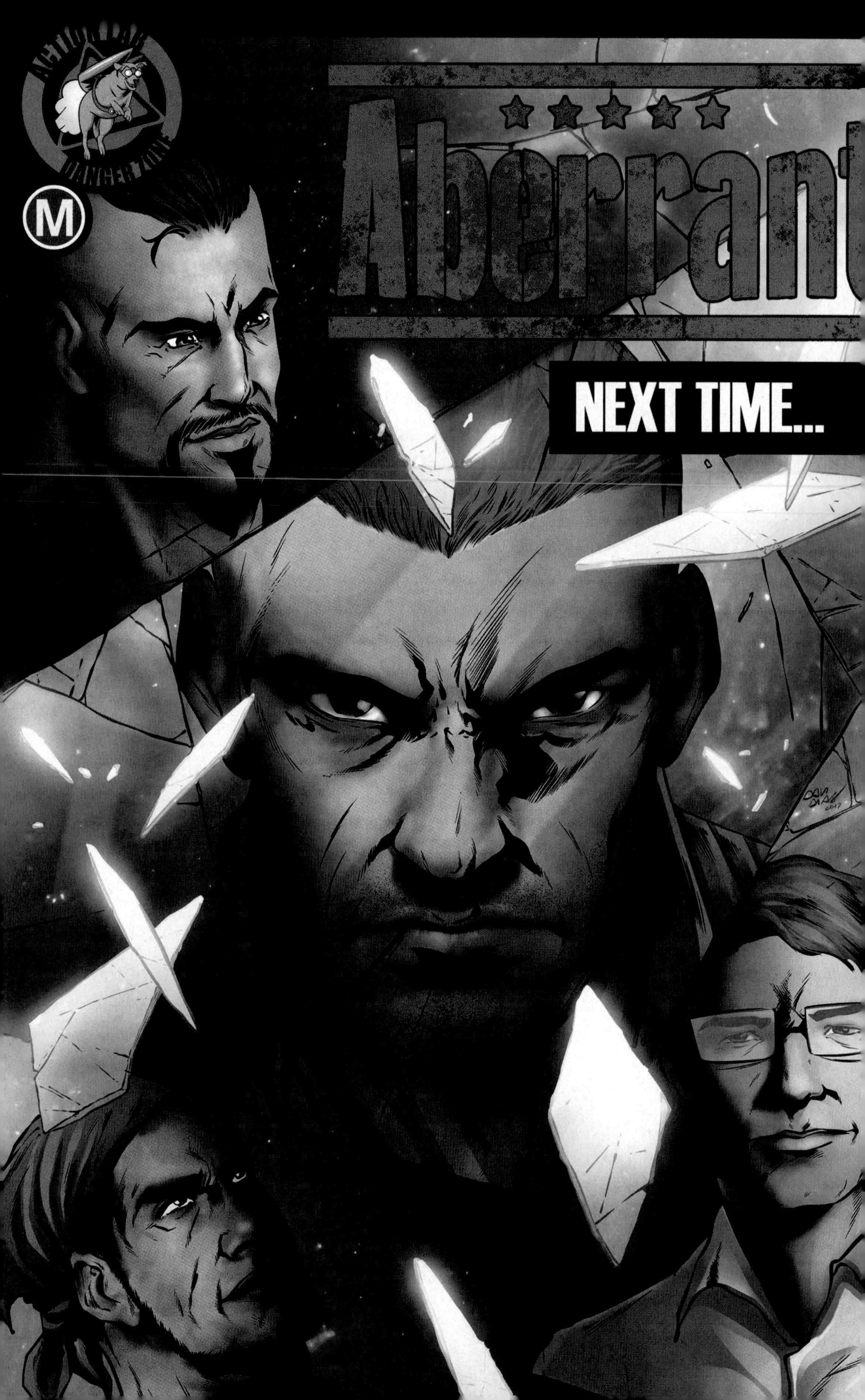
Aberrant
NEXT TIME...

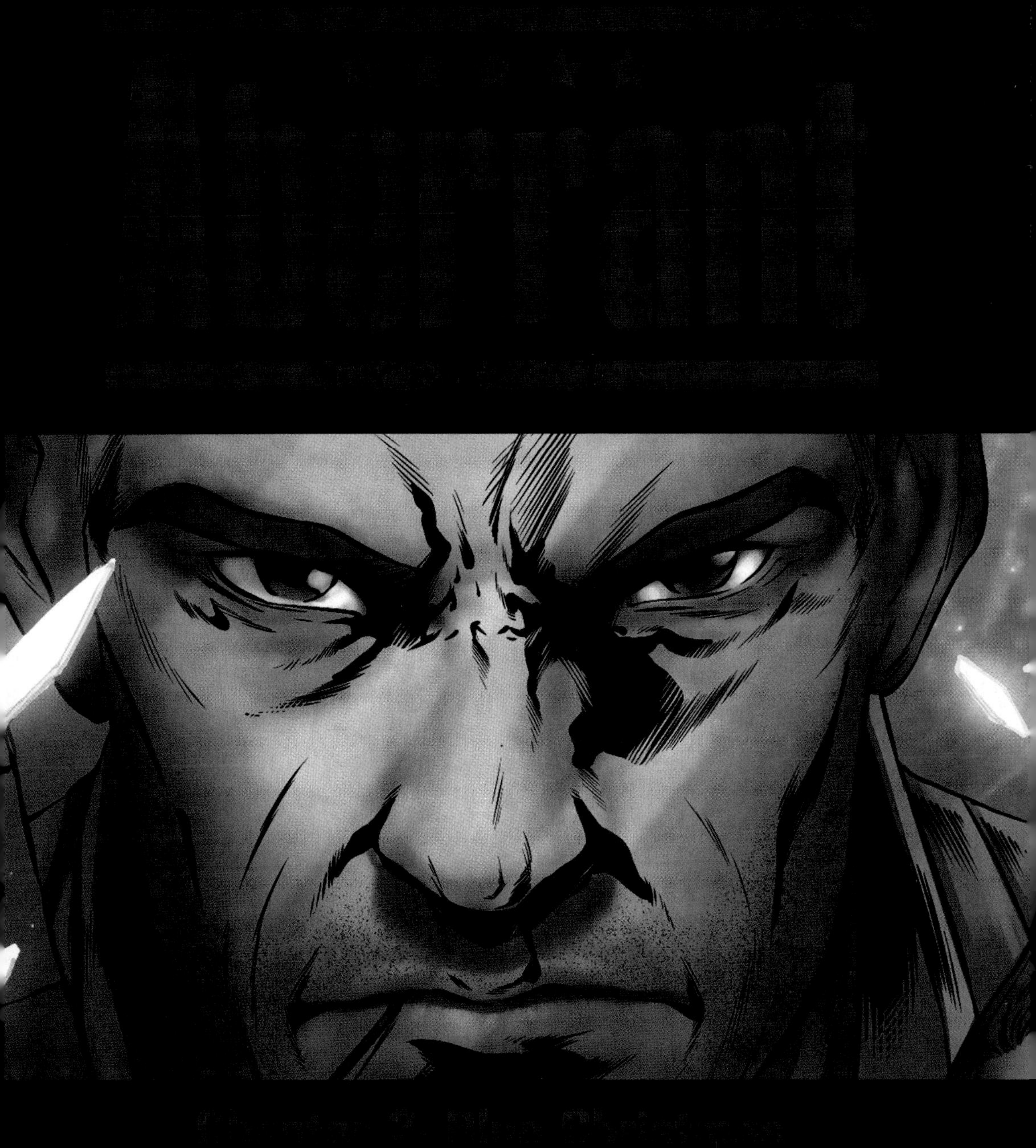

Special thanks to Karla Nappi, Jeff Leeds, Steven Prince, Karol Wisniewski, Jim Higgins and everyone at Meltdown Comics

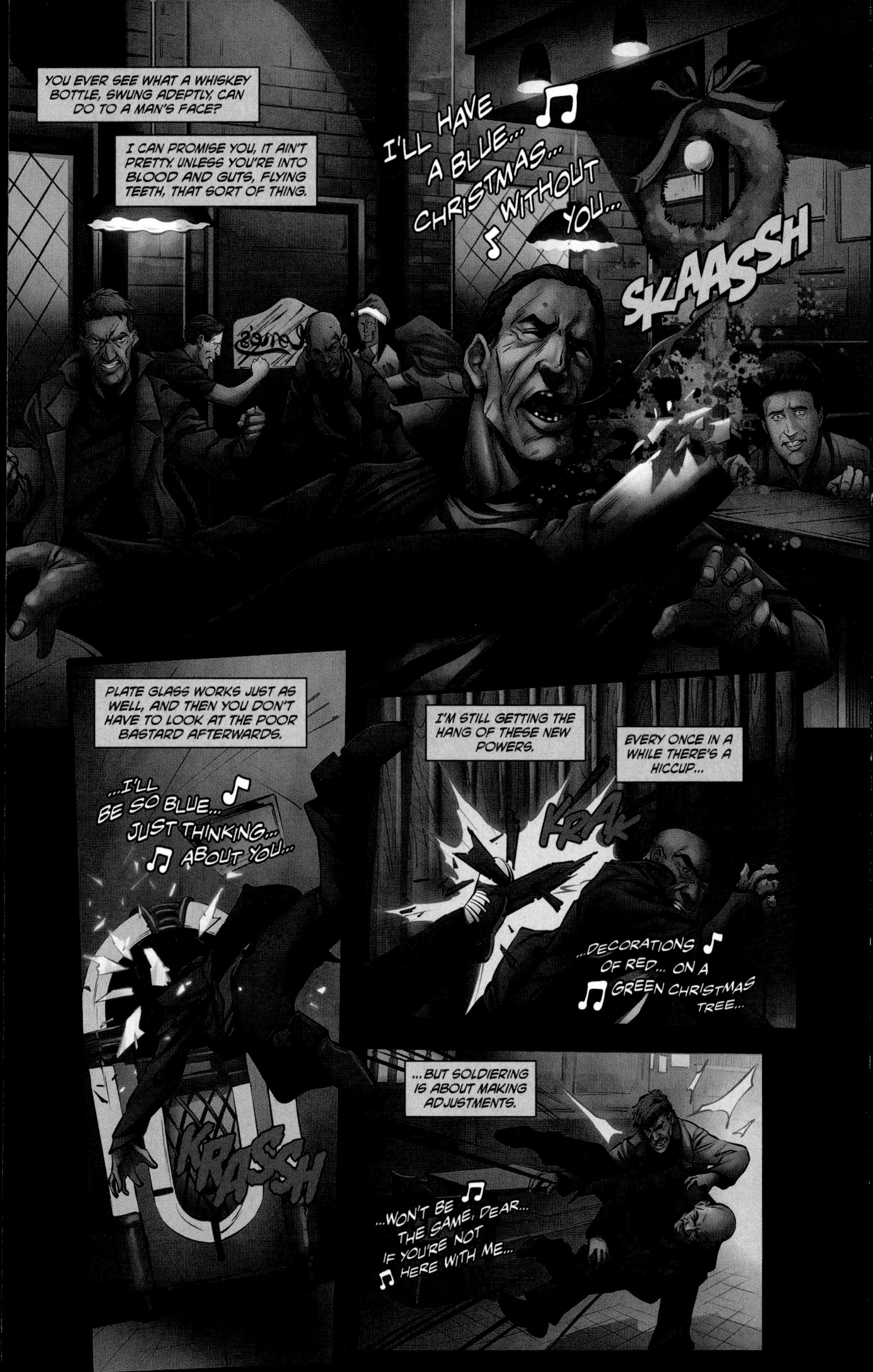
YOU EVER SEE WHAT A WHISKEY BOTTLE, SWUNG ADEPTLY, CAN DO TO A MAN'S FACE?
I CAN PROMISE YOU, IT AIN'T PRETTY. UNLESS YOU'RE INTO BLOOD AND GUTS, FLYING TEETH, THAT SORT OF THING.
I'LL HAVE A BLUE... CHRISTMAS... WITHOUT YOU...
SKAASSH
PLATE GLASS WORKS JUST AS WELL, AND THEN YOU DON'T HAVE TO LOOK AT THE POOR BASTARD AFTERWARDS.
...I'LL BE SO BLUE... JUST THINKING... ABOUT YOU...
KRASSH
I'M STILL GETTING THE HANG OF THESE NEW POWERS.
EVERY ONCE IN A WHILE THERE'S A HICCUP...
KRAK
...DECORATIONS OF RED... ON A GREEN CHRISTMAS TREE...
...BUT SOLDIERING IS ABOUT MAKING ADJUSTMENTS.
...WON'T BE THE SAME, DEAR... IF YOU'RE NOT HERE WITH ME...

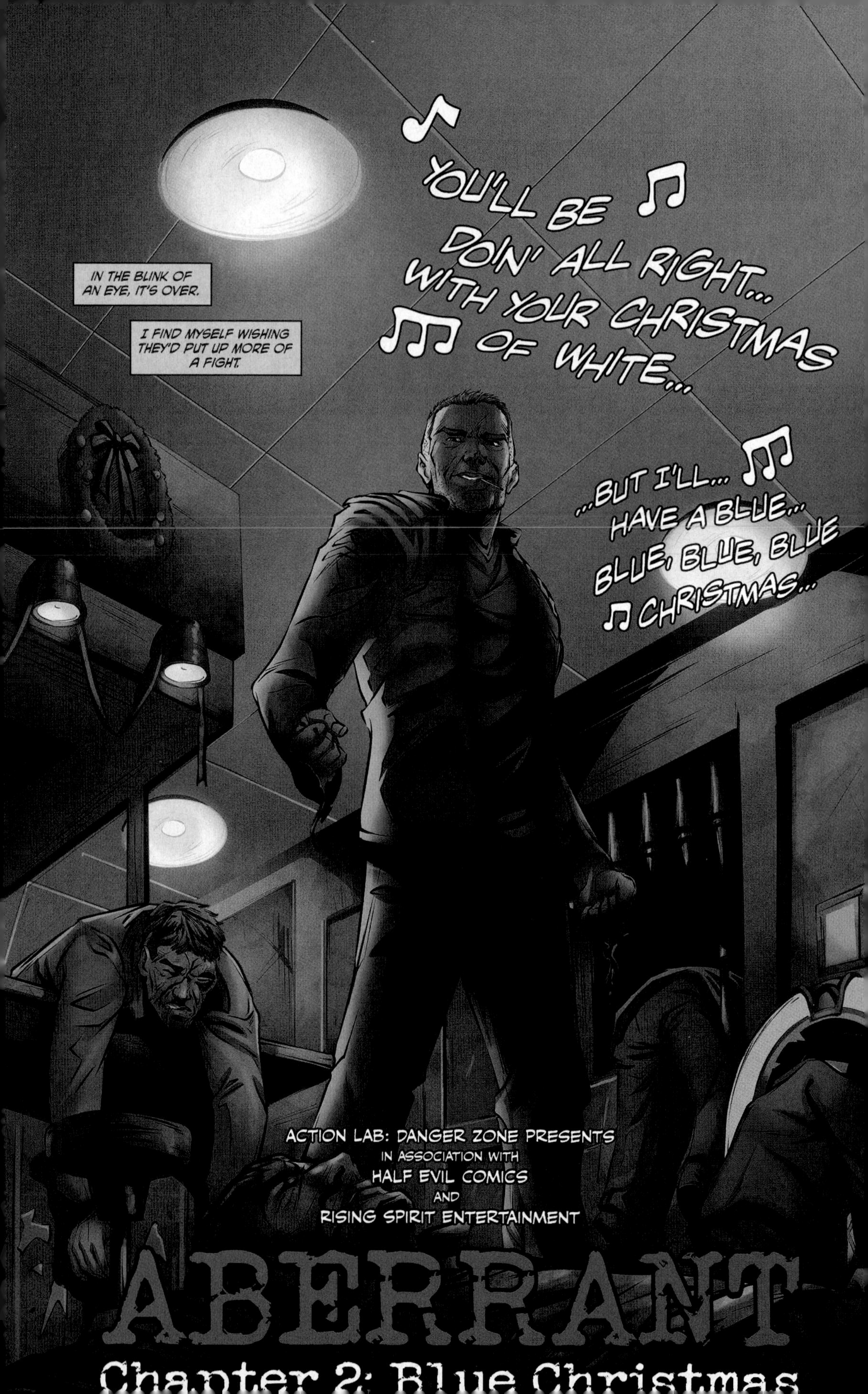
IN THE BLINK OF AN EYE, IT'S OVER.
I FIND MYSELF WISHING THEY'D PUT UP MORE OF A FIGHT.
YOU'LL BE DOIN' ALL RIGHT... WITH YOUR CHRISTMAS OF WHITE...
...BUT I'LL... HAVE A BLUE... BLUE, BLUE, BLUE CHRISTMAS...
ACTION LAB: DANGER ZONE PRESENTS
IN ASSOCIATION WITH
HALF EVIL COMICS
AND
RISING SPIRIT ENTERTAINMENT
ABERRANT
Chapter 2: Blue Christmas

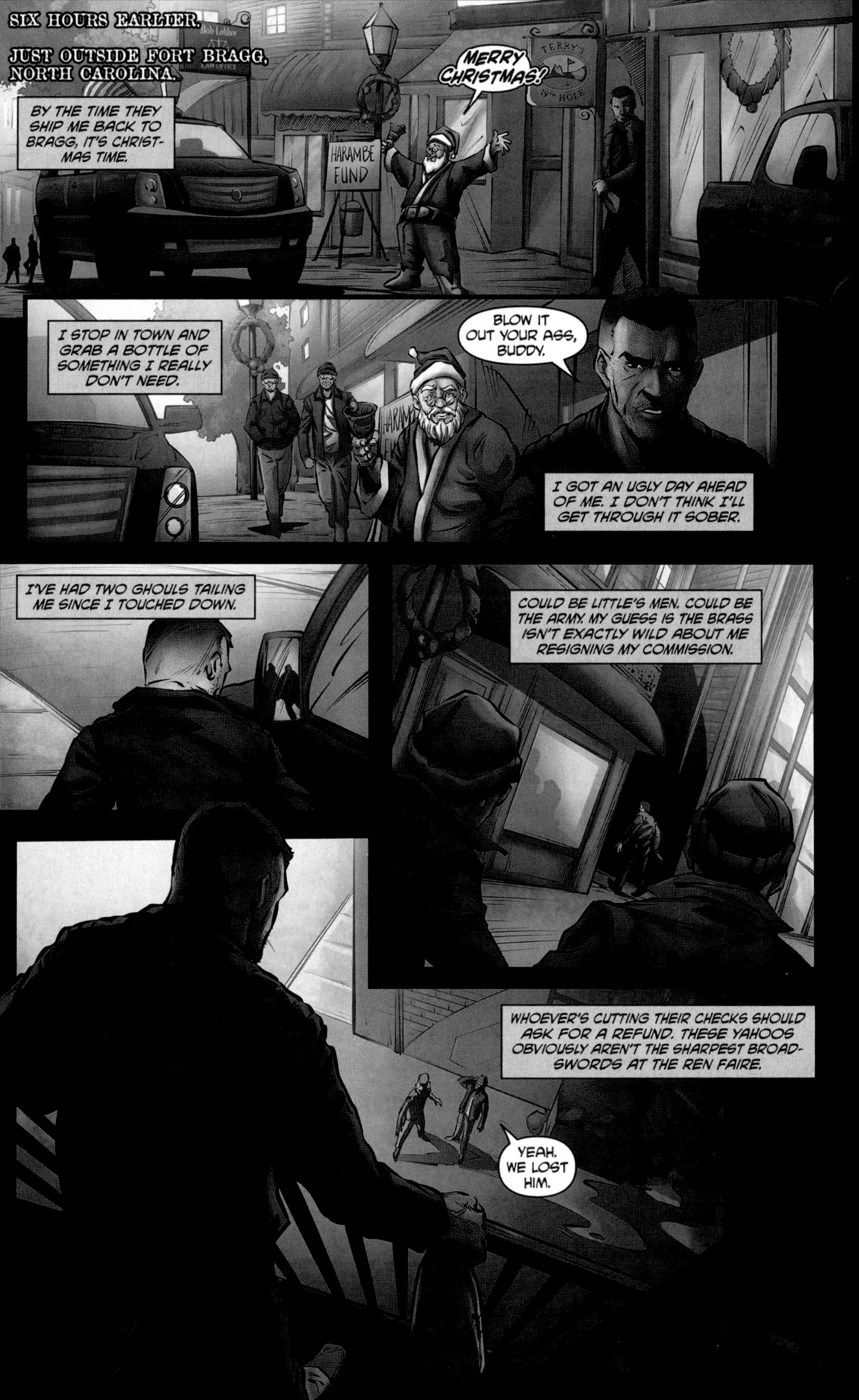
SIX HOURS EARLIER.
JUST OUTSIDE FORT BRAGG, NORTH CAROLINA.
Bob Loblaw LAW OFFICE
TERRY'S 19TH HOLE
BY THE TIME THEY SHIP ME BACK TO BRAGG, IT'S CHRISTMAS TIME.
MERRY CHRISTMAS!
HARAMBE FUND
I STOP IN TOWN AND GRAB A BOTTLE OF SOMETHING I REALLY DON'T NEED.
BLOW IT OUT YOUR ASS, BUDDY.
I GOT AN UGLY DAY AHEAD OF ME. I DON'T THINK I'LL GET THROUGH IT SOBER.
I'VE HAD TWO GHOULS TAILING ME SINCE I TOUCHED DOWN.
COULD BE LITTLE'S MEN. COULD BE THE ARMY. MY GUESS IS THE BRASS ISN'T EXACTLY WILD ABOUT ME RESIGNING MY COMMISSION.
WHOEVER'S CUTTING THEIR CHECKS SHOULD ASK FOR A REFUND. THESE YAHOOS OBVIOUSLY AREN'T THE SHARPEST BROADSWORDS AT THE REN FAIRE.
YEAH. WE LOST HIM.

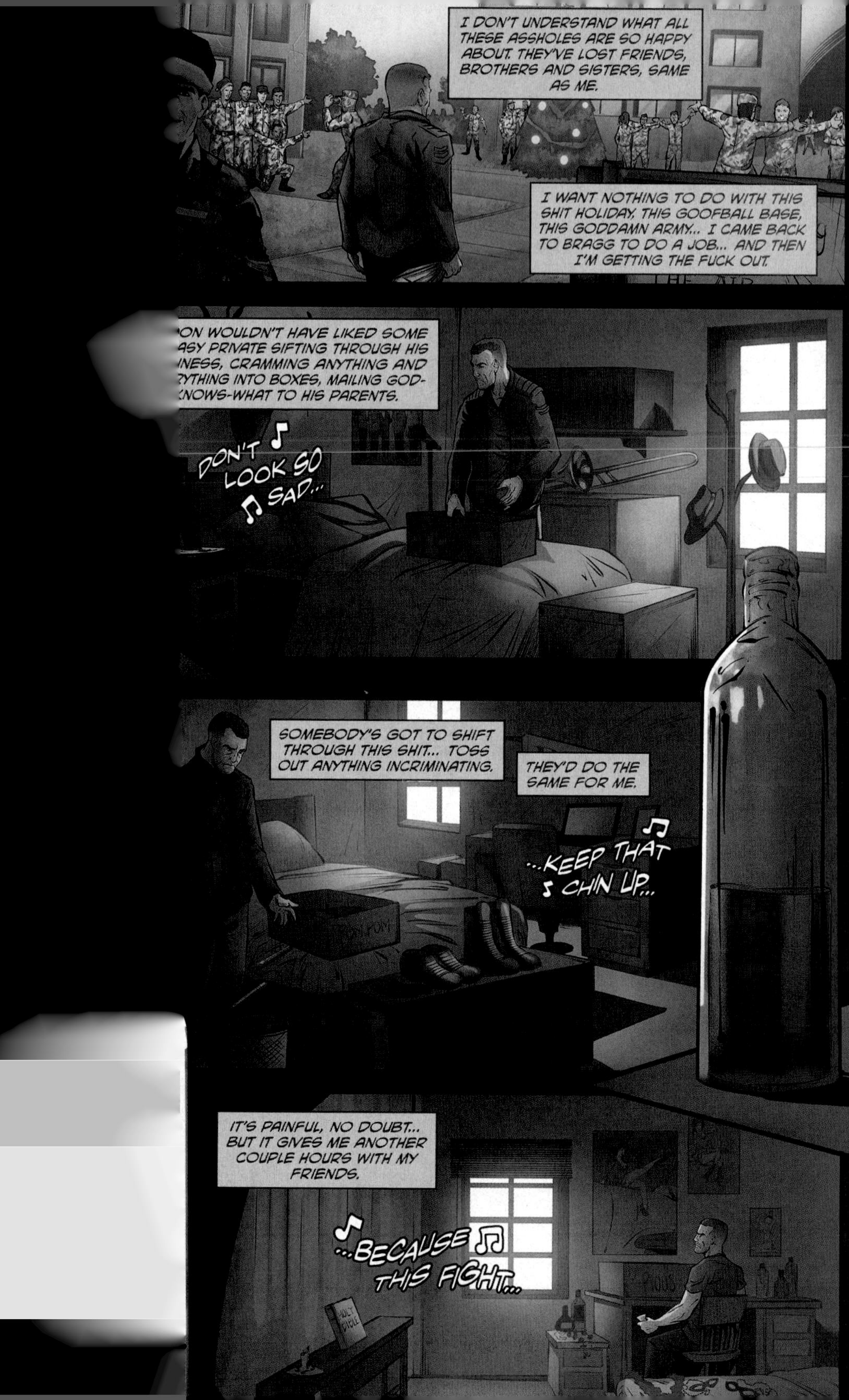

I DON'T UNDERSTAND WHAT ALL THESE ASSHOLES ARE SO HAPPY ABOUT. THEY'VE LOST FRIENDS, BROTHERS AND SISTERS, SAME AS ME.
I WANT NOTHING TO DO WITH THIS SHIT HOLIDAY, THIS GOOFBALL BASE, THIS GODDAMN ARMY... I CAME BACK TO BRAGG TO DO A JOB... AND THEN I'M GETTING THE FUCK OUT.
ON WOULDN'T HAVE LIKED SOME ASY PRIVATE SIFTING THROUGH HIS INESS, CRAMMING ANYTHING AND YTHING INTO BOXES, MAILING GOD-KNOWS-WHAT TO HIS PARENTS.
DON'T LOOK SO SAD...
SOMEBODY'S GOT TO SHIFT THROUGH THIS SHIT... TOSS OUT ANYTHING INCRIMINATING.
THEY'D DO THE SAME FOR ME.
...KEEP THAT CHIN UP...
IT'S PAINFUL, NO DOUBT... BUT IT GIVES ME ANOTHER COUPLE HOURS WITH MY FRIENDS.
...BECAUSE THIS FIGHT...

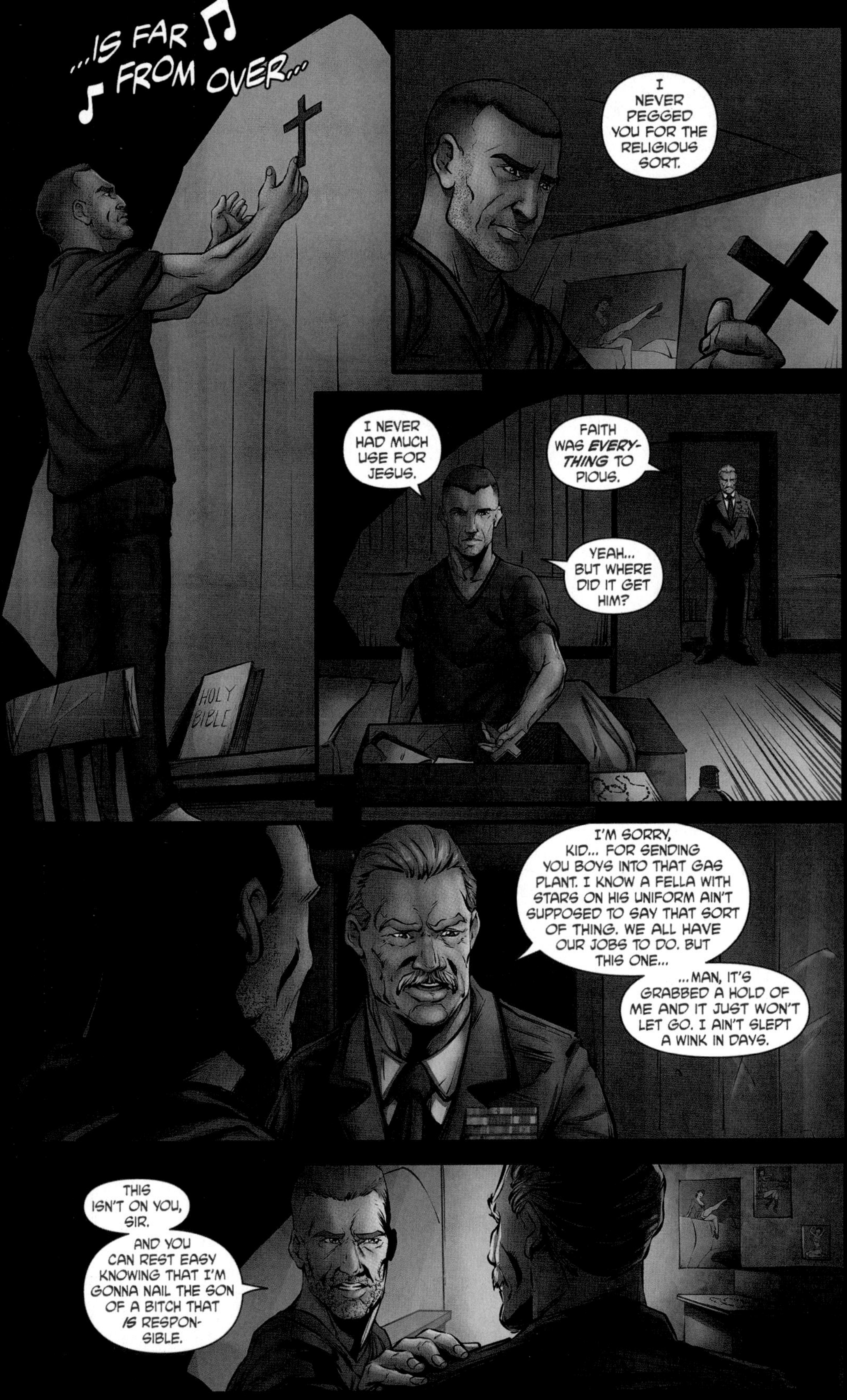
...IS FAR FROM OVER...
I NEVER PEGGED YOU FOR THE RELIGIOUS SORT.
I NEVER HAD MUCH USE FOR JESUS.
FAITH WAS EVERY-THING TO PIOUS.
YEAH... BUT WHERE DID IT GET HIM?
HOLY BIBLE
I'M SORRY, KID... FOR SENDING YOU BOYS INTO THAT GAS PLANT. I KNOW A FELLA WITH STARS ON HIS UNIFORM AIN'T SUPPOSED TO SAY THAT SORT OF THING. WE ALL HAVE OUR JOBS TO DO. BUT THIS ONE...
...MAN, IT'S GRABBED A HOLD OF ME AND IT JUST WON'T LET GO. I AIN'T SLEPT A WINK IN DAYS.
THIS ISN'T ON YOU, SIR.
AND YOU CAN REST EASY KNOWING THAT I'M GONNA NAIL THE SON OF A BITCH THAT IS RESPON-SIBLE.

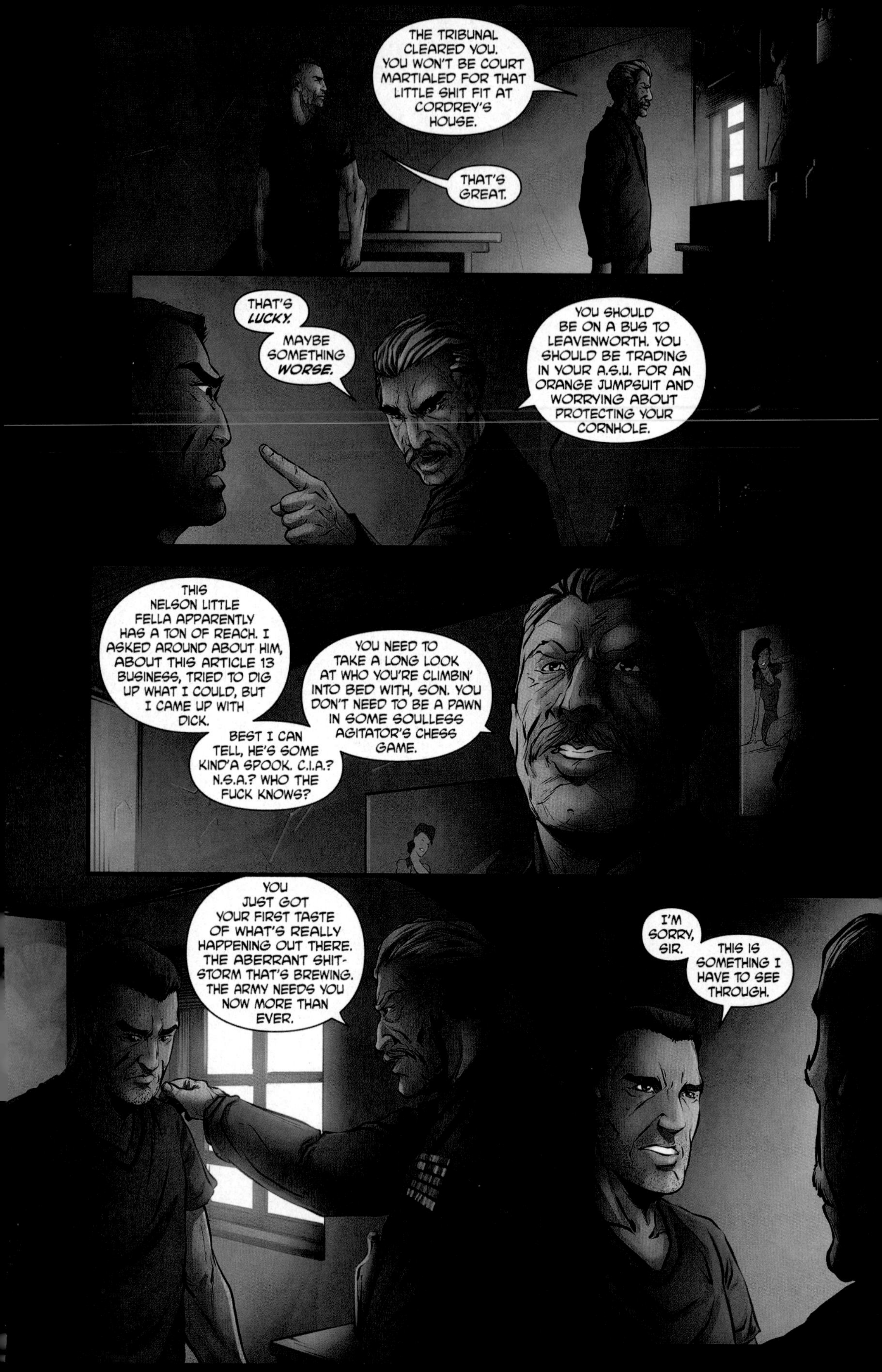
THE TRIBUNAL CLEARED YOU. YOU WON'T BE COURT MARTIALED FOR THAT LITTLE SHIT FIT AT CORDREY'S HOUSE.
THAT'S GREAT.
THAT'S *LUCKY.*
MAYBE SOMETHING *WORSE.*
YOU SHOULD BE ON A BUS TO LEAVENWORTH. YOU SHOULD BE TRADING IN YOUR A.S.U. FOR AN ORANGE JUMPSUIT AND WORRYING ABOUT PROTECTING YOUR CORNHOLE.
THIS NELSON LITTLE FELLA APPARENTLY HAS A TON OF REACH. I ASKED AROUND ABOUT HIM, ABOUT THIS ARTICLE 13 BUSINESS, TRIED TO DIG UP WHAT I COULD, BUT I CAME UP WITH DICK.
BEST I CAN TELL, HE'S SOME KIND'A SPOOK. C.I.A.? N.S.A.? WHO THE FUCK KNOWS?
YOU NEED TO TAKE A LONG LOOK AT WHO YOU'RE CLIMBIN' INTO BED WITH, SON. YOU DON'T NEED TO BE A PAWN IN SOME SOULLESS AGITATOR'S CHESS GAME.
YOU JUST GOT YOUR FIRST TASTE OF WHAT'S REALLY HAPPENING OUT THERE. THE ABERRANT SHIT-STORM THAT'S BREWING. THE ARMY NEEDS YOU NOW MORE THAN EVER.
I'M SORRY, SIR.
THIS IS SOMETHING I HAVE TO SEE THROUGH.

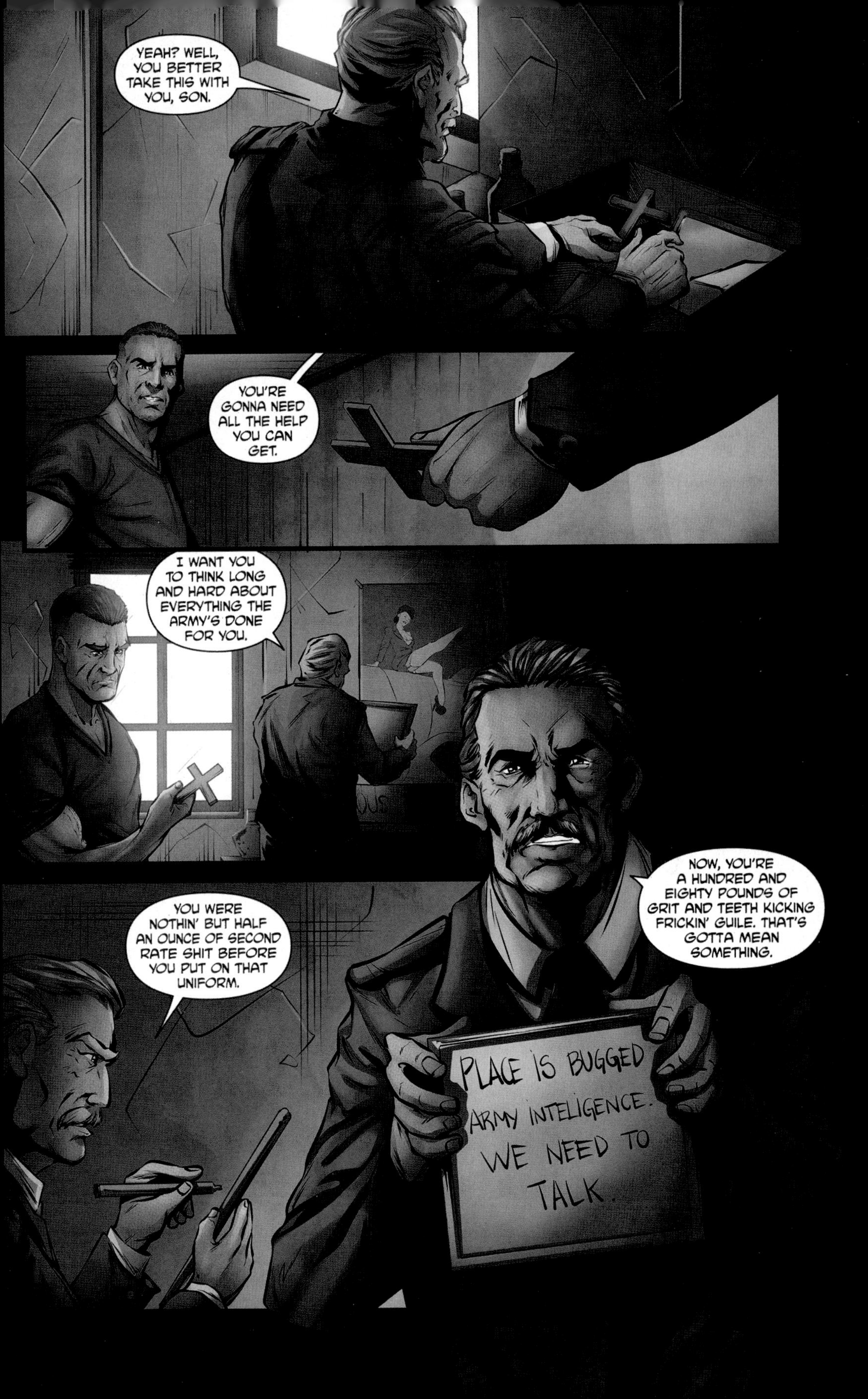
YEAH? WELL, YOU BETTER TAKE THIS WITH YOU, SON.
YOU'RE GONNA NEED ALL THE HELP YOU CAN GET.
I WANT YOU TO THINK LONG AND HARD ABOUT EVERYTHING THE ARMY'S DONE FOR YOU.
NOW, YOU'RE A HUNDRED AND EIGHTY POUNDS OF GRIT AND TEETH KICKING FRICKIN' GUILE. THAT'S GOTTA MEAN SOMETHING.
YOU WERE NOTHIN' BUT HALF AN OUNCE OF SECOND RATE SHIT BEFORE YOU PUT ON THAT UNIFORM.
PLACE IS BUGGED
ARMY INTELIGENCE.
WE NEED TO TALK.

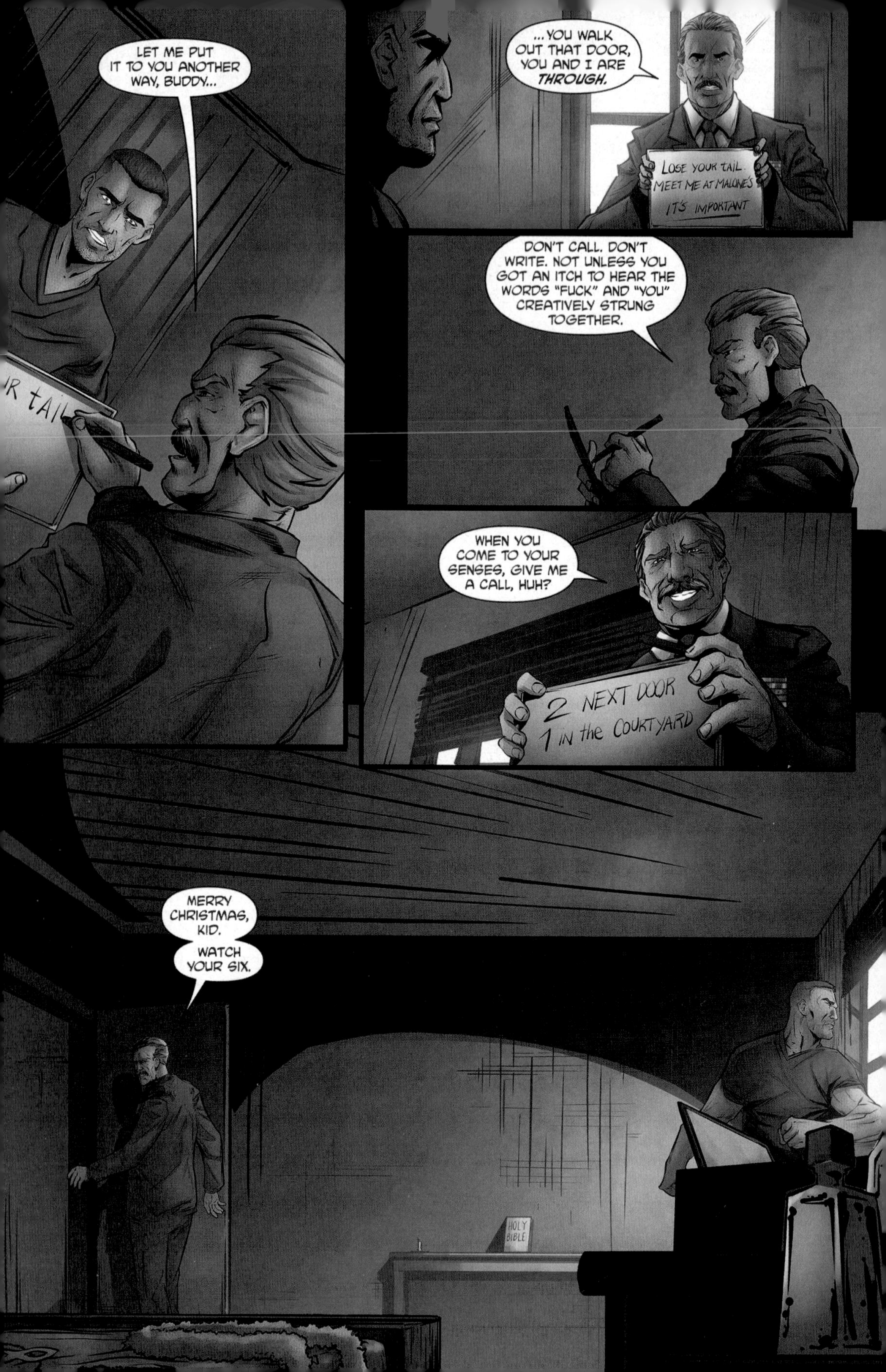
LET ME PUT IT TO YOU ANOTHER WAY, BUDDY...
...YOU WALK OUT THAT DOOR, YOU AND I ARE THROUGH.
LOSE YOUR TAIL. MEET ME AT MALONE'S IT'S IMPORTANT
DON'T CALL. DON'T WRITE. NOT UNLESS YOU GOT AN ITCH TO HEAR THE WORDS "FUCK" AND "YOU" CREATIVELY STRUNG TOGETHER.
WHEN YOU COME TO YOUR SENSES, GIVE ME A CALL, HUH?
2 NEXT DOOR 1 in the COURTYARD
MERRY CHRISTMAS, KID.
WATCH YOUR SIX.
HOLY BIBLE

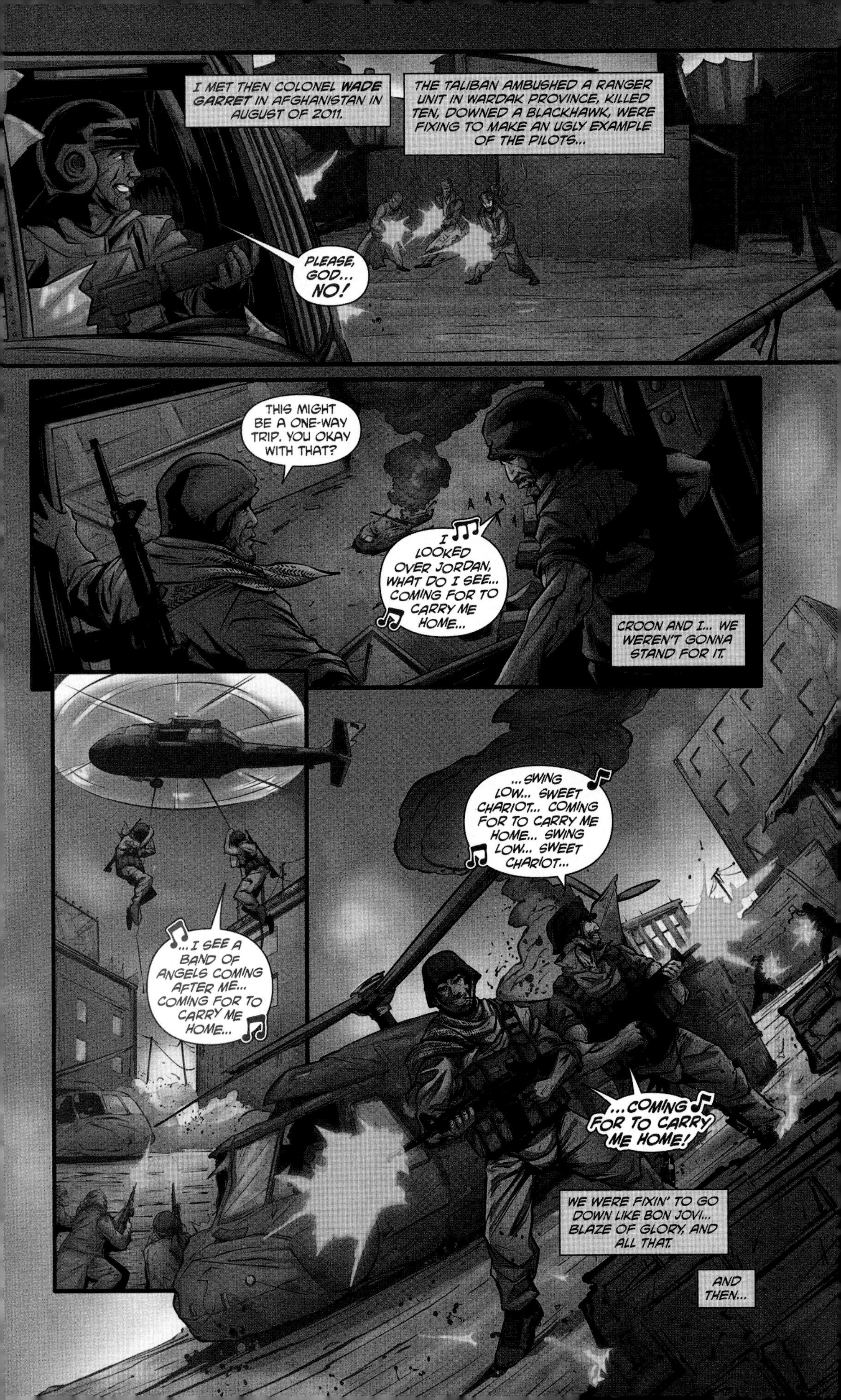

I MET THEN COLONEL WADE GARRET IN AFGHANISTAN IN AUGUST OF 2011.
THE TALIBAN AMBUSHED A RANGER UNIT IN WARDAK PROVINCE, KILLED TEN, DOWNED A BLACKHAWK, WERE FIXING TO MAKE AN UGLY EXAMPLE OF THE PILOTS...
PLEASE, GOD... NO!
THIS MIGHT BE A ONE-WAY TRIP. YOU OKAY WITH THAT?
I LOOKED OVER JORDAN, WHAT DO I SEE... COMING FOR TO CARRY ME HOME...
CROON AND I... WE WEREN'T GONNA STAND FOR IT.
...I SEE A BAND OF ANGELS COMING AFTER ME... COMING FOR TO CARRY ME HOME...
...SWING LOW... SWEET CHARIOT... COMING FOR TO CARRY ME HOME... SWING LOW... SWEET CHARIOT...
...COMING FOR TO CARRY ME HOME!
WE WERE FIXIN' TO GO DOWN LIKE BON JOVI... BLAZE OF GLORY, AND ALL THAT.
AND THEN...

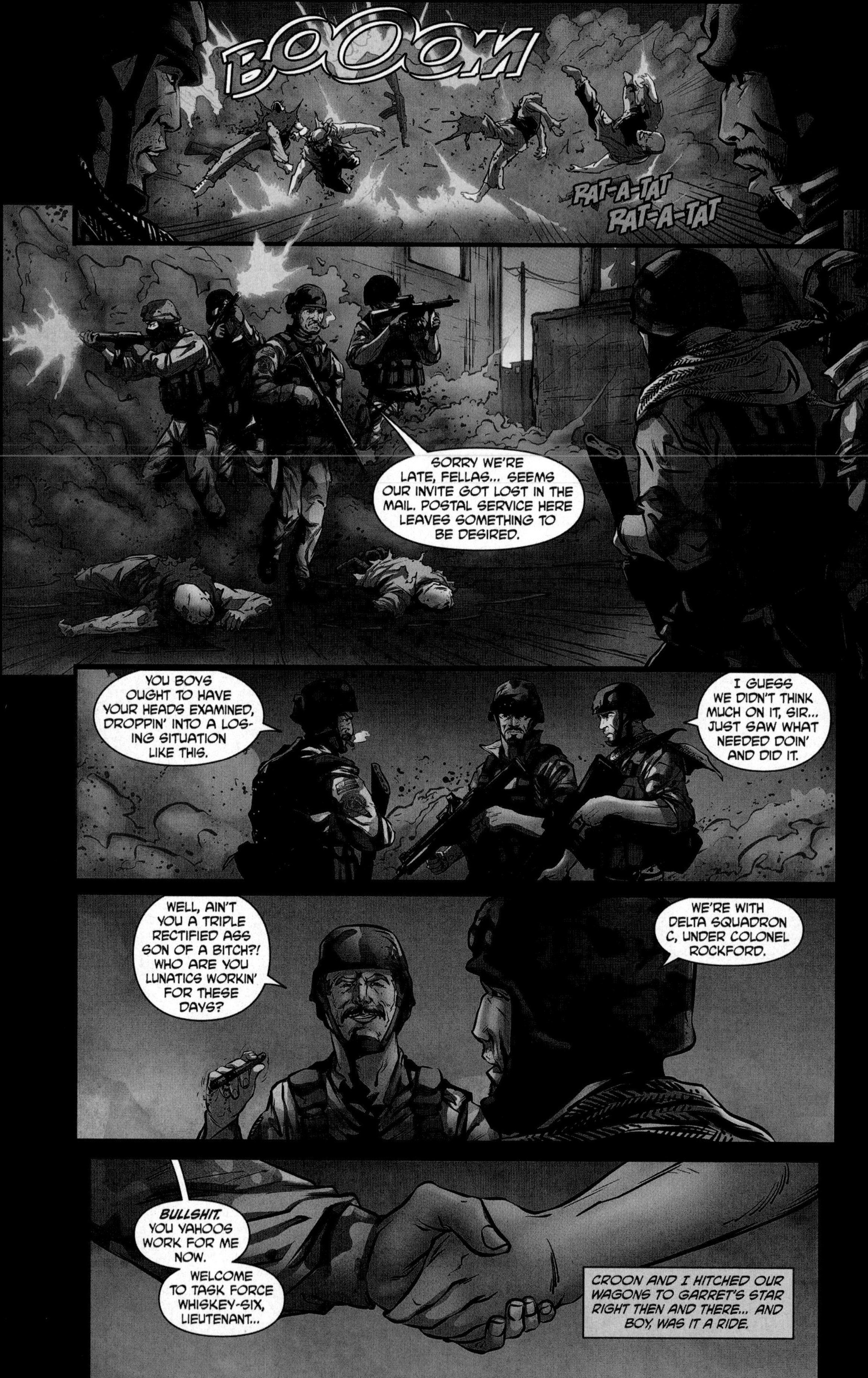
BOOOOM
RAT-A-TAT
RAT-A-TAT
SORRY WE'RE LATE, FELLAS... SEEMS OUR INVITE GOT LOST IN THE MAIL. POSTAL SERVICE HERE LEAVES SOMETHING TO BE DESIRED.
YOU BOYS OUGHT TO HAVE YOUR HEADS EXAMINED, DROPPIN' INTO A LOSING SITUATION LIKE THIS.
I GUESS WE DIDN'T THINK MUCH ON IT, SIR... JUST SAW WHAT NEEDED DOIN' AND DID IT.
WELL, AIN'T YOU A TRIPLE RECTIFIED ASS SON OF A BITCH?! WHO ARE YOU LUNATICS WORKIN' FOR THESE DAYS?
WE'RE WITH DELTA SQUADRON C, UNDER COLONEL ROCKFORD.
BULLSHIT. YOU YAHOOS WORK FOR ME NOW.
WELCOME TO TASK FORCE WHISKEY-SIX, LIEUTENANT...
CROON AND I HITCHED OUR WAGONS TO GARRET'S STAR RIGHT THEN AND THERE... AND BOY, WAS IT A RIDE.

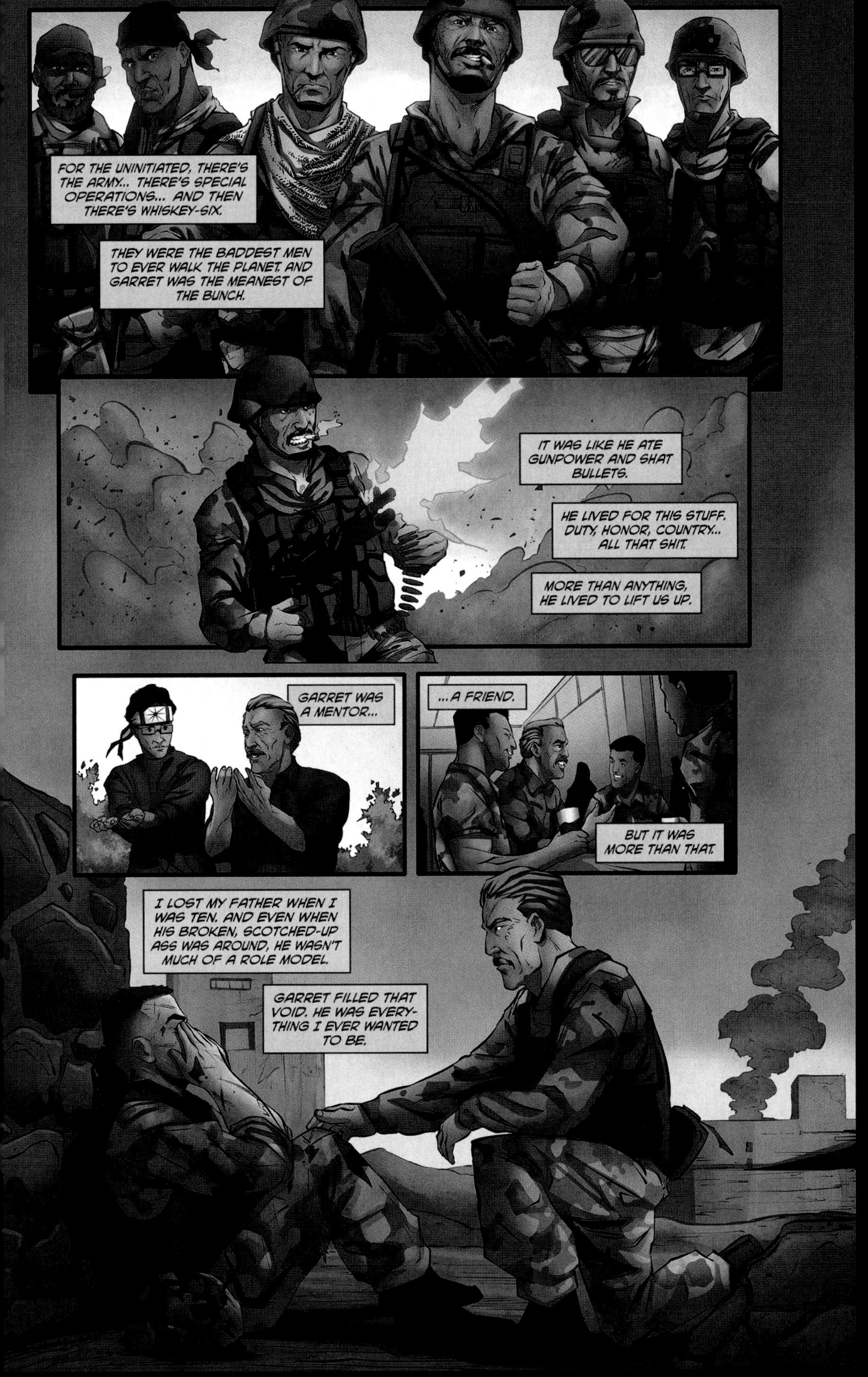
FOR THE UNINITIATED, THERE'S THE ARMY... THERE'S SPECIAL OPERATIONS... AND THEN THERE'S WHISKEY-SIX.
THEY WERE THE BADDEST MEN TO EVER WALK THE PLANET. AND GARRET WAS THE MEANEST OF THE BUNCH.
IT WAS LIKE HE ATE GUNPOWER AND SHAT BULLETS.
HE LIVED FOR THIS STUFF. DUTY, HONOR, COUNTRY... ALL THAT SHIT.
MORE THAN ANYTHING, HE LIVED TO LIFT US UP.
GARRET WAS A MENTOR...
...A FRIEND.
BUT IT WAS MORE THAN THAT.
I LOST MY FATHER WHEN I WAS TEN. AND EVEN WHEN HIS BROKEN, SCOTCHED-UP ASS WAS AROUND, HE WASN'T MUCH OF A ROLE MODEL.
GARRET FILLED THAT VOID. HE WAS EVERY-THING I EVER WANTED TO BE.

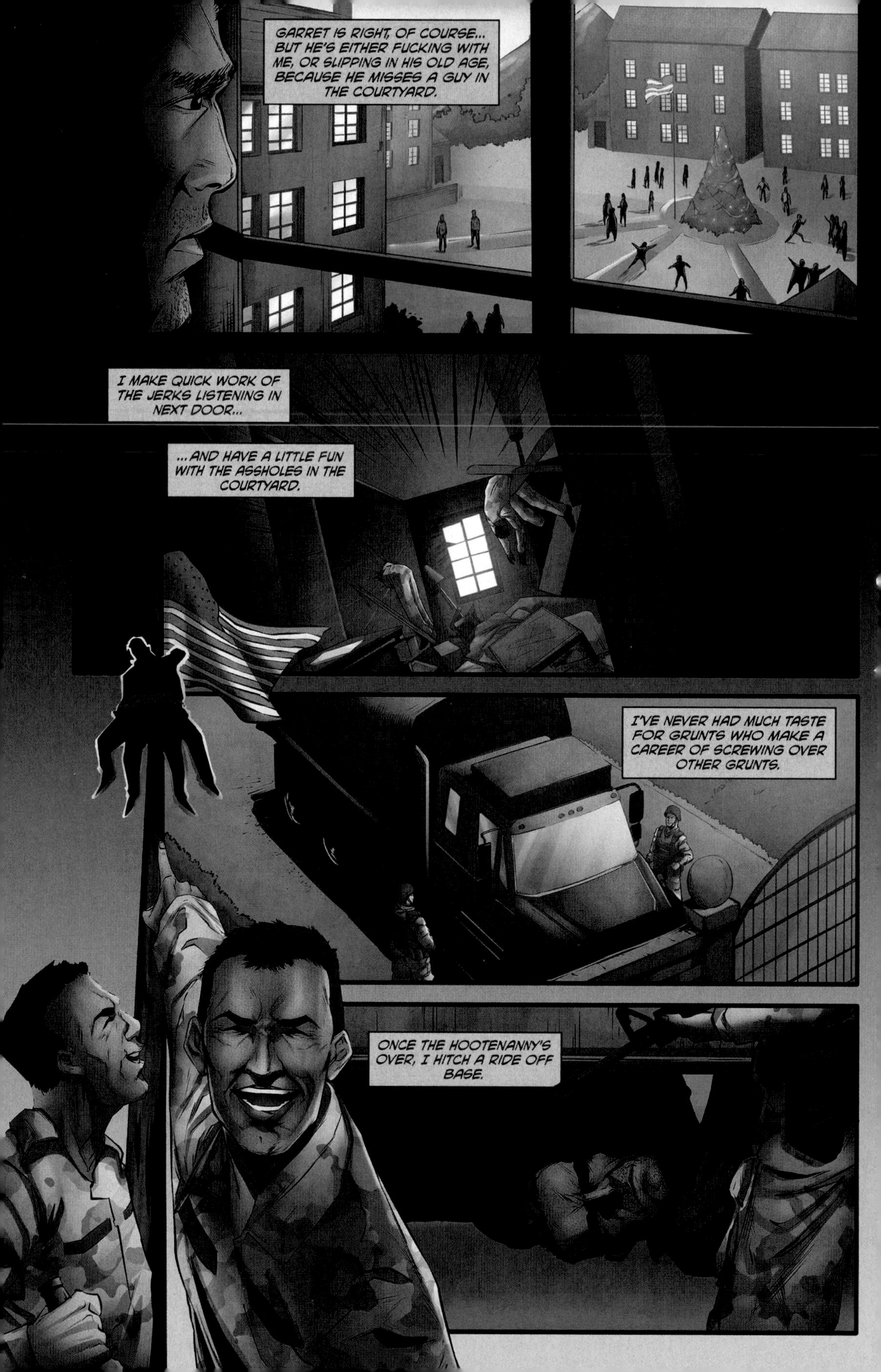
GARRET IS RIGHT, OF COURSE... BUT HE'S EITHER FUCKING WITH ME, OR SLIPPING IN HIS OLD AGE, BECAUSE HE MISSES A GUY IN THE COURTYARD.
I MAKE QUICK WORK OF THE JERKS LISTENING IN NEXT DOOR...
...AND HAVE A LITTLE FUN WITH THE ASSHOLES IN THE COURTYARD.
I'VE NEVER HAD MUCH TASTE FOR GRUNTS WHO MAKE A CAREER OF SCREWING OVER OTHER GRUNTS.
ONCE THE HOOTENANNY'S OVER, I HITCH A RIDE OFF BASE.

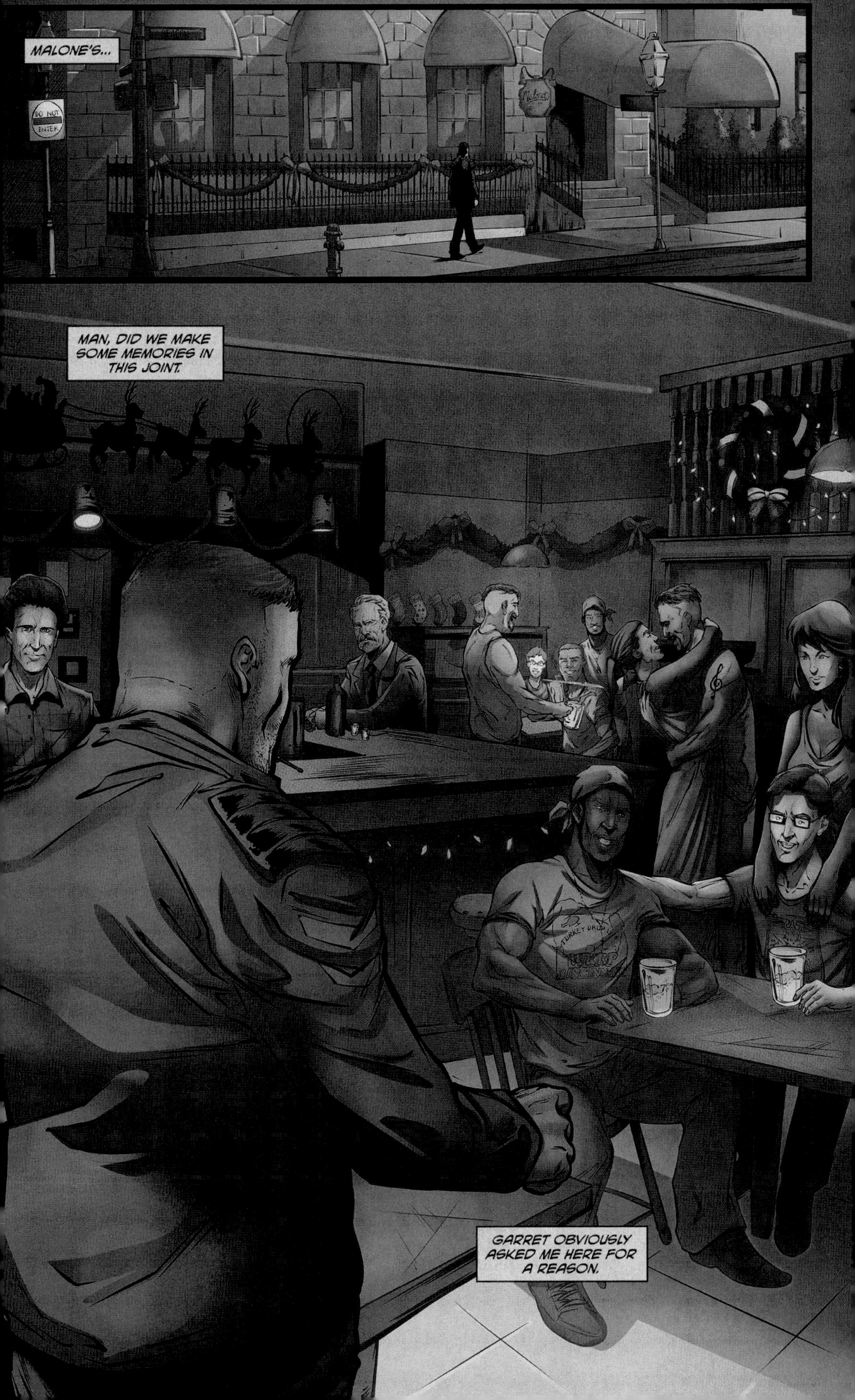
MALONE'S...
DO NOT ENTER
MAN, DID WE MAKE SOME MEMORIES IN THIS JOINT.
GARRET OBVIOUSLY ASKED ME HERE FOR A REASON.

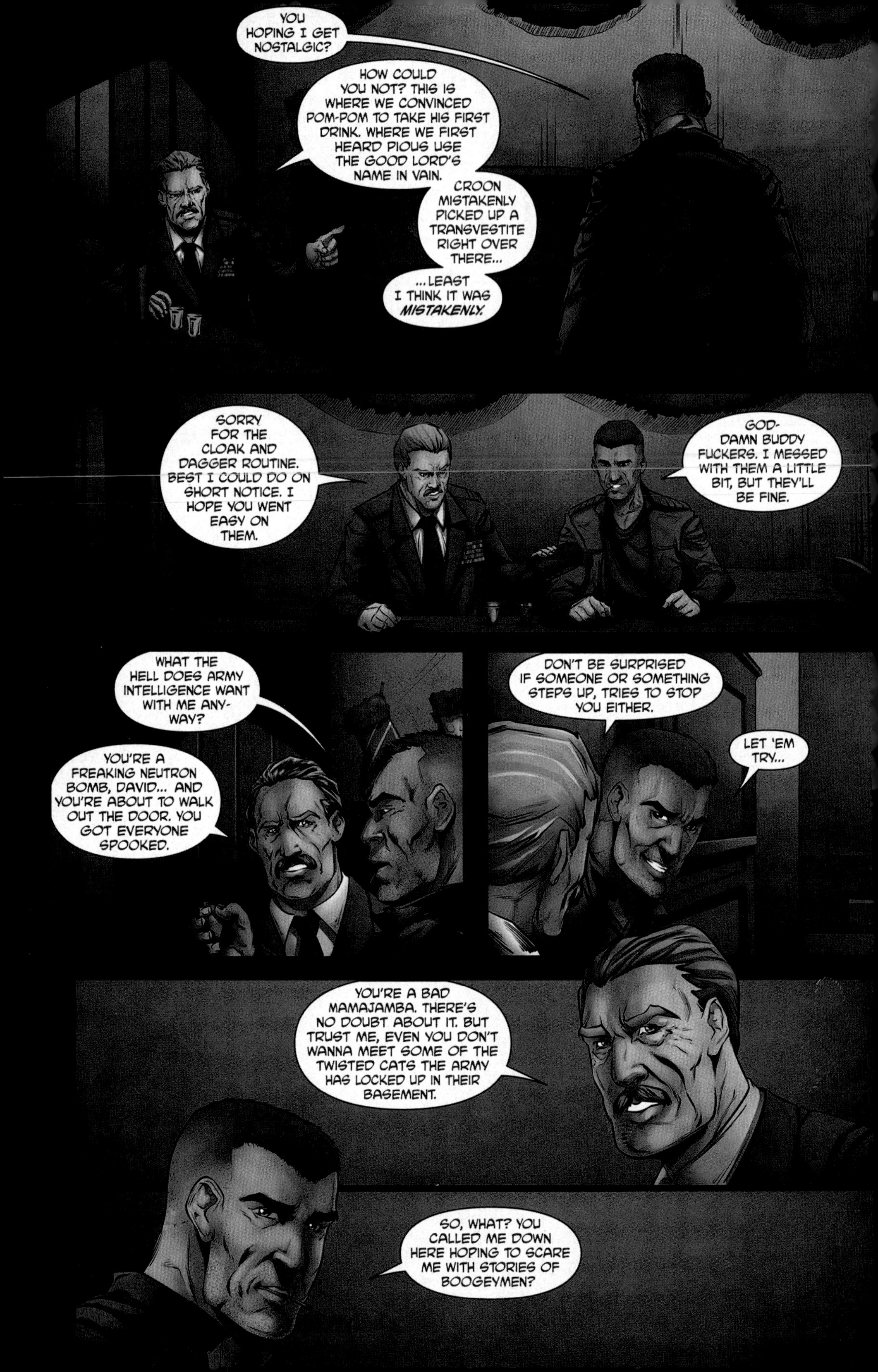
YOU HOPING I GET NOSTALGIC?
HOW COULD YOU NOT? THIS IS WHERE WE CONVINCED POM-POM TO TAKE HIS FIRST DRINK. WHERE WE FIRST HEARD PIOUS USE THE GOOD LORD'S NAME IN VAIN.
CROON MISTAKENLY PICKED UP A TRANSVESTITE RIGHT OVER THERE...
...LEAST I THINK IT WAS *MISTAKENLY.*
SORRY FOR THE CLOAK AND DAGGER ROUTINE. BEST I COULD DO ON SHORT NOTICE. I HOPE YOU WENT EASY ON THEM.
GOD-DAMN BUDDY FUCKERS. I MESSED WITH THEM A LITTLE BIT, BUT THEY'LL BE FINE.
WHAT THE HELL DOES ARMY INTELLIGENCE WANT WITH ME ANY-WAY?
YOU'RE A FREAKING NEUTRON BOMB, DAVID... AND YOU'RE ABOUT TO WALK OUT THE DOOR. YOU GOT EVERYONE SPOOKED.
DON'T BE SURPRISED IF SOMEONE OR SOMETHING STEPS UP, TRIES TO STOP YOU EITHER.
LET 'EM TRY...
YOU'RE A BAD MAMAJAMBA. THERE'S NO DOUBT ABOUT IT. BUT TRUST ME, EVEN YOU DON'T WANNA MEET SOME OF THE TWISTED CATS THE ARMY HAS LOCKED UP IN THEIR BASEMENT.
SO, WHAT? YOU CALLED ME DOWN HERE HOPING TO SCARE ME WITH STORIES OF BOOGEYMEN?

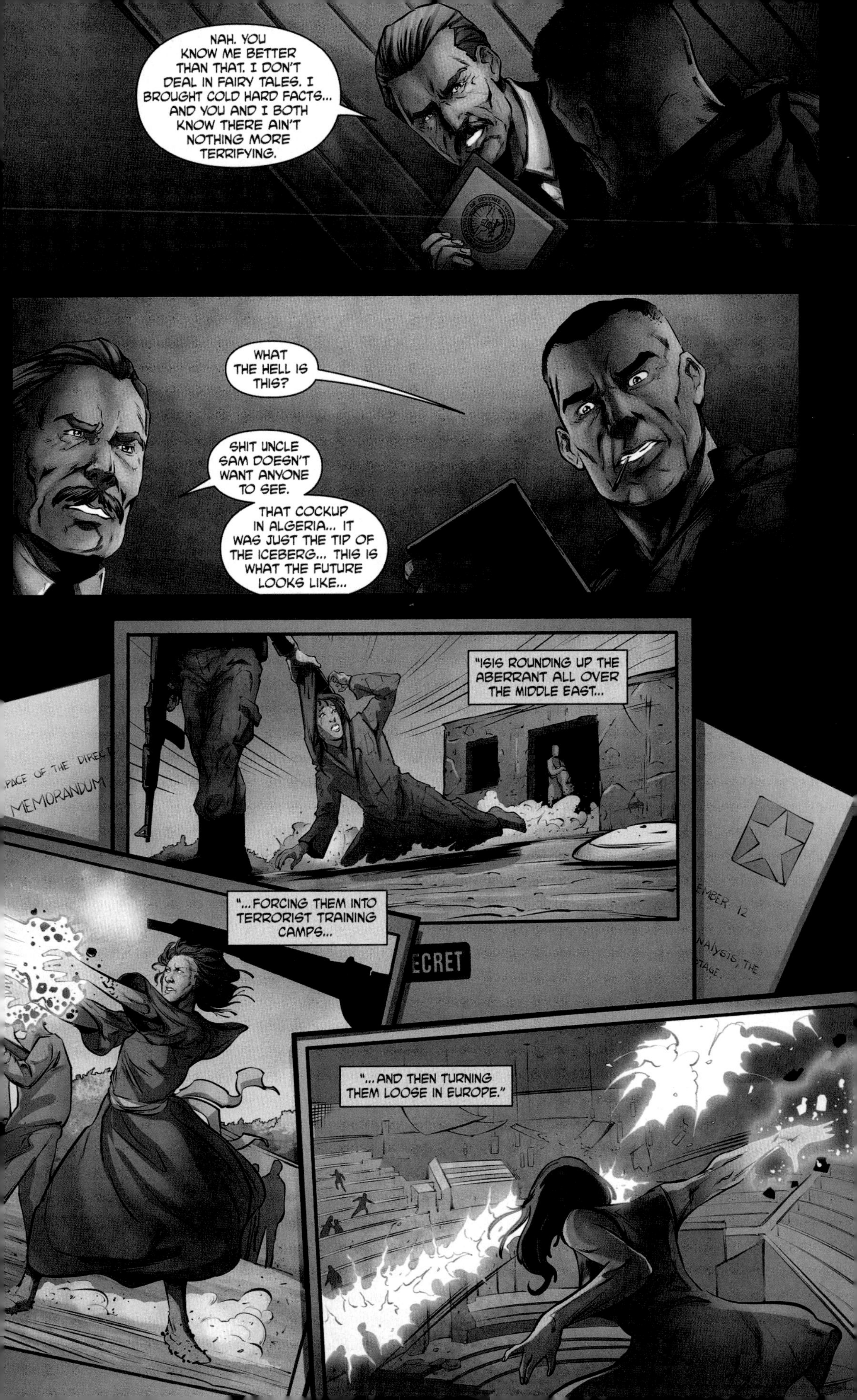
NAH. YOU KNOW ME BETTER THAN THAT. I DON'T DEAL IN FAIRY TALES. I BROUGHT COLD HARD FACTS... AND YOU AND I BOTH KNOW THERE AIN'T NOTHING MORE TERRIFYING.
WHAT THE HELL IS THIS?
SHIT UNCLE SAM DOESN'T WANT ANYONE TO SEE.
THAT COCKUP IN ALGERIA... IT WAS JUST THE TIP OF THE ICEBERG... THIS IS WHAT THE FUTURE LOOKS LIKE...
"ISIS ROUNDING UP THE ABERRANT ALL OVER THE MIDDLE EAST...
MEMORANDUM
"...FORCING THEM INTO TERRORIST TRAINING CAMPS...
"...AND THEN TURNING THEM LOOSE IN EUROPE."

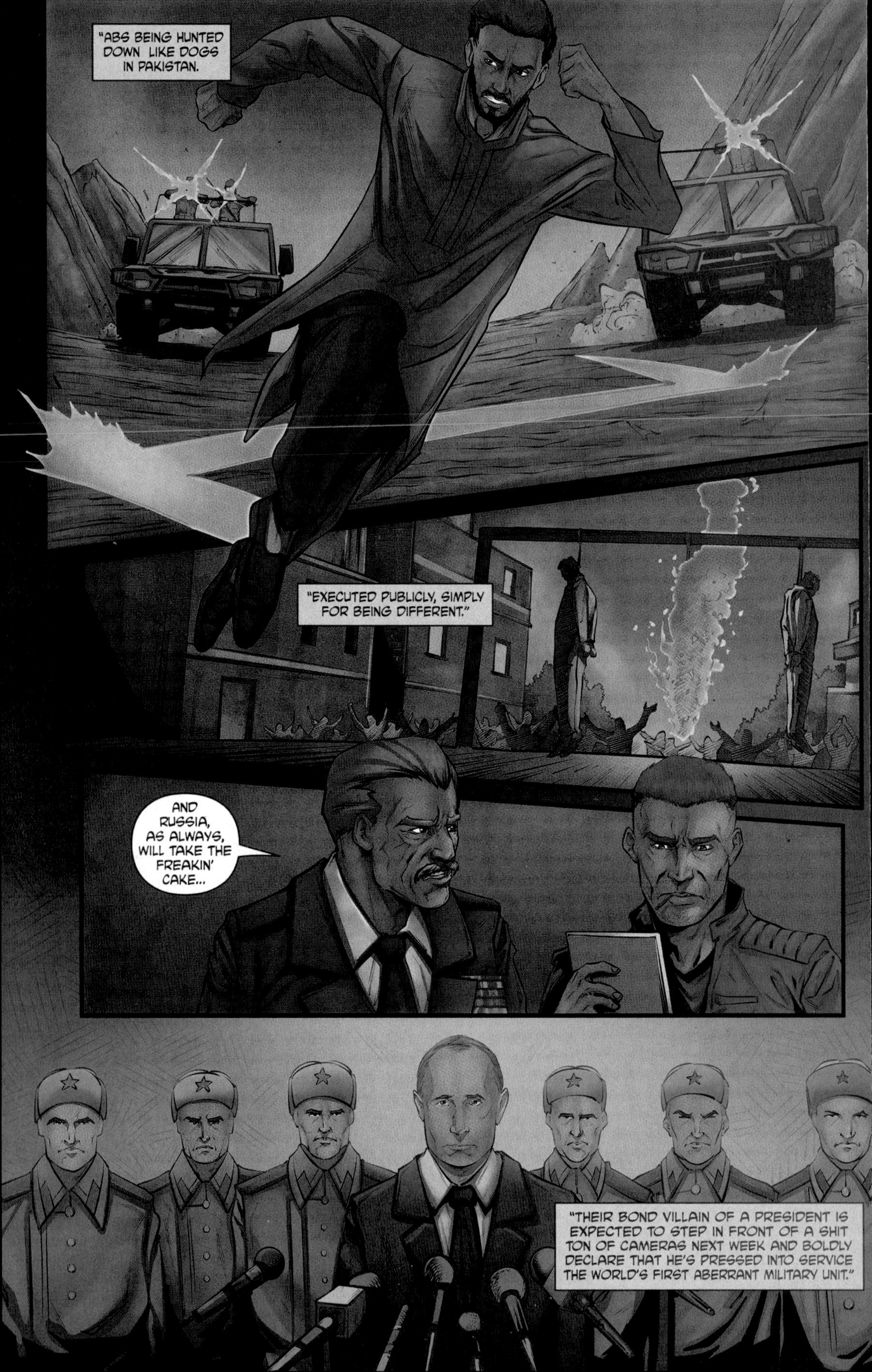
"ABS BEING HUNTED DOWN LIKE DOGS IN PAKISTAN.
"EXECUTED PUBLICLY, SIMPLY FOR BEING DIFFERENT."
AND RUSSIA, AS ALWAYS, WILL TAKE THE FREAKIN' CAKE...
"THEIR BOND VILLAIN OF A PRESIDENT IS EXPECTED TO STEP IN FRONT OF A SHIT TON OF CAMERAS NEXT WEEK AND BOLDLY DECLARE THAT HE'S PRESSED INTO SERVICE THE WORLD'S FIRST ABERRANT MILITARY UNIT."

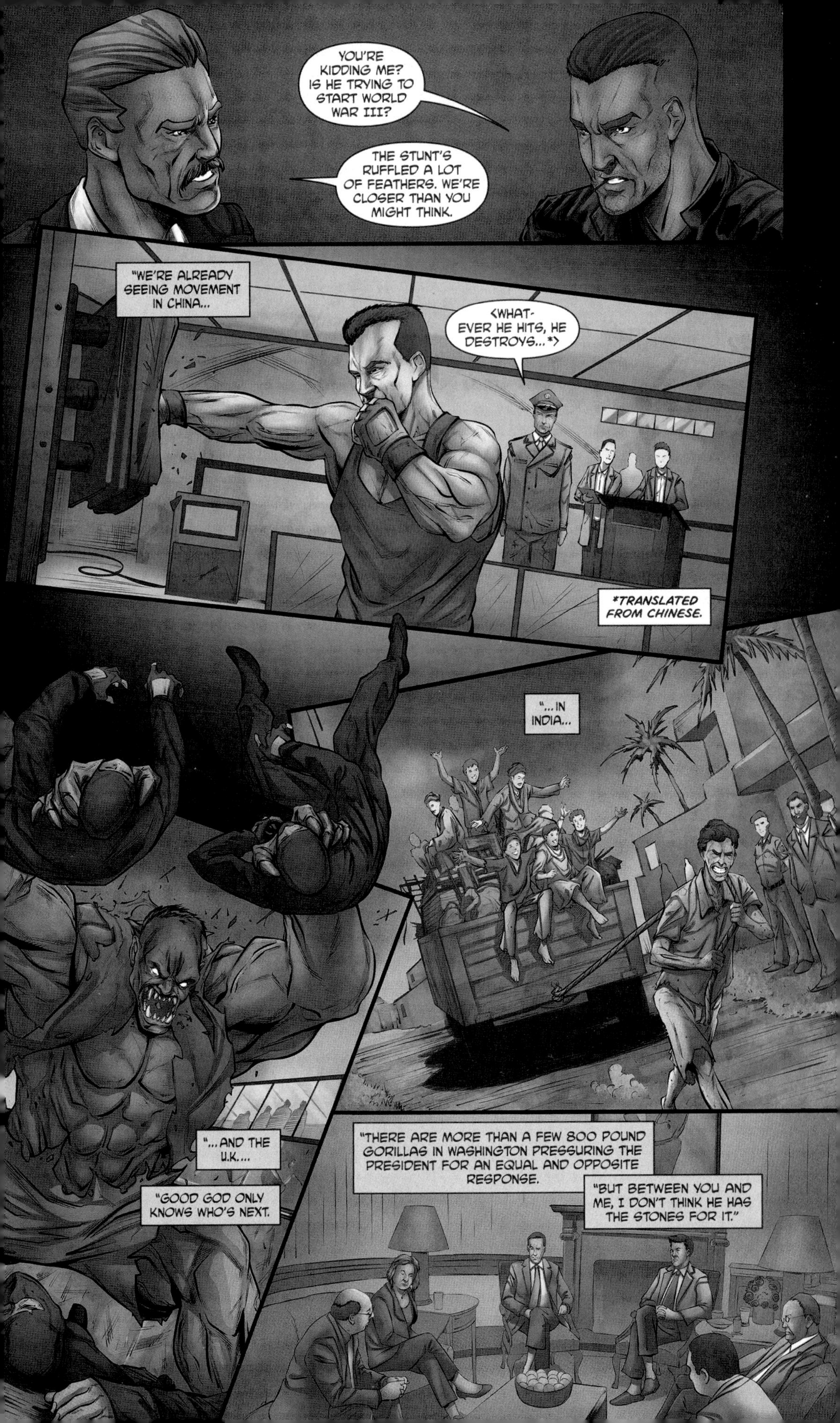
YOU'RE KIDDING ME? IS HE TRYING TO START WORLD WAR III?
THE STUNT'S RUFFLED A LOT OF FEATHERS. WE'RE CLOSER THAN YOU MIGHT THINK.
"WE'RE ALREADY SEEING MOVEMENT IN CHINA...
<WHAT-EVER HE HITS, HE DESTROYS...*>
*TRANSLATED FROM CHINESE.
"...IN INDIA...
"...AND THE U.K....
"GOOD GOD ONLY KNOWS WHO'S NEXT.
"THERE ARE MORE THAN A FEW 800 POUND GORILLAS IN WASHINGTON PRESSURING THE PRESIDENT FOR AN EQUAL AND OPPOSITE RESPONSE.
"BUT BETWEEN YOU AND ME, I DON'T THINK HE HAS THE STONES FOR IT."

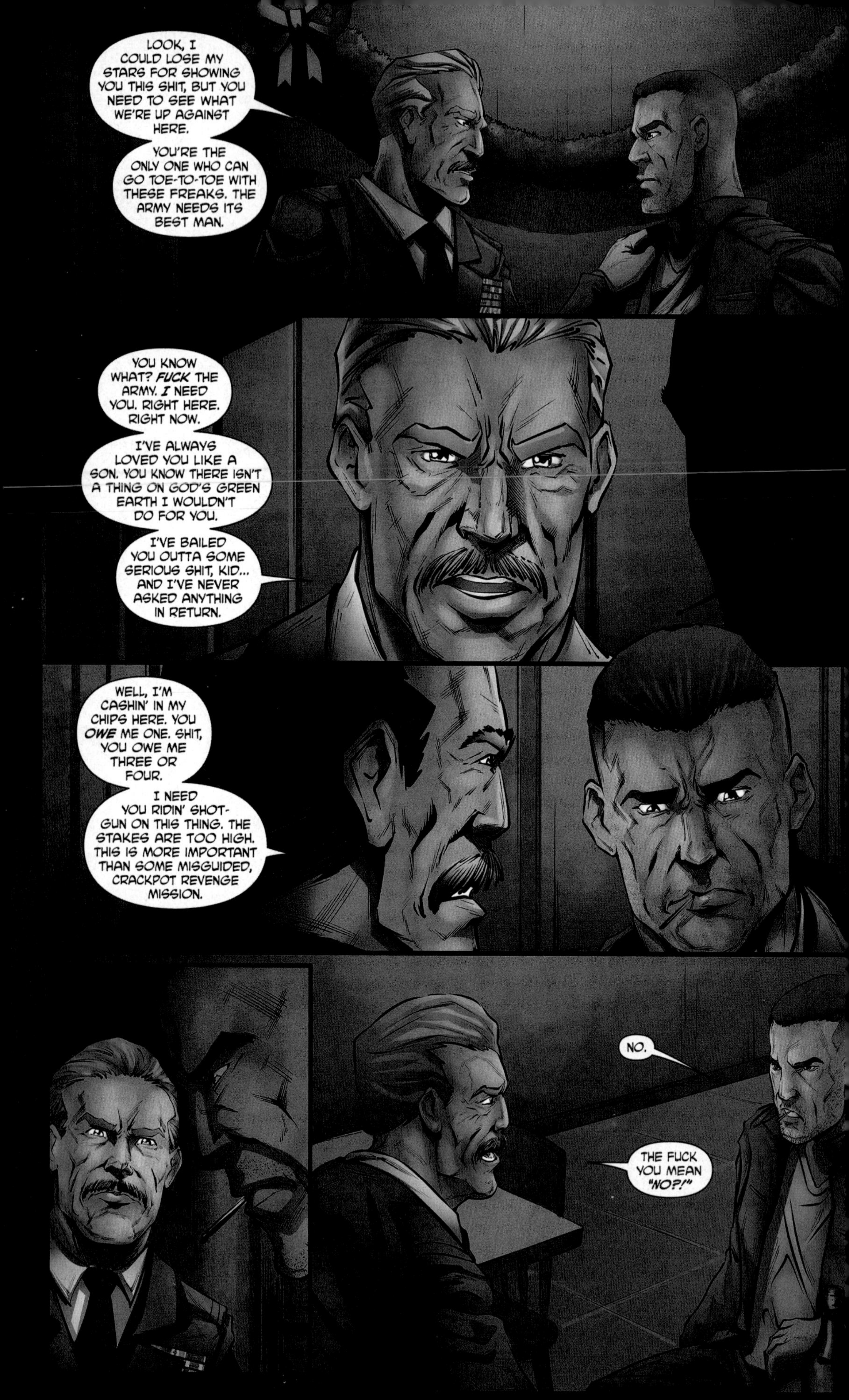
LOOK, I COULD LOSE MY STARS FOR SHOWING YOU THIS SHIT, BUT YOU NEED TO SEE WHAT WE'RE UP AGAINST HERE.
YOU'RE THE ONLY ONE WHO CAN GO TOE-TO-TOE WITH THESE FREAKS. THE ARMY NEEDS ITS BEST MAN.
YOU KNOW WHAT? FUCK THE ARMY. I NEED YOU. RIGHT HERE. RIGHT NOW.
I'VE ALWAYS LOVED YOU LIKE A SON. YOU KNOW THERE ISN'T A THING ON GOD'S GREEN EARTH I WOULDN'T DO FOR YOU.
I'VE BAILED YOU OUTTA SOME SERIOUS SHIT, KID... AND I'VE NEVER ASKED ANYTHING IN RETURN.
WELL, I'M CASHIN' IN MY CHIPS HERE. YOU OWE ME ONE. SHIT, YOU OWE ME THREE OR FOUR.
I NEED YOU RIDIN' SHOT-GUN ON THIS THING. THE STAKES ARE TOO HIGH. THIS IS MORE IMPORTANT THAN SOME MISGUIDED, CRACKPOT REVENGE MISSION.
NO.
THE FUCK YOU MEAN "NO?!"

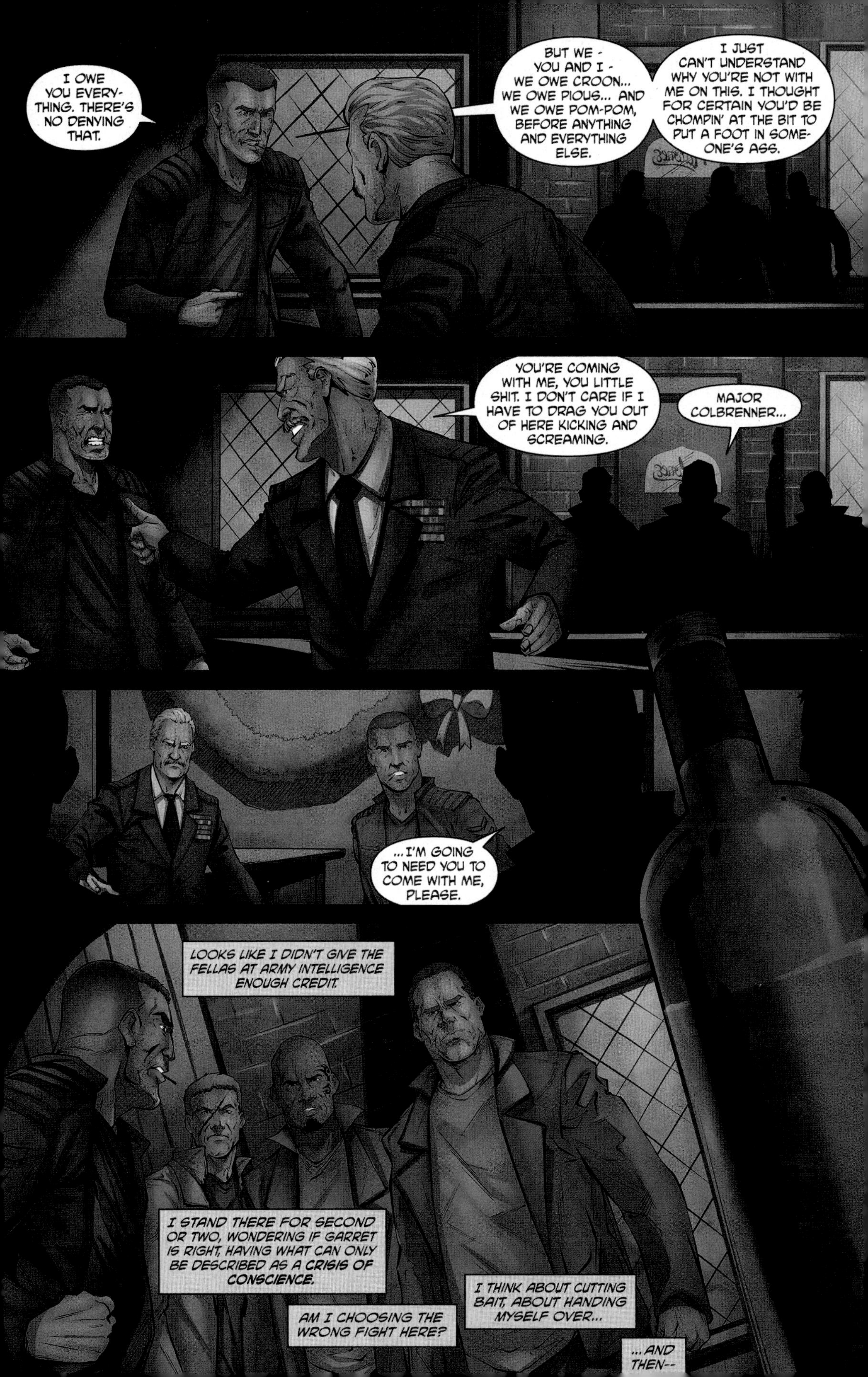
I OWE YOU EVERYTHING. THERE'S NO DENYING THAT.
BUT WE - YOU AND I - WE OWE CROON... WE OWE PIOUS... AND WE OWE POM-POM, BEFORE ANYTHING AND EVERYTHING ELSE.
I JUST CAN'T UNDERSTAND WHY YOU'RE NOT WITH ME ON THIS. I THOUGHT FOR CERTAIN YOU'D BE CHOMPIN' AT THE BIT TO PUT A FOOT IN SOMEONE'S ASS.
YOU'RE COMING WITH ME, YOU LITTLE SHIT. I DON'T CARE IF I HAVE TO DRAG YOU OUT OF HERE KICKING AND SCREAMING.
MAJOR COLBRENNER...
...I'M GOING TO NEED YOU TO COME WITH ME, PLEASE.
LOOKS LIKE I DIDN'T GIVE THE FELLAS AT ARMY INTELLIGENCE ENOUGH CREDIT.
I STAND THERE FOR SECOND OR TWO, WONDERING IF GARRET IS RIGHT, HAVING WHAT CAN ONLY BE DESCRIBED AS A CRISIS OF CONSCIENCE.
AM I CHOOSING THE WRONG FIGHT HERE?
I THINK ABOUT CUTTING BAIT, ABOUT HANDING MYSELF OVER...
...AND THEN--

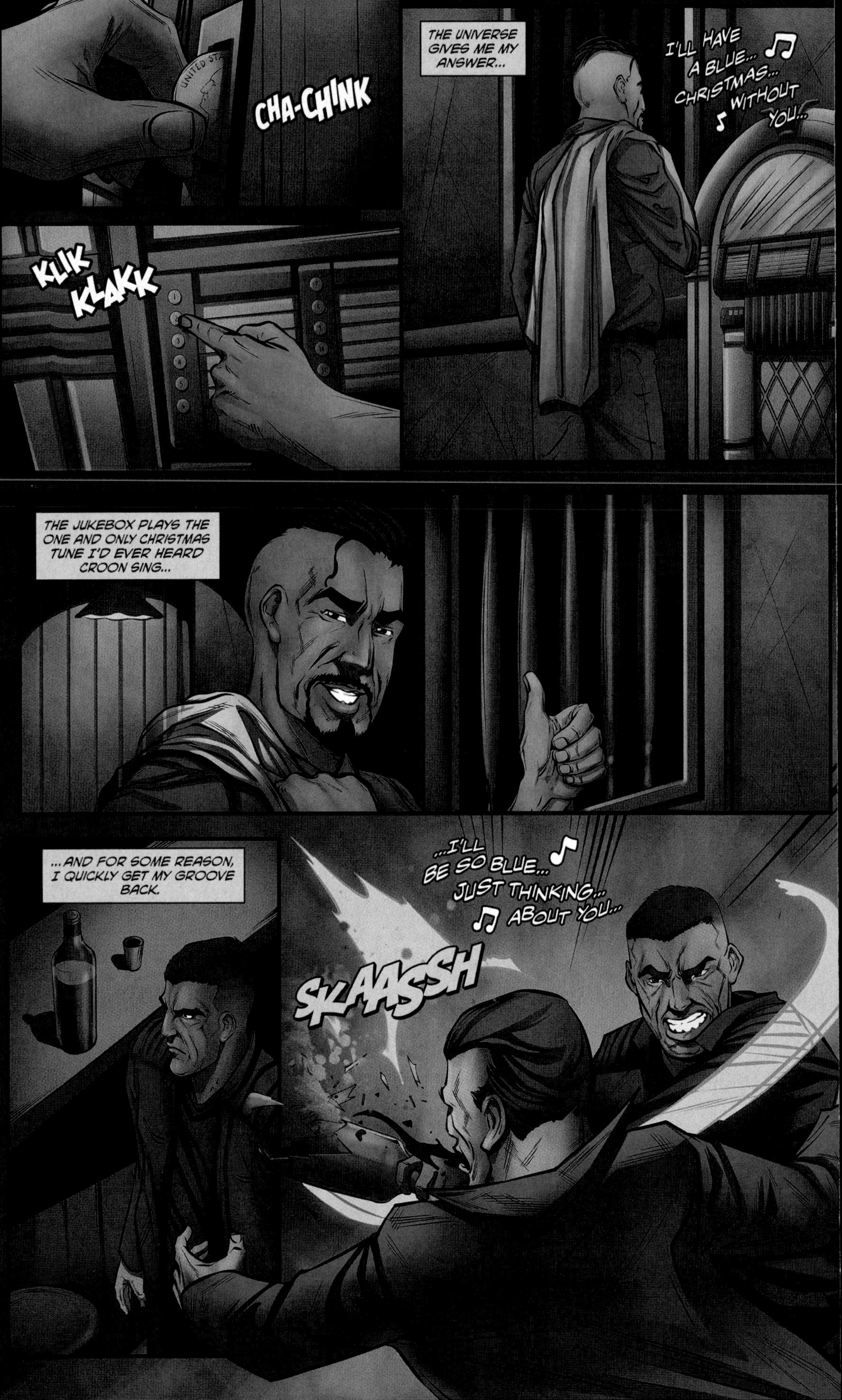
CHA-CHINK
THE UNIVERSE GIVES ME MY ANSWER...
I'LL HAVE A BLUE... CHRISTMAS... WITHOUT YOU...
KLIK KLAKK
THE JUKEBOX PLAYS THE ONE AND ONLY CHRISTMAS TUNE I'D EVER HEARD CROON SING...
...AND FOR SOME REASON, I QUICKLY GET MY GROOVE BACK.
...I'LL BE SO BLUE... JUST THINKING... ABOUT YOU...
SKAASSH

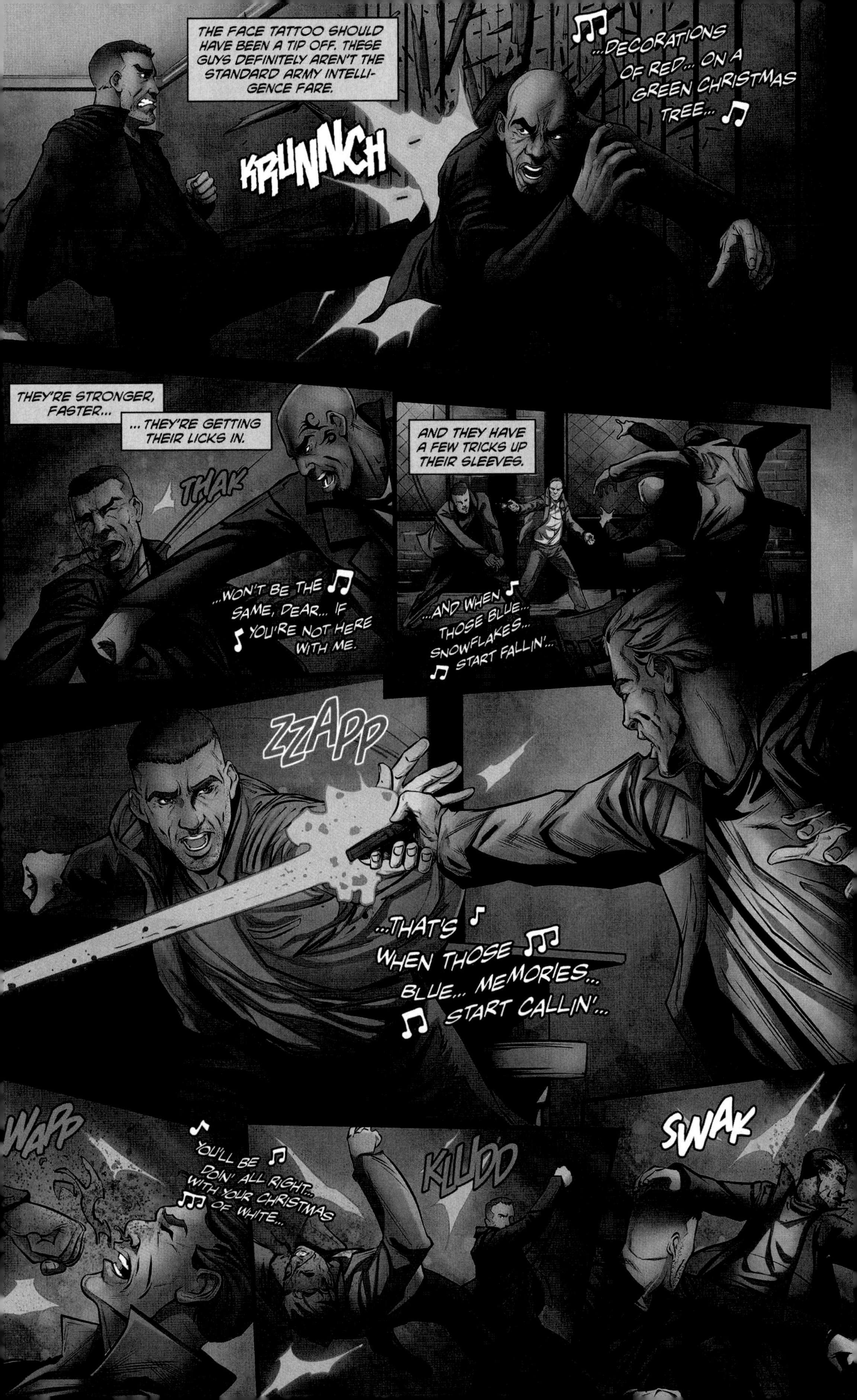
THE FACE TATTOO SHOULD HAVE BEEN A TIP OFF. THESE GUYS DEFINITELY AREN'T THE STANDARD ARMY INTELLIGENCE FARE.
♫ ...DECORATIONS OF RED... ON A GREEN CHRISTMAS TREE... ♫
KRUNNCH
THEY'RE STRONGER, FASTER...
...THEY'RE GETTING THEIR LICKS IN.
THAK
...WON'T BE THE ♫ SAME, DEAR... IF ♪ YOU'RE NOT HERE WITH ME.
AND THEY HAVE A FEW TRICKS UP THEIR SLEEVES.
...AND WHEN ♪ THOSE BLUE... SNOWFLAKES... ♫ START FALLIN'...
ZZAPP
...THAT'S ♪ WHEN THOSE ♫ BLUE... MEMORIES... ♫ START CALLIN'...
WAPP
♪ YOU'LL BE ♫ DOIN' ALL RIGHT... WITH YOUR CHRISTMAS ♫ OF WHITE...
KLUDD
SWAK

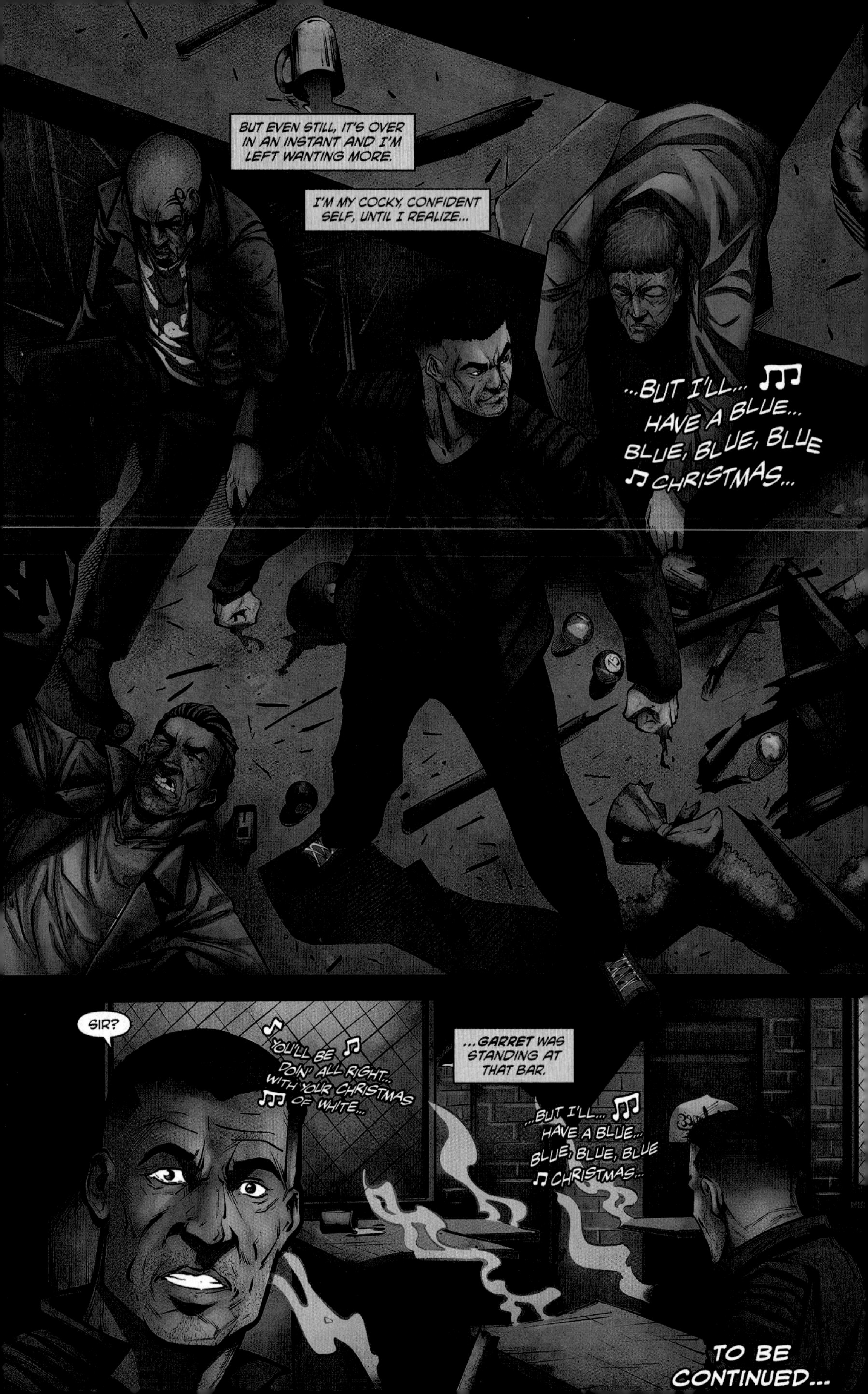
BUT EVEN STILL, IT'S OVER IN AN INSTANT AND I'M LEFT WANTING MORE.
I'M MY COCKY, CONFIDENT SELF, UNTIL I REALIZE...
...BUT I'LL... HAVE A BLUE... BLUE, BLUE, BLUE CHRISTMAS...
SIR?
YOU'LL BE DOIN' ALL RIGHT... WITH YOUR CHRISTMAS OF WHITE...
...GARRET WAS STANDING AT THAT BAR.
...BUT I'LL... HAVE A BLUE... BLUE, BLUE, BLUE CHRISTMAS...
TO BE CONTINUED...

Aberrant

GOT ABERRANT-RELATED RANTS, RAVES, FULMINATIONS, VOCIFERATIONS, INVECTIVES, OR OBLOQUIES? GOT FAN ART? KNOW WHERE JIMMY HOFFA IS BURIED? KNOW HOW IN THE HELL TUPAC KEEPS RELEASING ALBUMS?

SEND ALL BUSINESS FIT TO PRINT TO: HALFEVILCOMICS@GMAIL.COM

This Month's Music:

Blue Christmas
Words and Music by Bill Hayes and
Jay Johnson
Copyright © 1948 Universal - Polygram
International Publishing, Inc. and
Judy J. Olmstead Trust
Copyright Renewed
All Rights for Judy J. Olmstead Trust Controlled
and Administered by Lichelle Music Company
All Rights Reserved
Used by Permission
Reprinted by Permission of Hal Leonard LLC

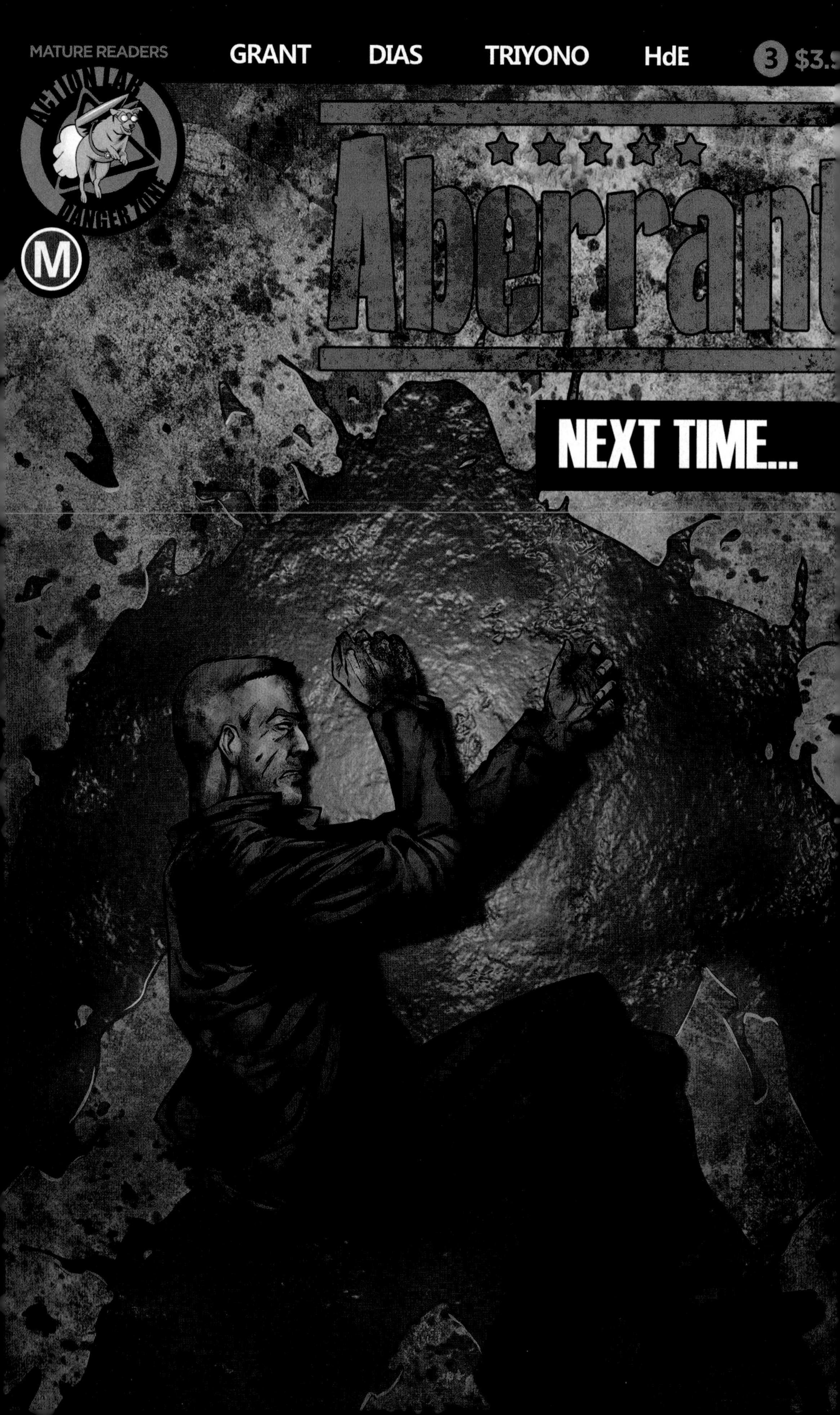
MATURE READERS
GRANT
DIAS
TRIYONO
HdE
3
ACTION LAB
DANGER ZONE
M
Aberrant
NEXT TIME...

Aberrant

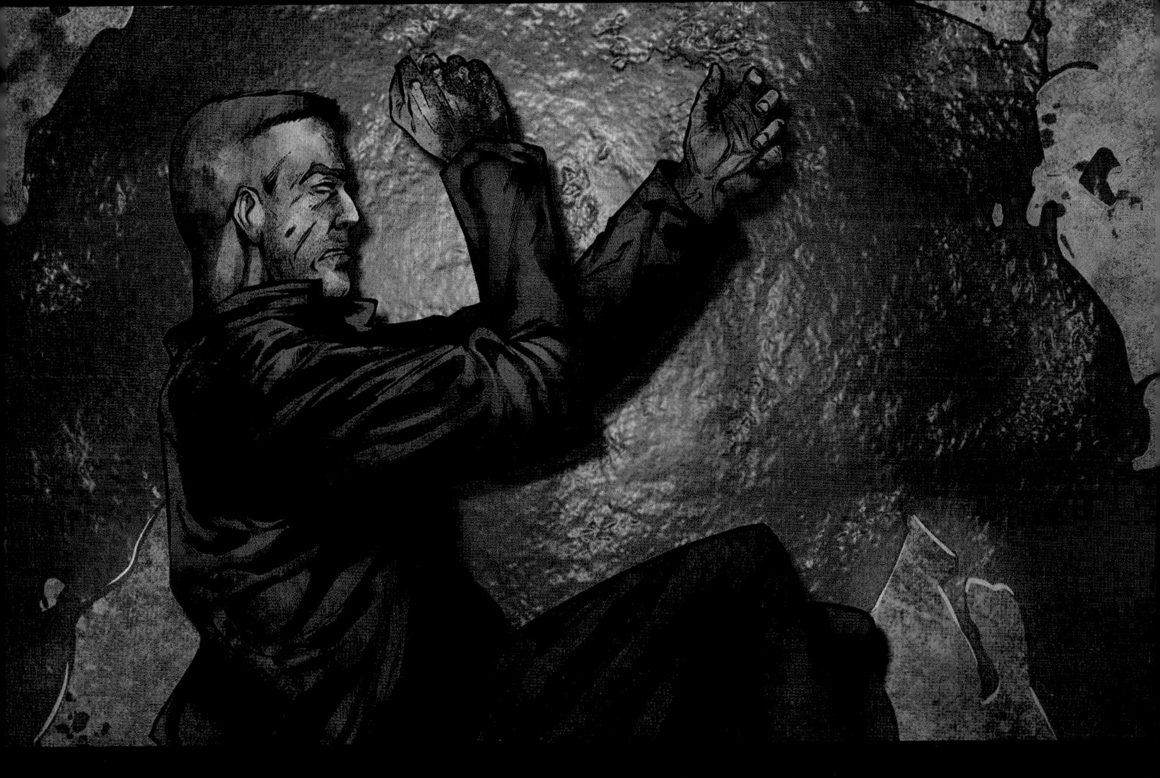

Chapter 3: Hold On For One More Day

Rylend Grant
Writer/Director
@rylendgrant

Davi Leon Dias
Artist
@davileon

Iwan Joko Triyono
Colorist

HdE
Letterer

R.J. Hendricks
Executive Producer

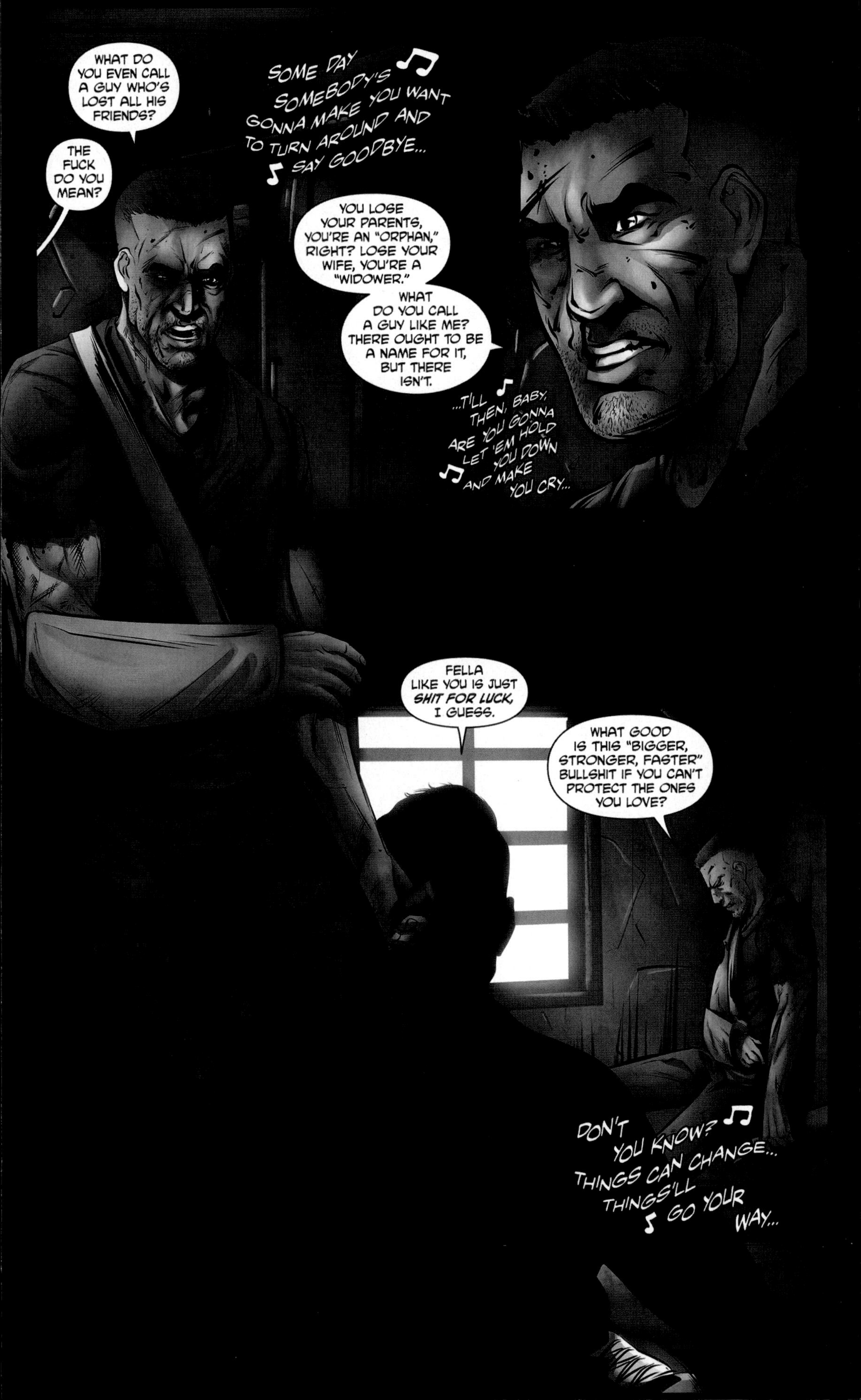
WHAT DO YOU EVEN CALL A GUY WHO'S LOST ALL HIS FRIENDS?
THE FUCK DO YOU MEAN?
SOME DAY SOMEBODY'S GONNA MAKE YOU WANT TO TURN AROUND AND SAY GOODBYE...
YOU LOSE YOUR PARENTS, YOU'RE AN "ORPHAN," RIGHT? LOSE YOUR WIFE, YOU'RE A "WIDOWER."
WHAT DO YOU CALL A GUY LIKE ME? THERE OUGHT TO BE A NAME FOR IT, BUT THERE ISN'T.
...T'ILL THEN, BABY, ARE YOU GONNA LET 'EM HOLD YOU DOWN AND MAKE YOU CRY...
FELLA LIKE YOU IS JUST *SHIT FOR LUCK*, I GUESS.
WHAT GOOD IS THIS "BIGGER, STRONGER, FASTER" BULLSHIT IF YOU CAN'T PROTECT THE ONES YOU LOVE?
DON'T YOU KNOW? THINGS CAN CHANGE... THINGS'LL GO YOUR WAY...

ACTION LAB: DANGER ZONE PRESENTS
IN ASSOCIATION WITH
HALF EVIL COMICS
AND
RISING SPIRIT ENTERTAINMENT

ABERRANT

Chapter 3: Hold On For One More Day

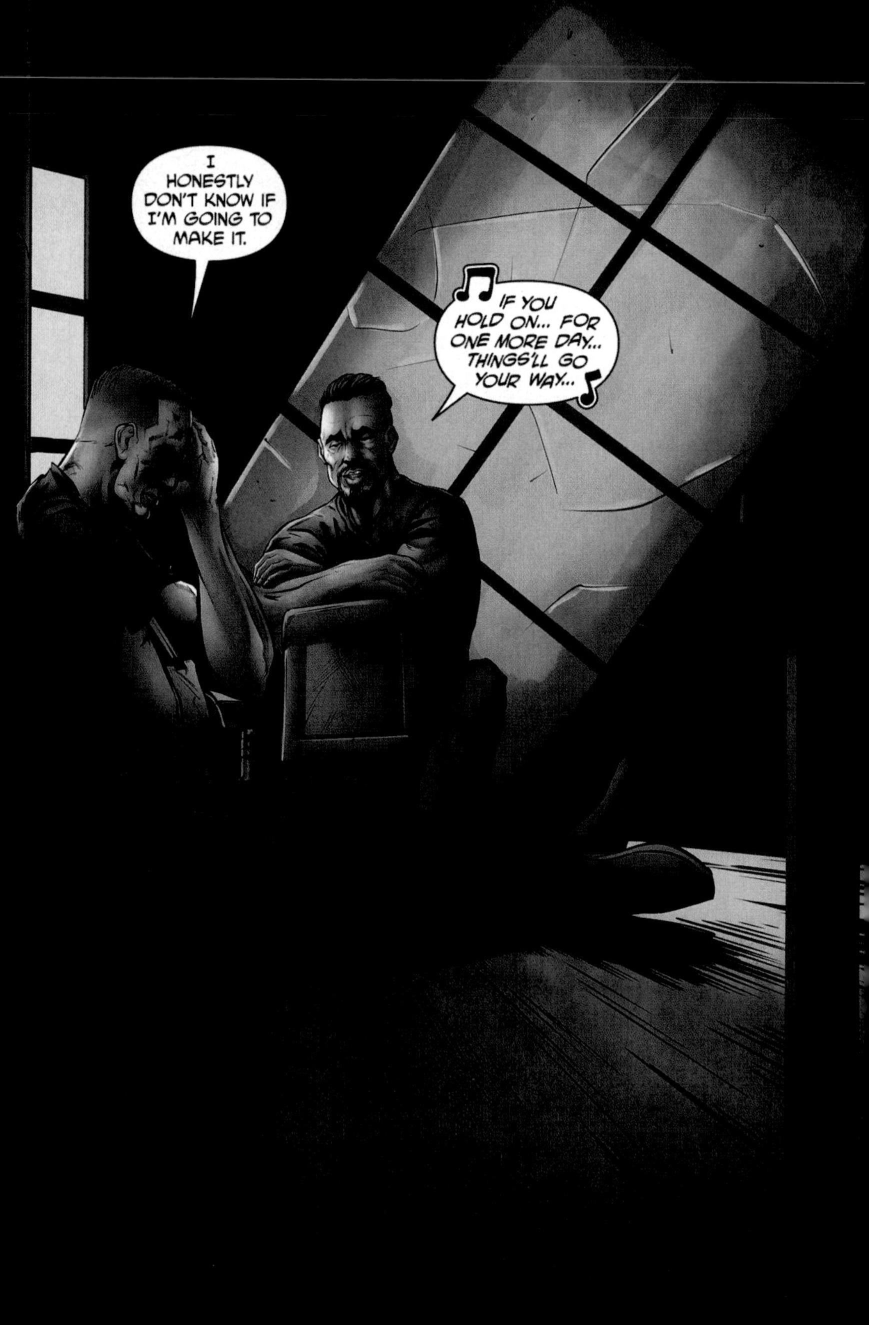
I HONESTLY DON'T KNOW IF I'M GOING TO MAKE IT.
IF YOU HOLD ON... FOR ONE MORE DAY... THINGS'LL GO YOUR WAY...

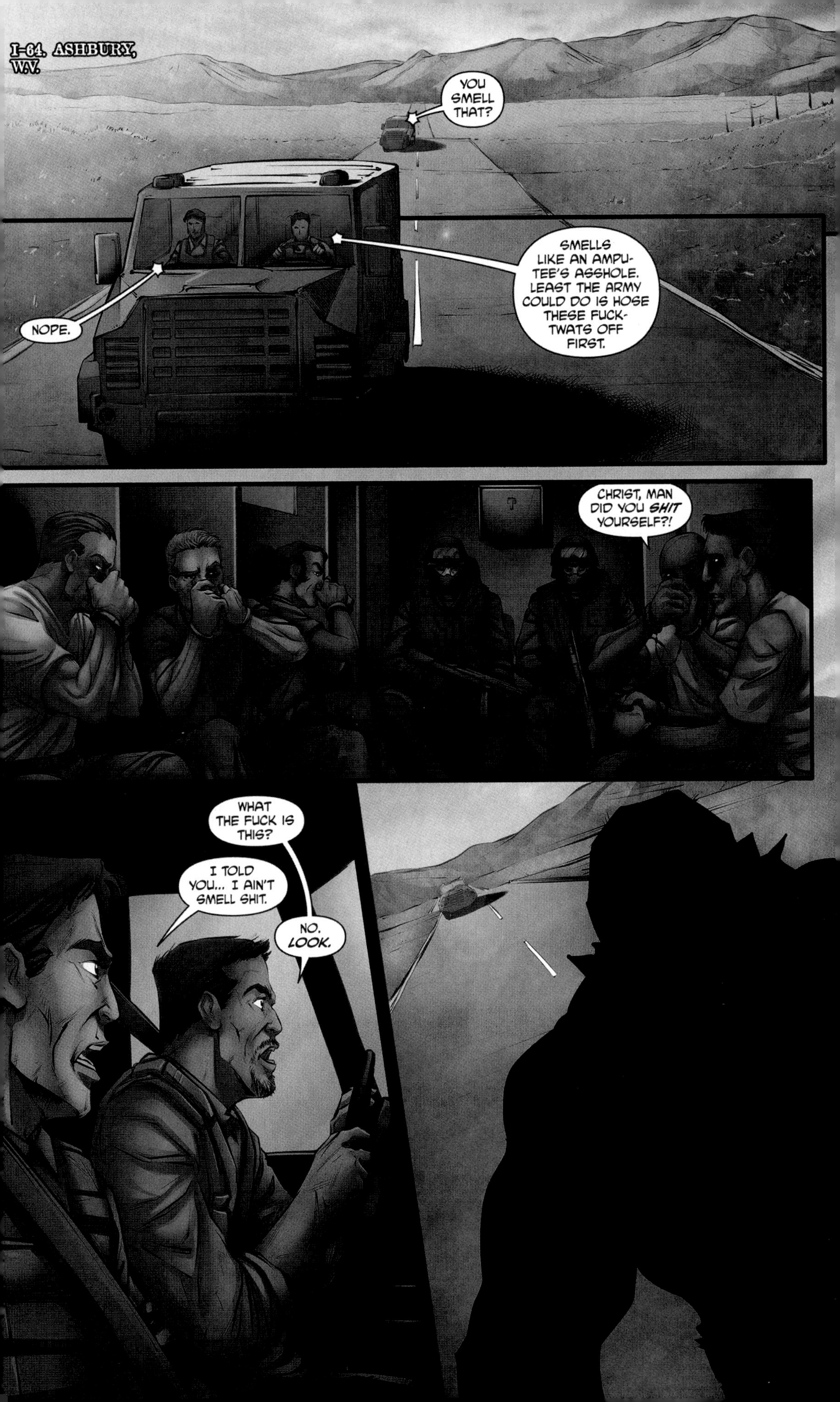
I-64. ASHBURY, W.V.
YOU SMELL THAT?
NOPE.
SMELLS LIKE AN AMPU-TEE'S ASSHOLE. LEAST THE ARMY COULD DO IS HOSE THESE FUCK-TWATS OFF FIRST.
CHRIST, MAN DID YOU SHIT YOURSELF?!
WHAT THE FUCK IS THIS?
I TOLD YOU... I AIN'T SMELL SHIT.
NO. LOOK.

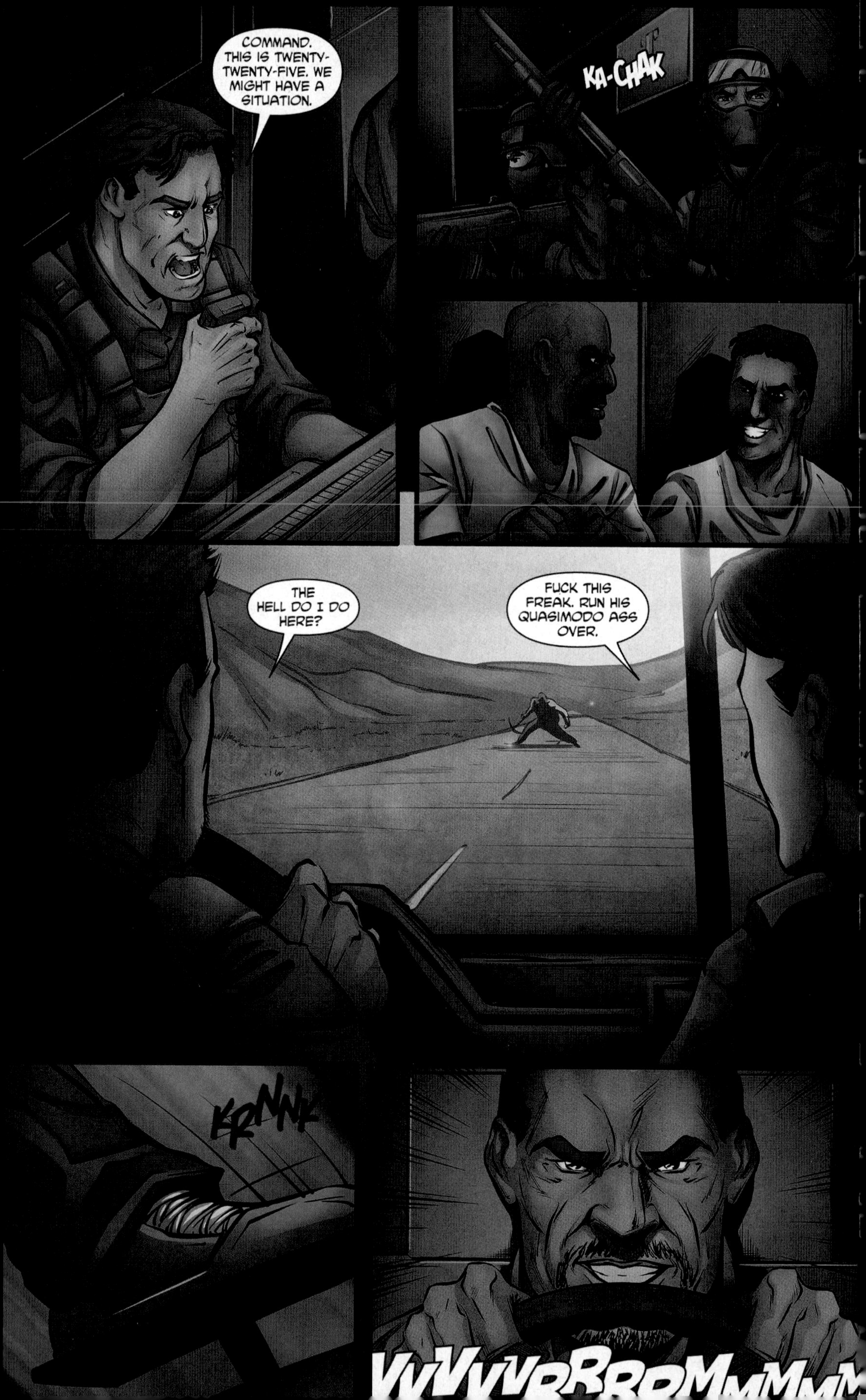
COMMAND. THIS IS TWENTY-TWENTY-FIVE. WE MIGHT HAVE A SITUATION.
KA-CHAK
THE HELL DO I DO HERE?
FUCK THIS FREAK. RUN HIS QUASIMODO ASS OVER.
KRNNK
VVVVVVRRRRMMMMM

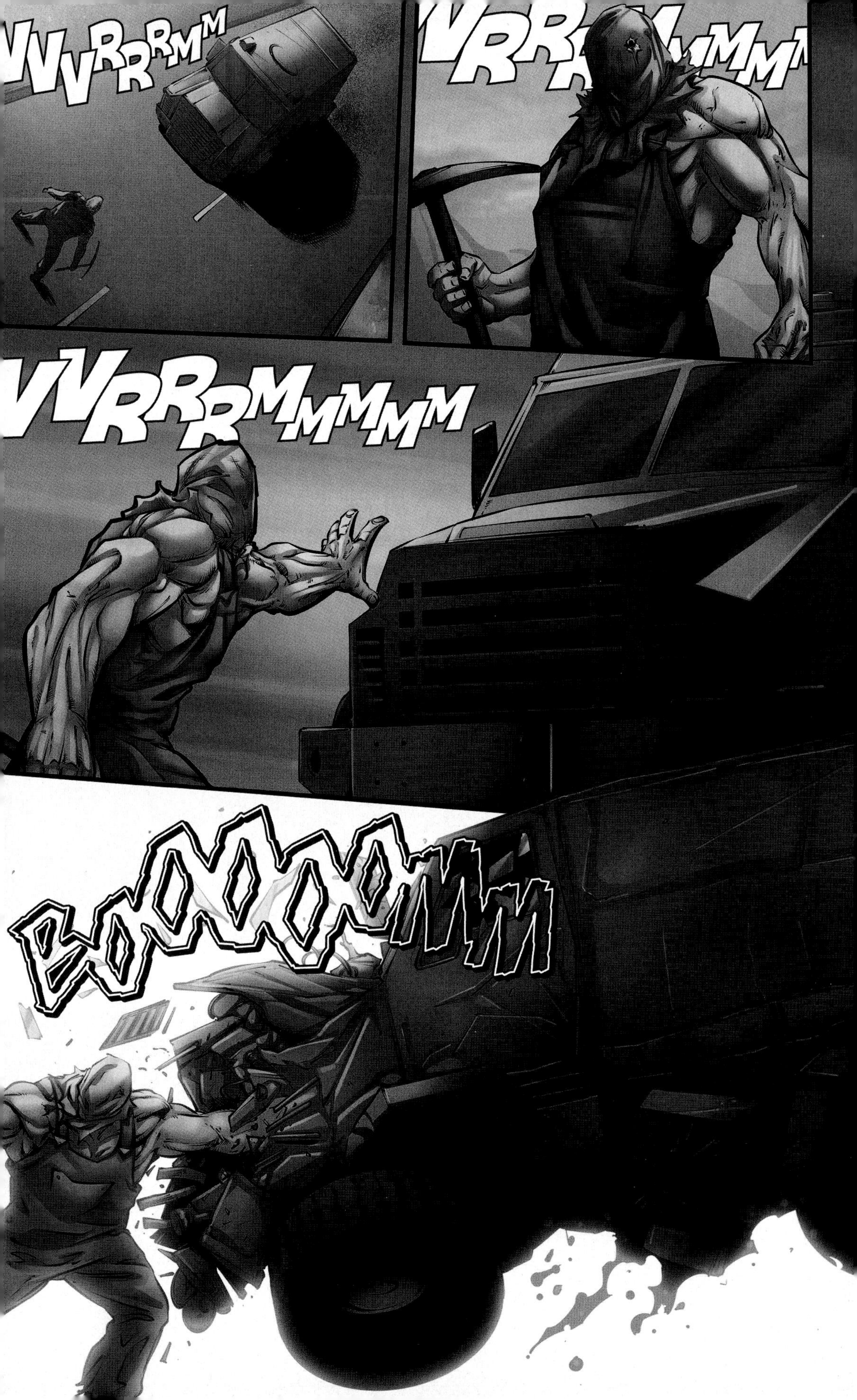
VVVRRRRMM
VRRRRMMMM
VVRRRMMMMM
BOOOOMMM

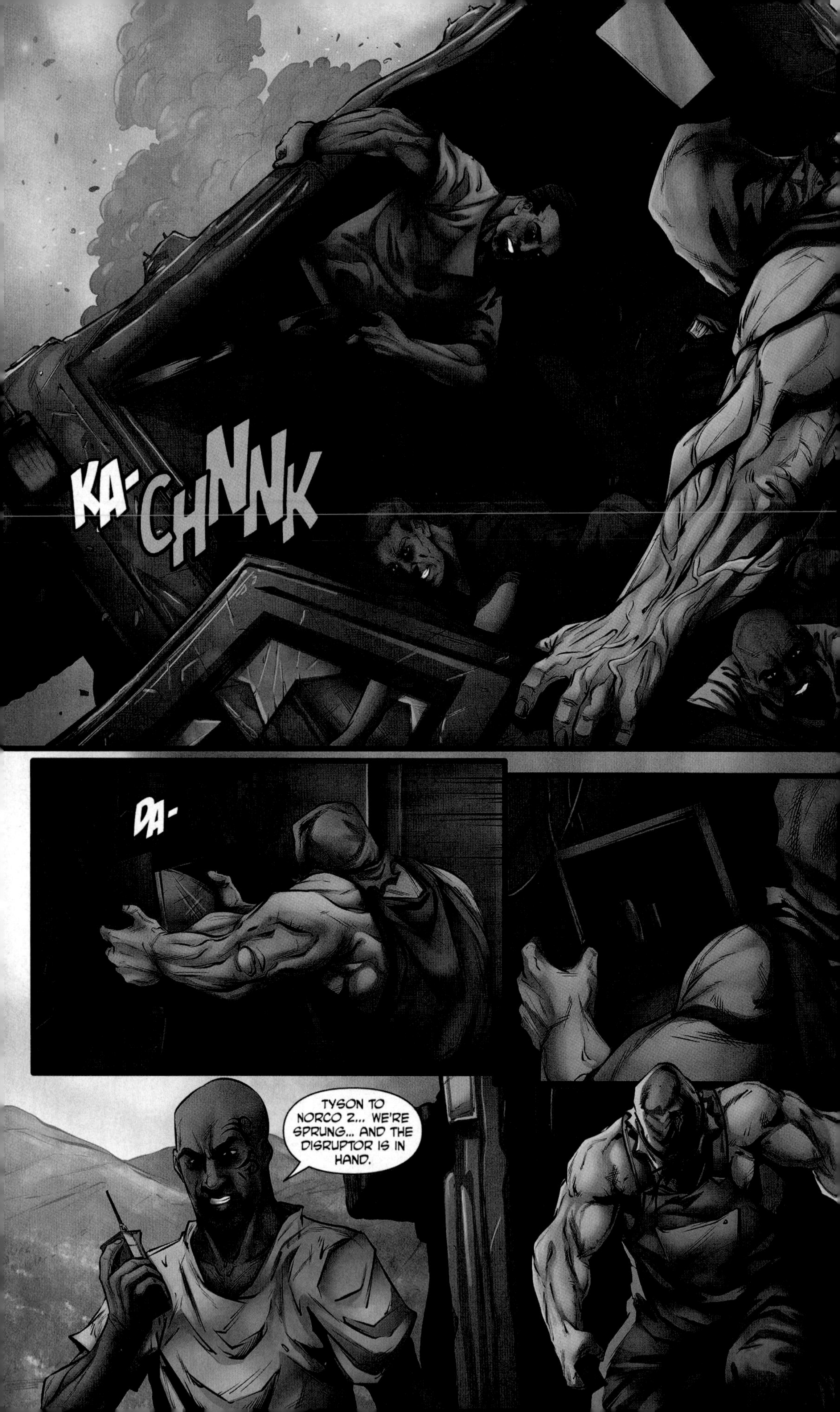
KA-CHNNK
DA-
TYSON TO NORCO 2... WE'RE SPRUNG... AND THE DISRUPTOR IS IN HAND.

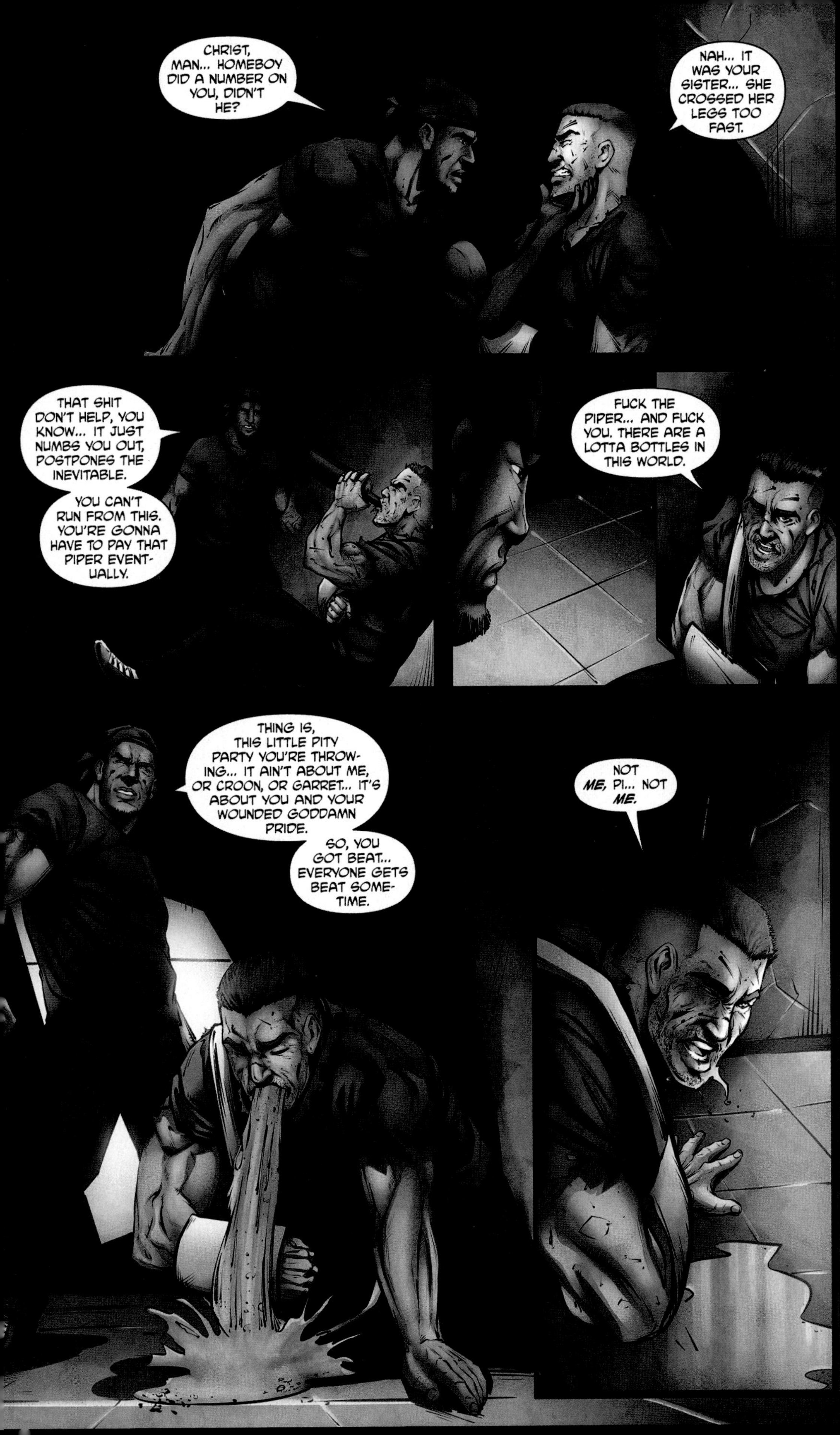
CHRIST, MAN... HOMEBOY DID A NUMBER ON YOU, DIDN'T HE?
NAH... IT WAS YOUR SISTER... SHE CROSSED HER LEGS TOO FAST.
THAT SHIT DON'T HELP, YOU KNOW... IT JUST NUMBS YOU OUT, POSTPONES THE INEVITABLE.
YOU CAN'T RUN FROM THIS. YOU'RE GONNA HAVE TO PAY THAT PIPER EVENT-UALLY.
FUCK THE PIPER... AND FUCK YOU. THERE ARE A LOTTA BOTTLES IN THIS WORLD.
THING IS, THIS LITTLE PITY PARTY YOU'RE THROW-ING... IT AIN'T ABOUT ME, OR CROON, OR GARRET... IT'S ABOUT YOU AND YOUR WOUNDED GODDAMN PRIDE.
SO, YOU GOT BEAT... EVERYONE GETS BEAT SOME-TIME.
NOT *ME,* PI... NOT *ME.*

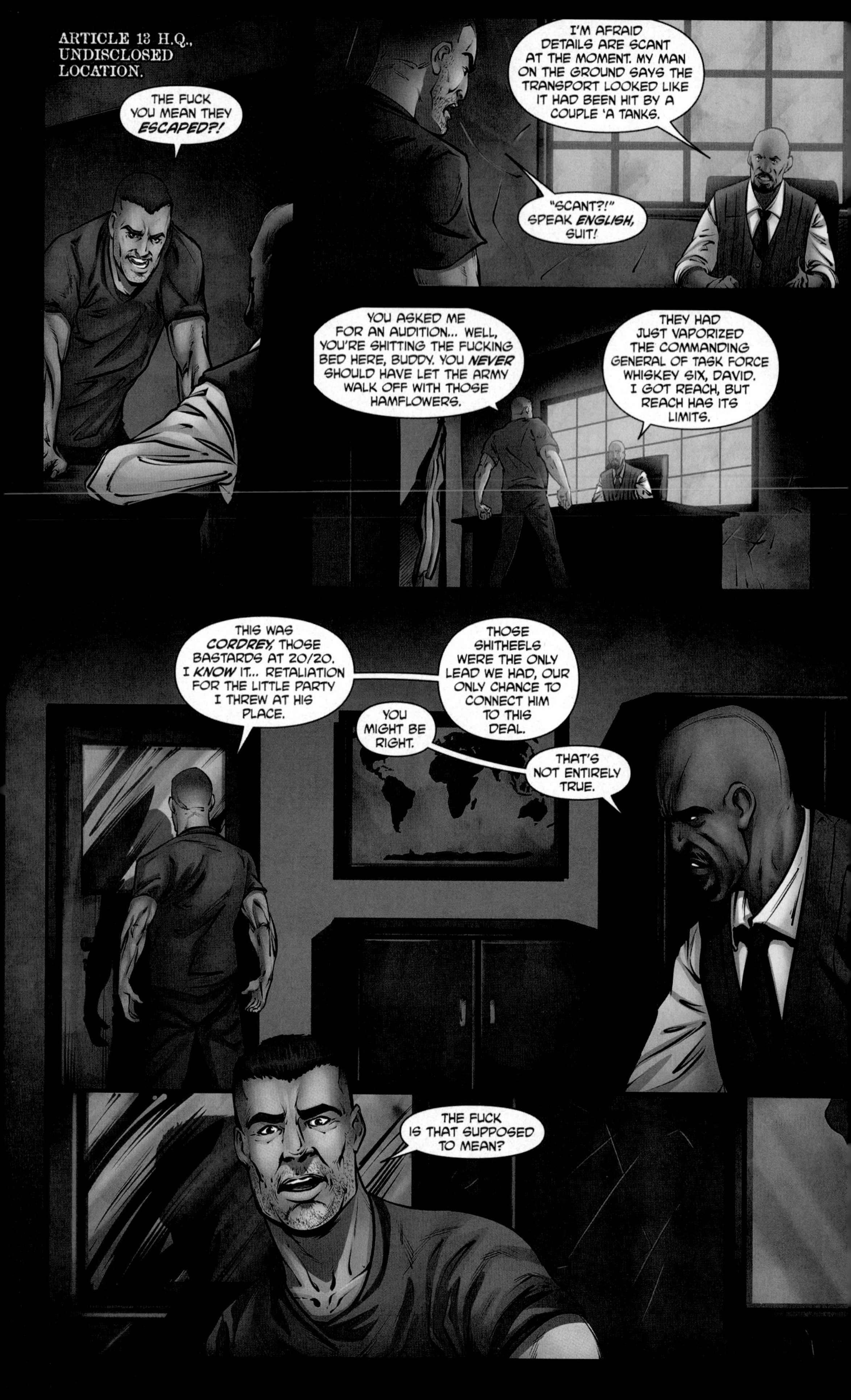
ARTICLE 13 H.Q., UNDISCLOSED LOCATION.
THE FUCK YOU MEAN THEY *ESCAPED?!*
I'M AFRAID DETAILS ARE SCANT AT THE MOMENT. MY MAN ON THE GROUND SAYS THE TRANSPORT LOOKED LIKE IT HAD BEEN HIT BY A COUPLE 'A TANKS.
"SCANT?!" SPEAK *ENGLISH,* SUIT!
YOU ASKED ME FOR AN AUDITION... WELL, YOU'RE SHITTING THE FUCKING BED HERE, BUDDY. YOU *NEVER* SHOULD HAVE LET THE ARMY WALK OFF WITH THOSE HAMFLOWERS.
THEY HAD JUST VAPORIZED THE COMMANDING GENERAL OF TASK FORCE WHISKEY SIX, DAVID. I GOT REACH, BUT REACH HAS ITS LIMITS.
THIS WAS *CORDREY,* THOSE BASTARDS AT 20/20. I *KNOW* IT... RETALIATION FOR THE LITTLE PARTY I THREW AT HIS PLACE.
THOSE SHITHEELS WERE THE ONLY LEAD WE HAD, OUR ONLY CHANCE TO CONNECT HIM TO THIS DEAL.
YOU MIGHT BE RIGHT.
THAT'S NOT ENTIRELY TRUE.
THE FUCK IS THAT SUPPOSED TO MEAN?

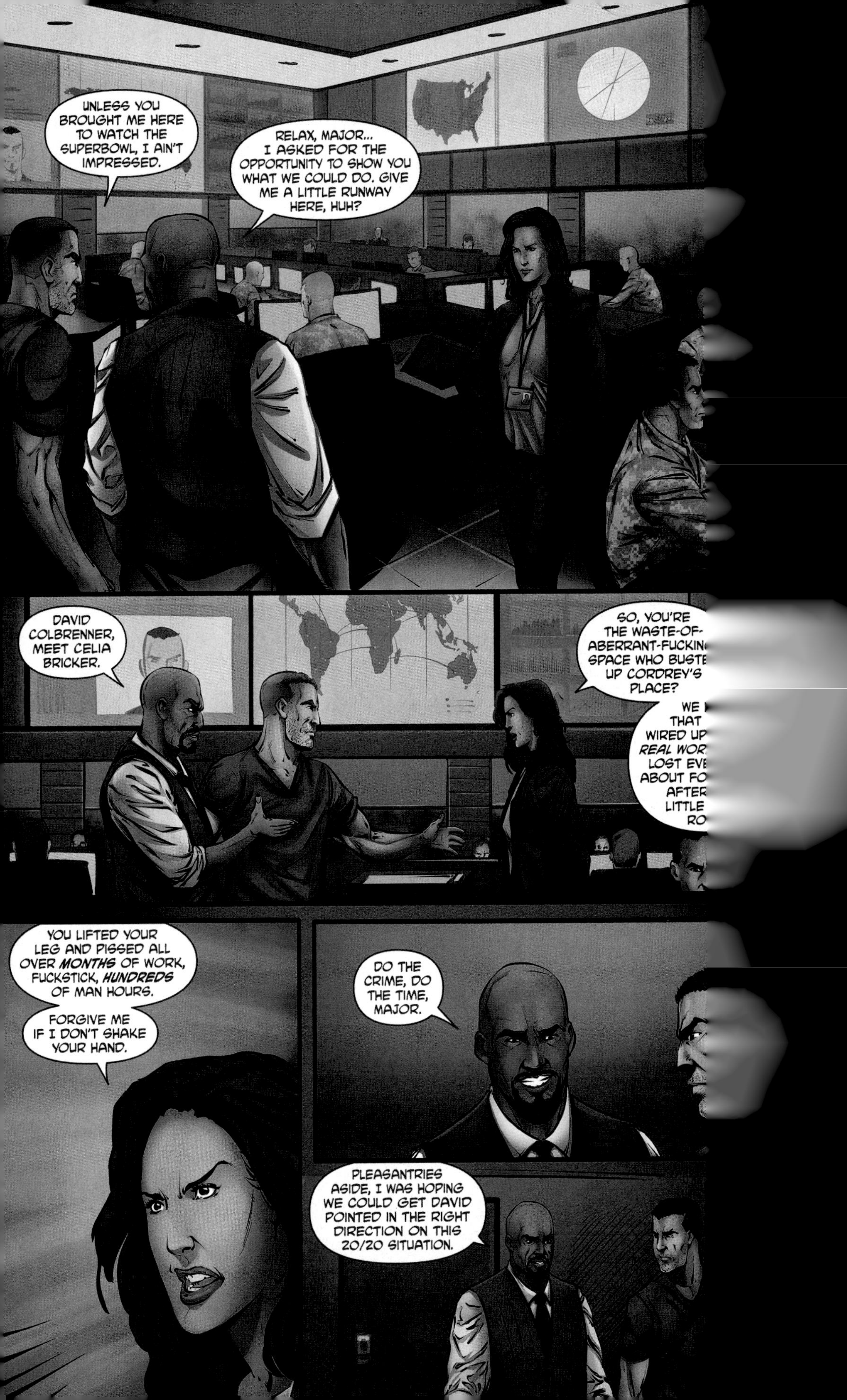

UNLESS YOU BROUGHT ME HERE TO WATCH THE SUPERBOWL, I AIN'T IMPRESSED.
RELAX, MAJOR... I ASKED FOR THE OPPORTUNITY TO SHOW YOU WHAT WE COULD DO. GIVE ME A LITTLE RUNWAY HERE, HUH?
DAVID COLBRENNER, MEET CELIA BRICKER.
SO, YOU'RE THE WASTE-OF-ABERRANT-FUCKIN SPACE WHO BUSTE UP CORDREY'S PLACE?
WE THAT WIRED UP REAL WOR LOST EVE ABOUT FO AFTER LITTLE RO
YOU LIFTED YOUR LEG AND PISSED ALL OVER MONTHS OF WORK, FUCKSTICK, HUNDREDS OF MAN HOURS.
FORGIVE ME IF I DON'T SHAKE YOUR HAND.
DO THE CRIME, DO THE TIME, MAJOR.
PLEASANTRIES ASIDE, I WAS HOPING WE COULD GET DAVID POINTED IN THE RIGHT DIRECTION ON THIS 20/20 SITUATION.

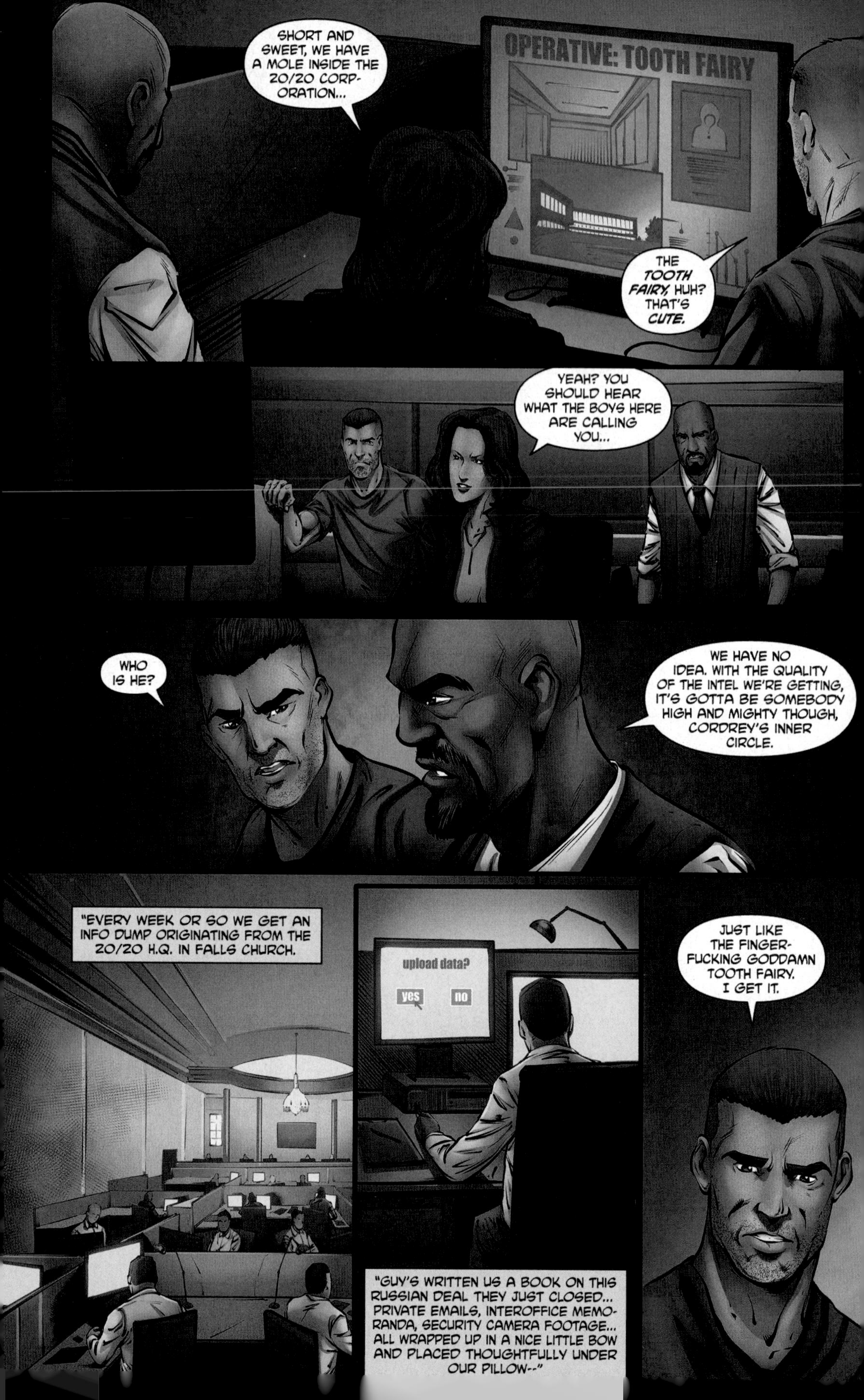
SHORT AND SWEET, WE HAVE A MOLE INSIDE THE 20/20 CORPORATION...
OPERATIVE: TOOTH FAIRY
THE TOOTH FAIRY, HUH? THAT'S CUTE.
YEAH? YOU SHOULD HEAR WHAT THE BOYS HERE ARE CALLING YOU...
WHO IS HE?
WE HAVE NO IDEA. WITH THE QUALITY OF THE INTEL WE'RE GETTING, IT'S GOTTA BE SOMEBODY HIGH AND MIGHTY THOUGH, CORDREY'S INNER CIRCLE.
"EVERY WEEK OR SO WE GET AN INFO DUMP ORIGINATING FROM THE 20/20 H.Q. IN FALLS CHURCH.
upload data?
yes
no
"GUY'S WRITTEN US A BOOK ON THIS RUSSIAN DEAL THEY JUST CLOSED... PRIVATE EMAILS, INTEROFFICE MEMORANDA, SECURITY CAMERA FOOTAGE... ALL WRAPPED UP IN A NICE LITTLE BOW AND PLACED THOUGHTFULLY UNDER OUR PILLOW--"
JUST LIKE THE FINGER-FUCKING GODDAMN TOOTH FAIRY. I GET IT.

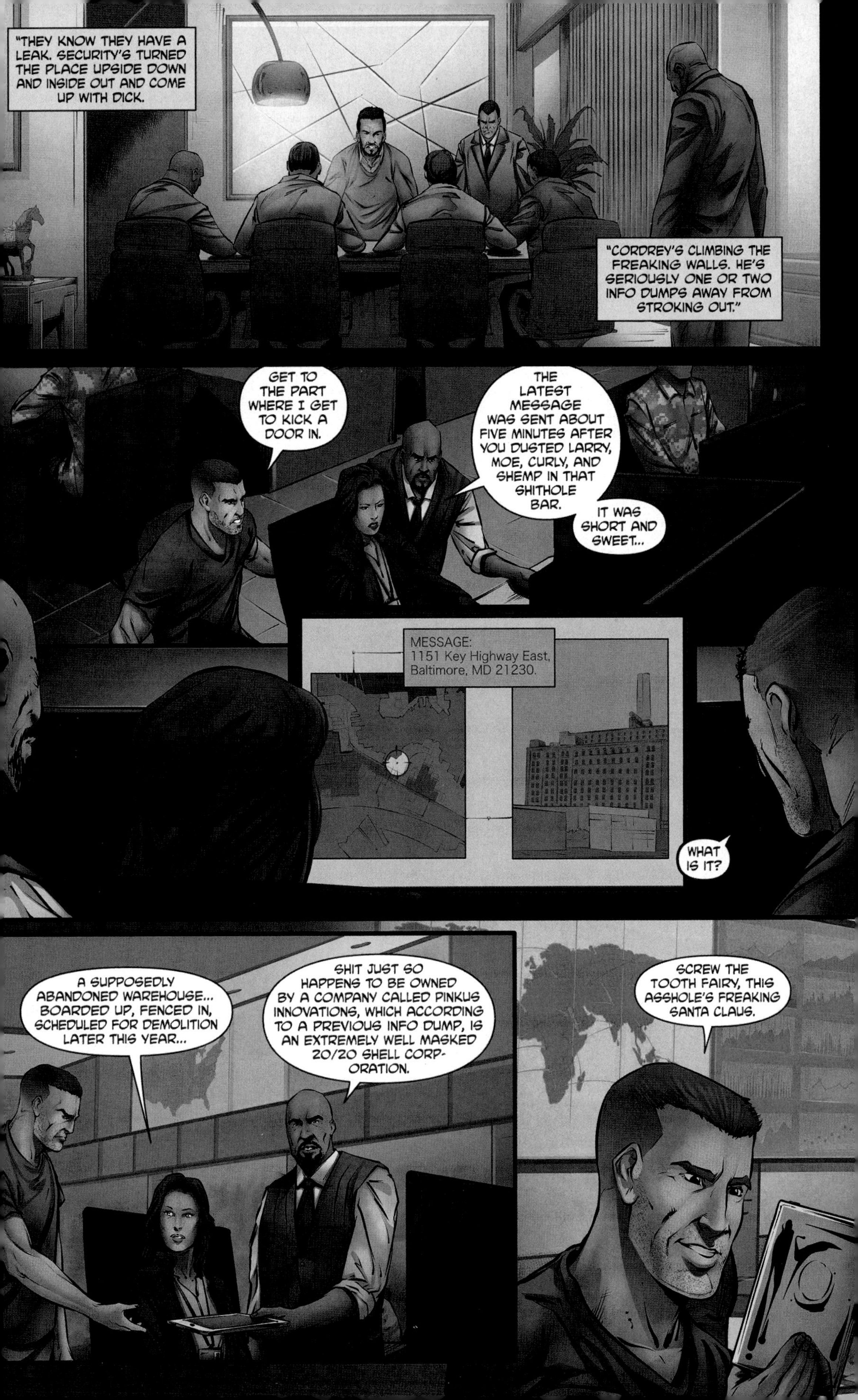
"THEY KNOW THEY HAVE A LEAK. SECURITY'S TURNED THE PLACE UPSIDE DOWN AND INSIDE OUT AND COME UP WITH DICK.
"CORDREY'S CLIMBING THE FREAKING WALLS. HE'S SERIOUSLY ONE OR TWO INFO DUMPS AWAY FROM STROKING OUT."
GET TO THE PART WHERE I GET TO KICK A DOOR IN.
THE LATEST MESSAGE WAS SENT ABOUT FIVE MINUTES AFTER YOU DUSTED LARRY, MOE, CURLY, AND SHEMP IN THAT SHITHOLE BAR.
IT WAS SHORT AND SWEET...
MESSAGE:
1151 Key Highway East,
Baltimore, MD 21230.
WHAT IS IT?
A SUPPOSEDLY ABANDONED WAREHOUSE... BOARDED UP, FENCED IN, SCHEDULED FOR DEMOLITION LATER THIS YEAR...
SHIT JUST SO HAPPENS TO BE OWNED BY A COMPANY CALLED PINKUS INNOVATIONS, WHICH ACCORDING TO A PREVIOUS INFO DUMP, IS AN EXTREMELY WELL MASKED 20/20 SHELL CORP-ORATION.
SCREW THE TOOTH FAIRY, THIS ASSHOLE'S FREAKING SANTA CLAUS.

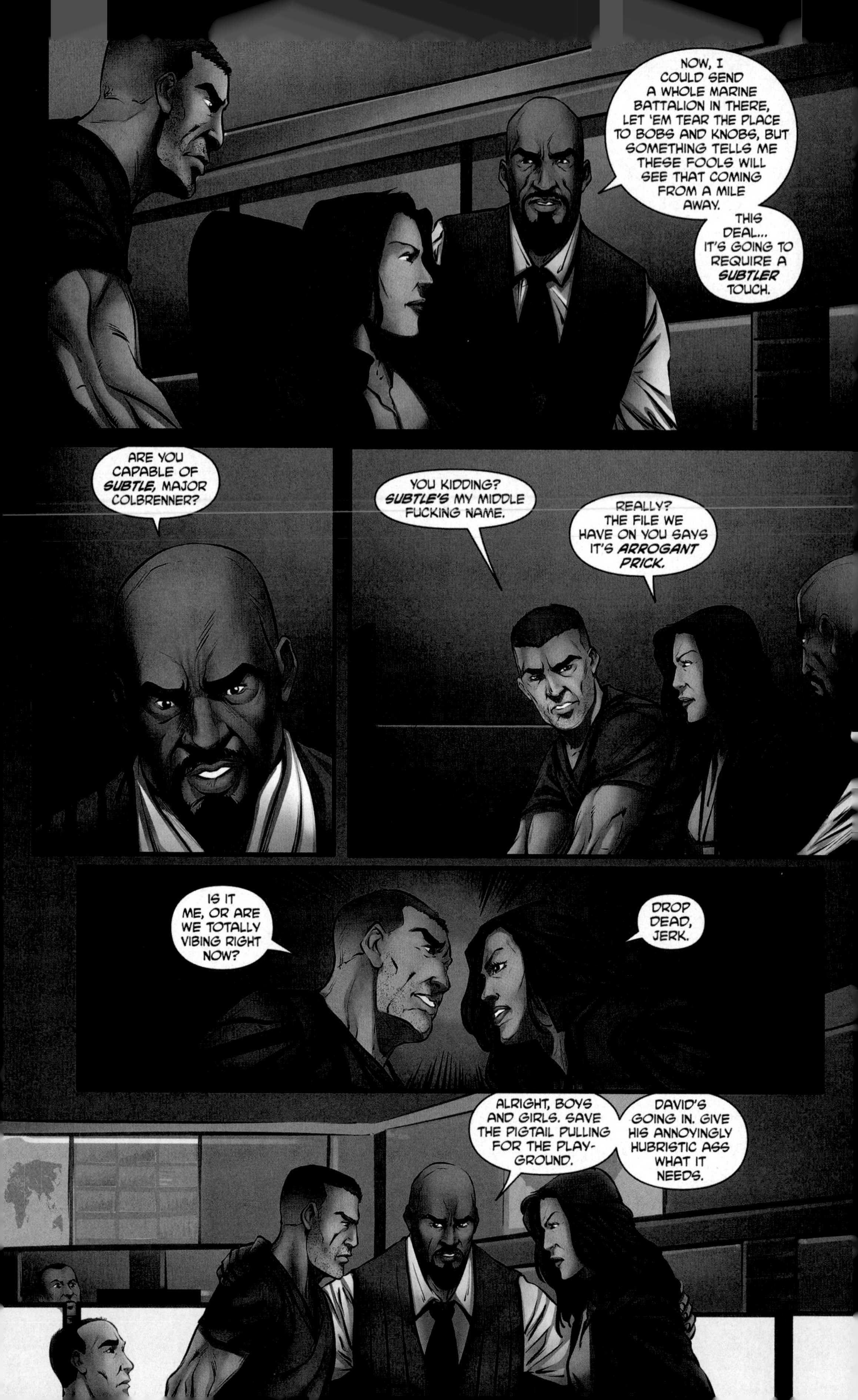
NOW, I COULD SEND A WHOLE MARINE BATTALION IN THERE, LET 'EM TEAR THE PLACE TO BOBS AND KNOBS, BUT SOMETHING TELLS ME THESE FOOLS WILL SEE THAT COMING FROM A MILE AWAY.
THIS DEAL... IT'S GOING TO REQUIRE A *SUBTLER* TOUCH.
ARE YOU CAPABLE OF *SUBTLE,* MAJOR COLBRENNER?
YOU KIDDING? *SUBTLE'S* MY MIDDLE FUCKING NAME.
REALLY? THE FILE WE HAVE ON YOU SAYS IT'S *ARROGANT PRICK.*
IS IT ME, OR ARE WE TOTALLY VIBING RIGHT NOW?
DROP DEAD, JERK.
ALRIGHT, BOYS AND GIRLS. SAVE THE PIGTAIL PULLING FOR THE PLAY-GROUND.
DAVID'S GOING IN. GIVE HIS ANNOYINGLY HUBRISTIC ASS WHAT IT NEEDS.

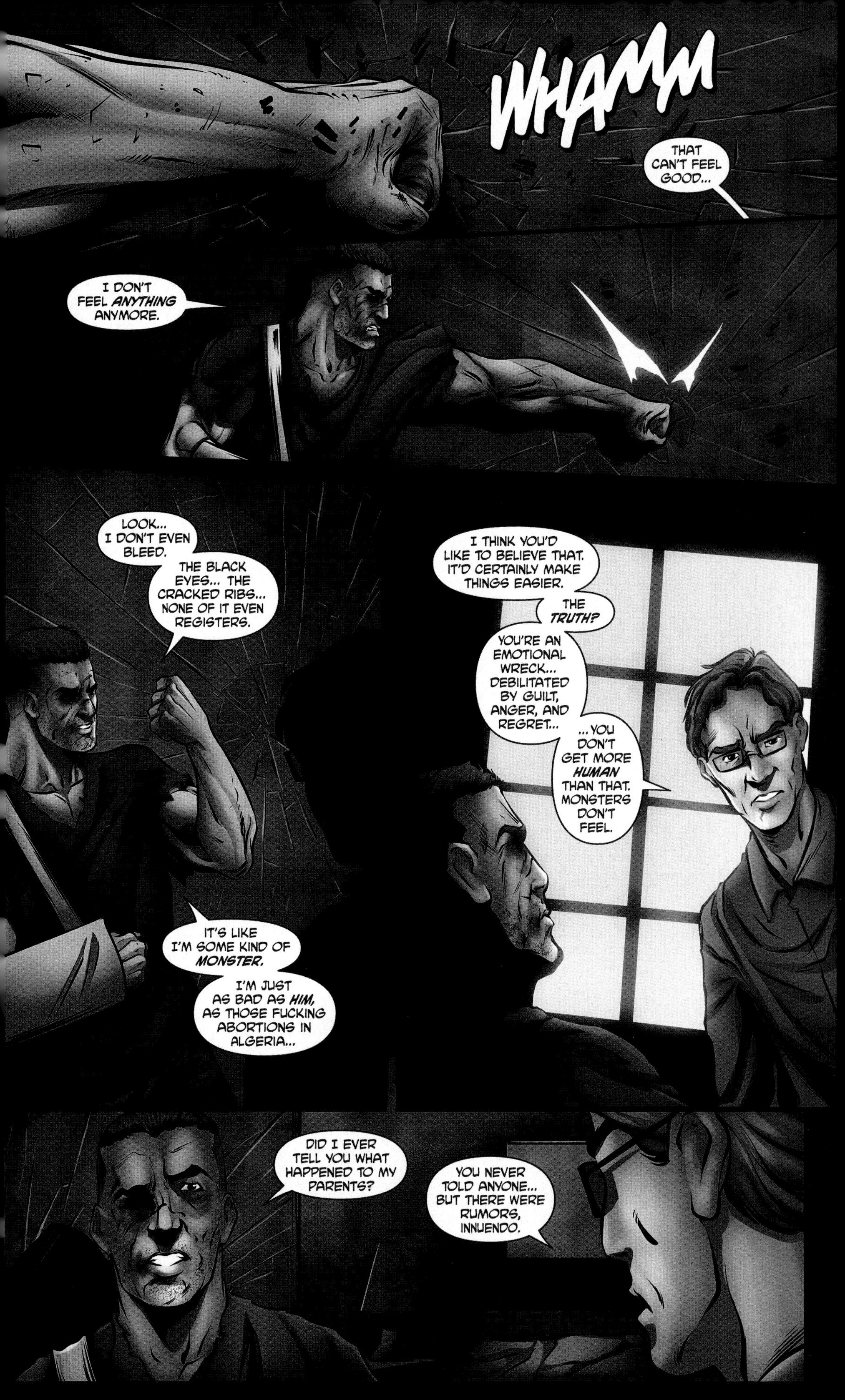
WHAMM
THAT CAN'T FEEL GOOD...
I DON'T FEEL *ANYTHING* ANYMORE.
LOOK... I DON'T EVEN BLEED.
THE BLACK EYES... THE CRACKED RIBS... NONE OF IT EVEN REGISTERS.
IT'S LIKE I'M SOME KIND OF *MONSTER.*
I'M JUST AS BAD AS *HIM,* AS THOSE FUCKING ABORTIONS IN ALGERIA...
I THINK YOU'D LIKE TO BELIEVE THAT. IT'D CERTAINLY MAKE THINGS EASIER.
THE *TRUTH?*
YOU'RE AN EMOTIONAL WRECK... DEBILITATED BY GUILT, ANGER, AND REGRET...
...YOU DON'T GET MORE *HUMAN* THAN THAT. MONSTERS DON'T FEEL.
DID I EVER TELL YOU WHAT HAPPENED TO MY PARENTS?
YOU NEVER TOLD ANYONE... BUT THERE WERE RUMORS, INNUENDO.

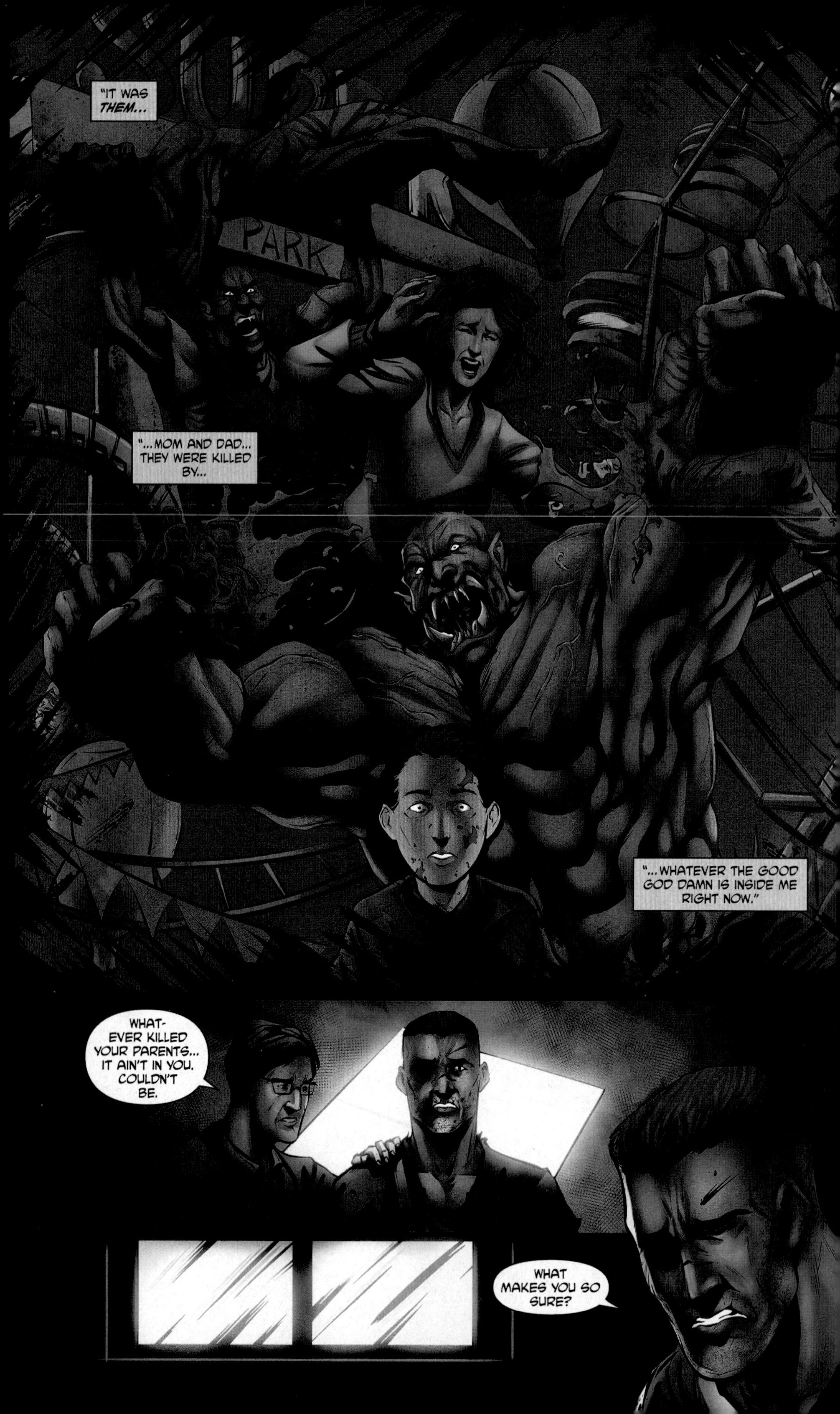

"IT WAS THEM...
PARK
"...MOM AND DAD... THEY WERE KILLED BY...
"...WHATEVER THE GOOD GOD DAMN IS INSIDE ME RIGHT NOW."
WHAT-EVER KILLED YOUR PARENTS... IT AIN'T IN YOU. COULDN'T BE.
WHAT MAKES YOU SO SURE?

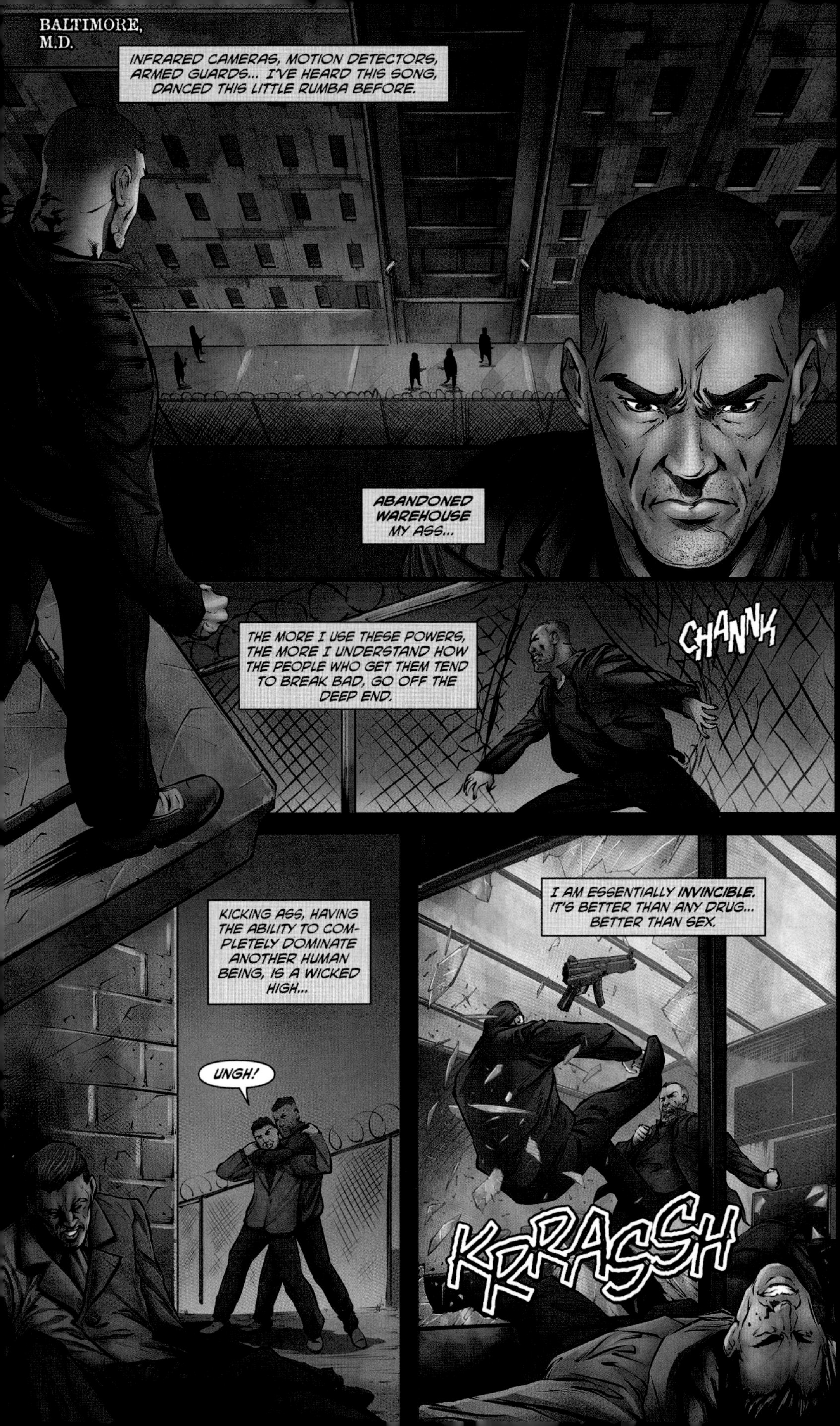
BALTIMORE, M.D.
INFRARED CAMERAS, MOTION DETECTORS, ARMED GUARDS... I'VE HEARD THIS SONG, DANCED THIS LITTLE RUMBA BEFORE.
ABANDONED WAREHOUSE MY ASS...
THE MORE I USE THESE POWERS, THE MORE I UNDERSTAND HOW THE PEOPLE WHO GET THEM TEND TO BREAK BAD, GO OFF THE DEEP END.
CHANNK
KICKING ASS, HAVING THE ABILITY TO COM-PLETELY DOMINATE ANOTHER HUMAN BEING, IS A WICKED HIGH...
UNGH!
I AM ESSENTIALLY INVINCIBLE. IT'S BETTER THAN ANY DRUG... BETTER THAN SEX.
KRASSH

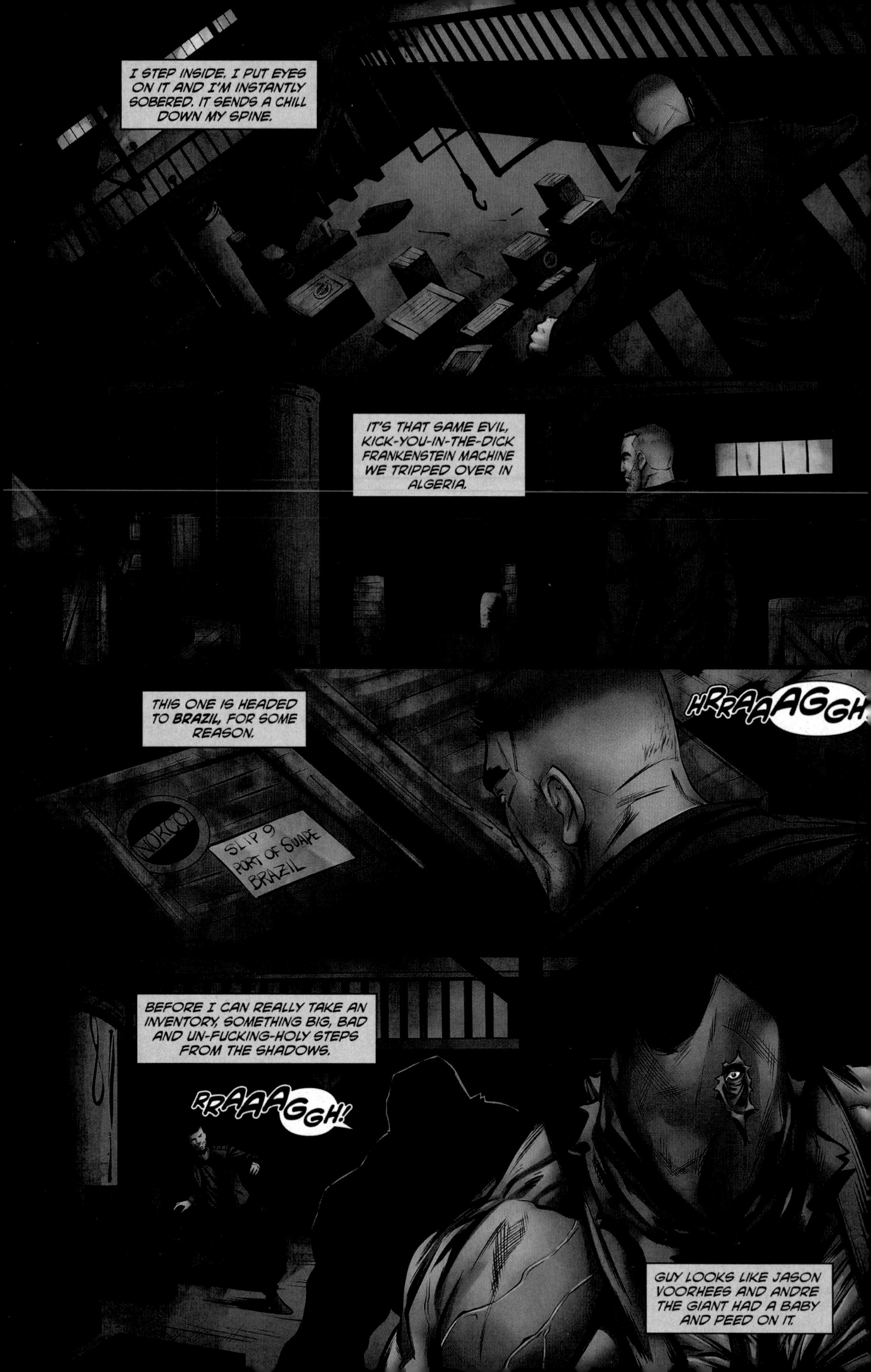
I STEP INSIDE. I PUT EYES ON IT AND I'M INSTANTLY SOBERED. IT SENDS A CHILL DOWN MY SPINE.
IT'S THAT SAME EVIL, KICK-YOU-IN-THE-DICK FRANKENSTEIN MACHINE WE TRIPPED OVER IN ALGERIA.
THIS ONE IS HEADED TO BRAZIL, FOR SOME REASON.
NORCO
SLIP 9 PORT OF SUAPE BRAZIL
HRRAAAAGGH
BEFORE I CAN REALLY TAKE AN INVENTORY, SOMETHING BIG, BAD AND UN-FUCKING-HOLY STEPS FROM THE SHADOWS.
RRAAAAGGH!
GUY LOOKS LIKE JASON VOORHEES AND ANDRE THE GIANT HAD A BABY AND PEED ON IT.

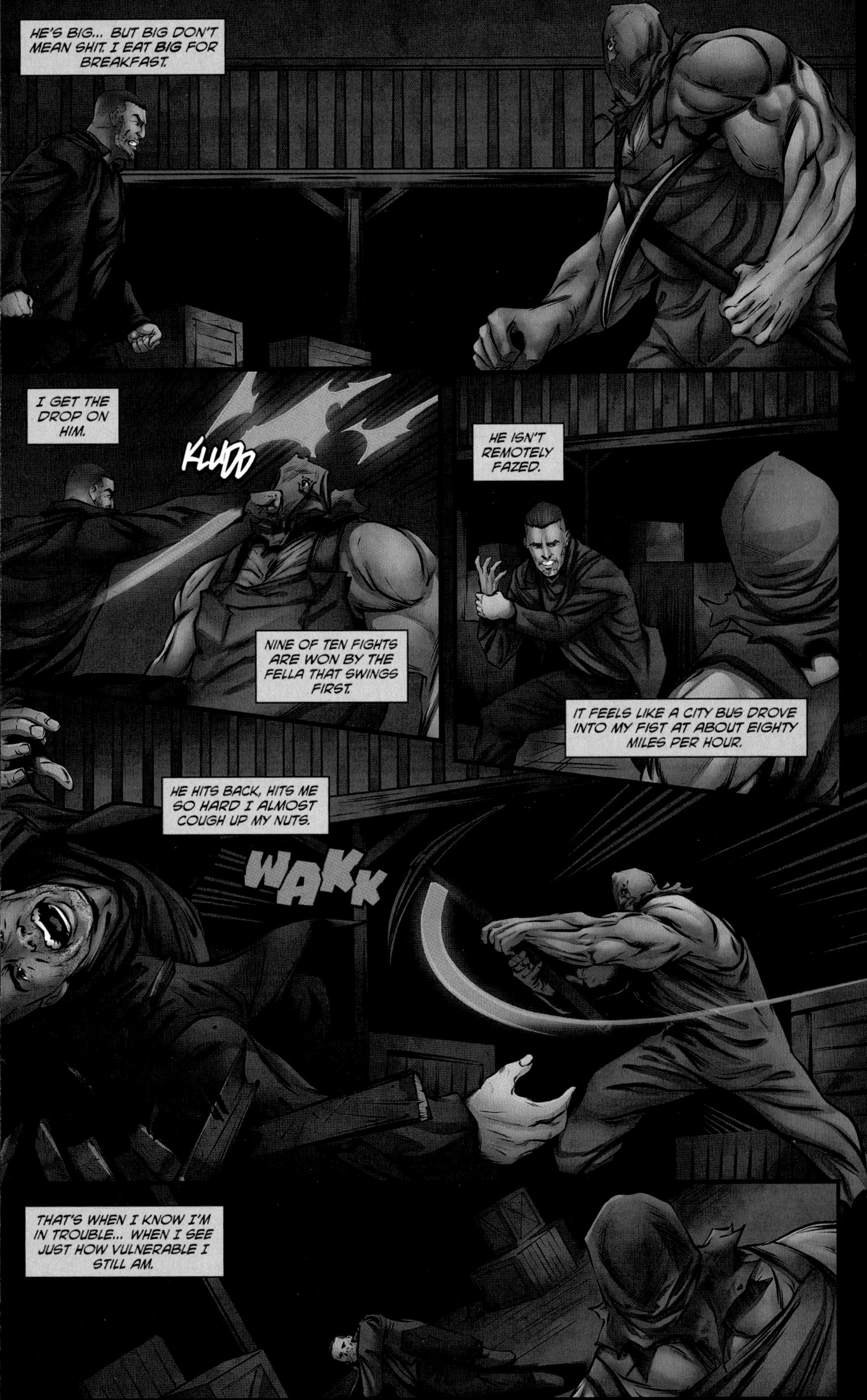
HE'S BIG... BUT BIG DON'T MEAN SHIT. I EAT BIG FOR BREAKFAST.
I GET THE DROP ON HIM.
KLUDD
NINE OF TEN FIGHTS ARE WON BY THE FELLA THAT SWINGS FIRST.
HE ISN'T REMOTELY FAZED.
IT FEELS LIKE A CITY BUS DROVE INTO MY FIST AT ABOUT EIGHTY MILES PER HOUR.
HE HITS BACK, HITS ME SO HARD I ALMOST COUGH UP MY NUTS.
WAKK
THAT'S WHEN I KNOW I'M IN TROUBLE... WHEN I SEE JUST HOW VULNERABLE I STILL AM.

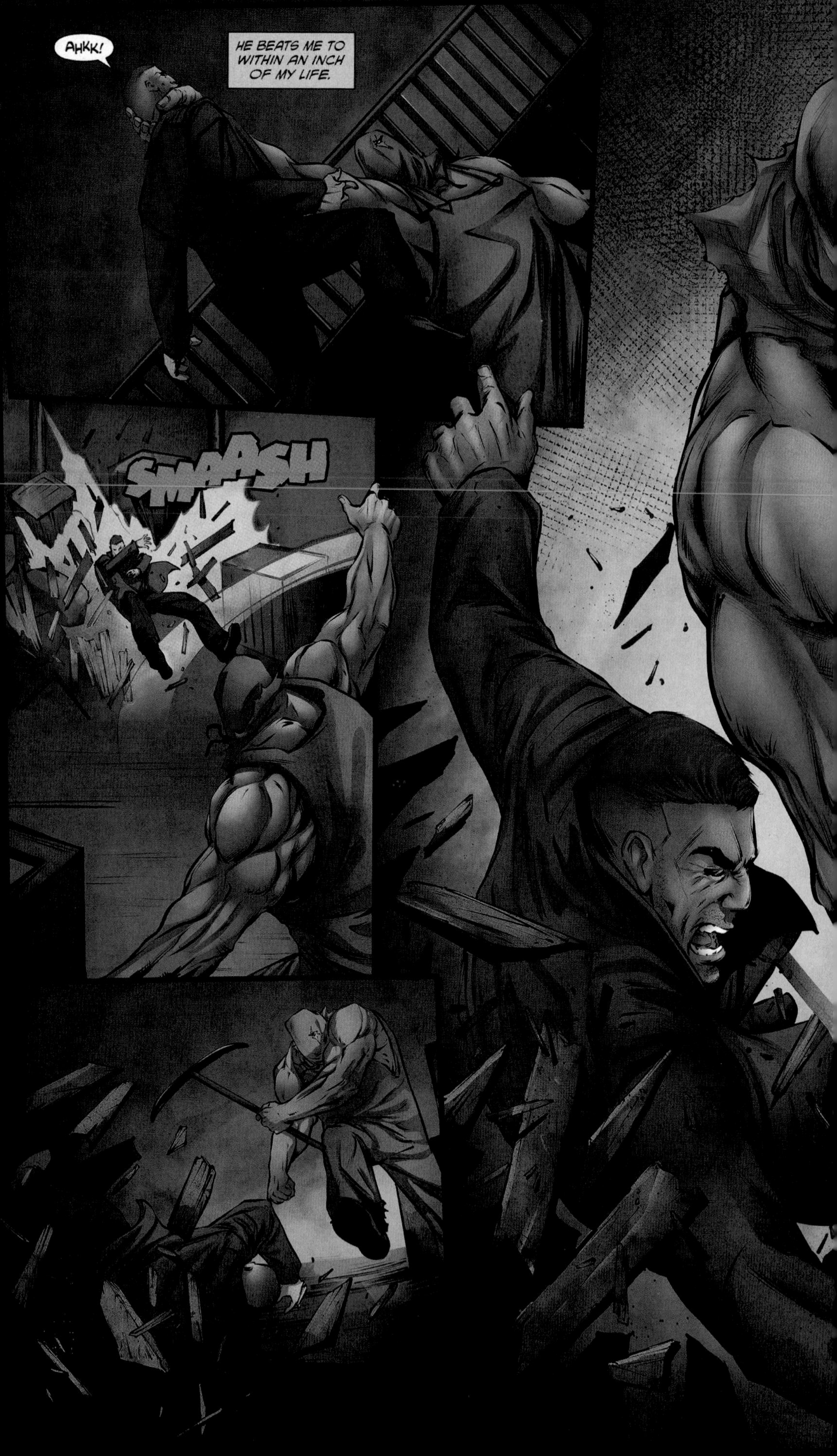
AHKK!
HE BEATS ME TO WITHIN AN INCH OF MY LIFE.
SMAASH

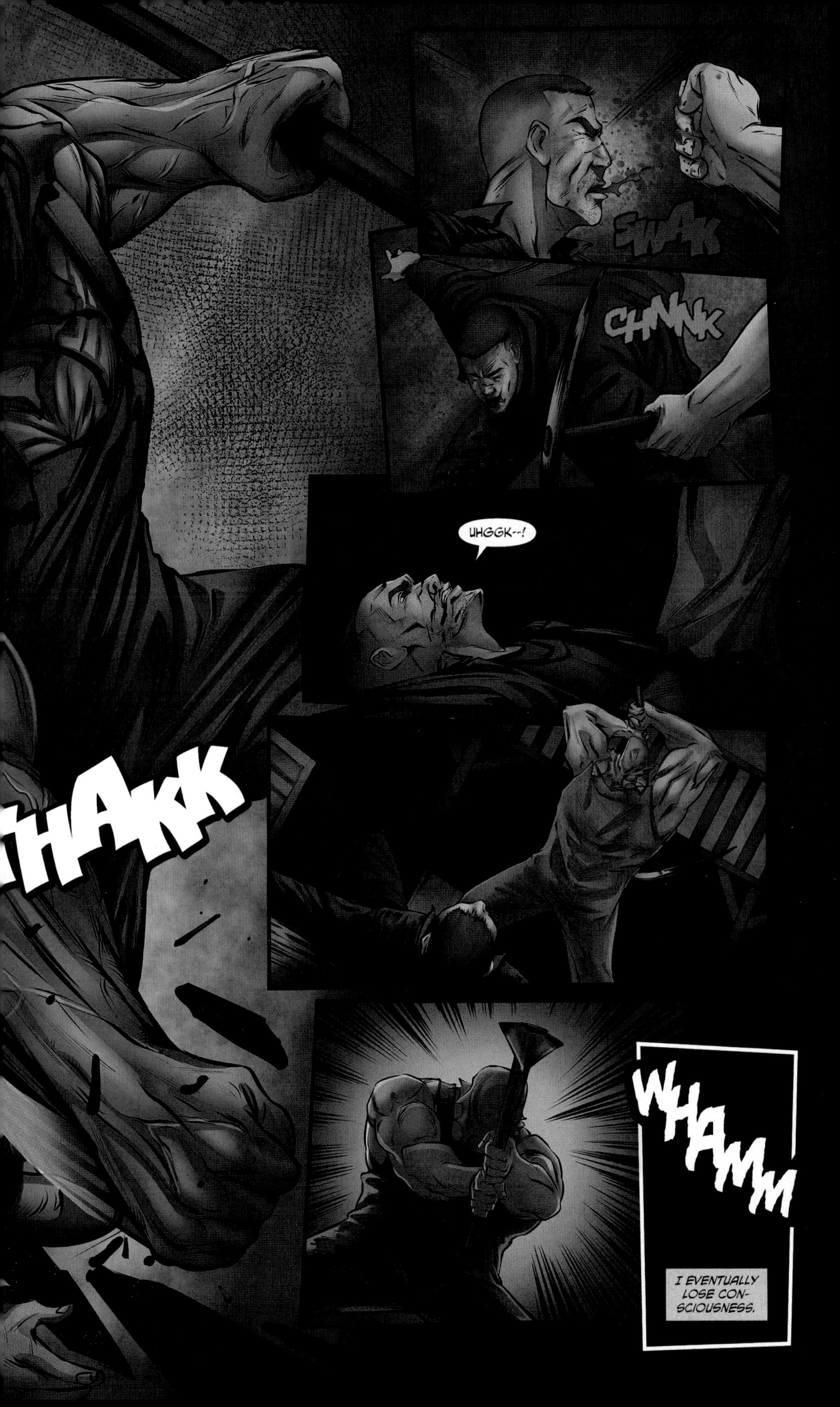
SWAK
CHNNK
UHGGK--!
THAKK
WHAMM
I EVENTUALLY LOSE CON- SCIOUSNESS.

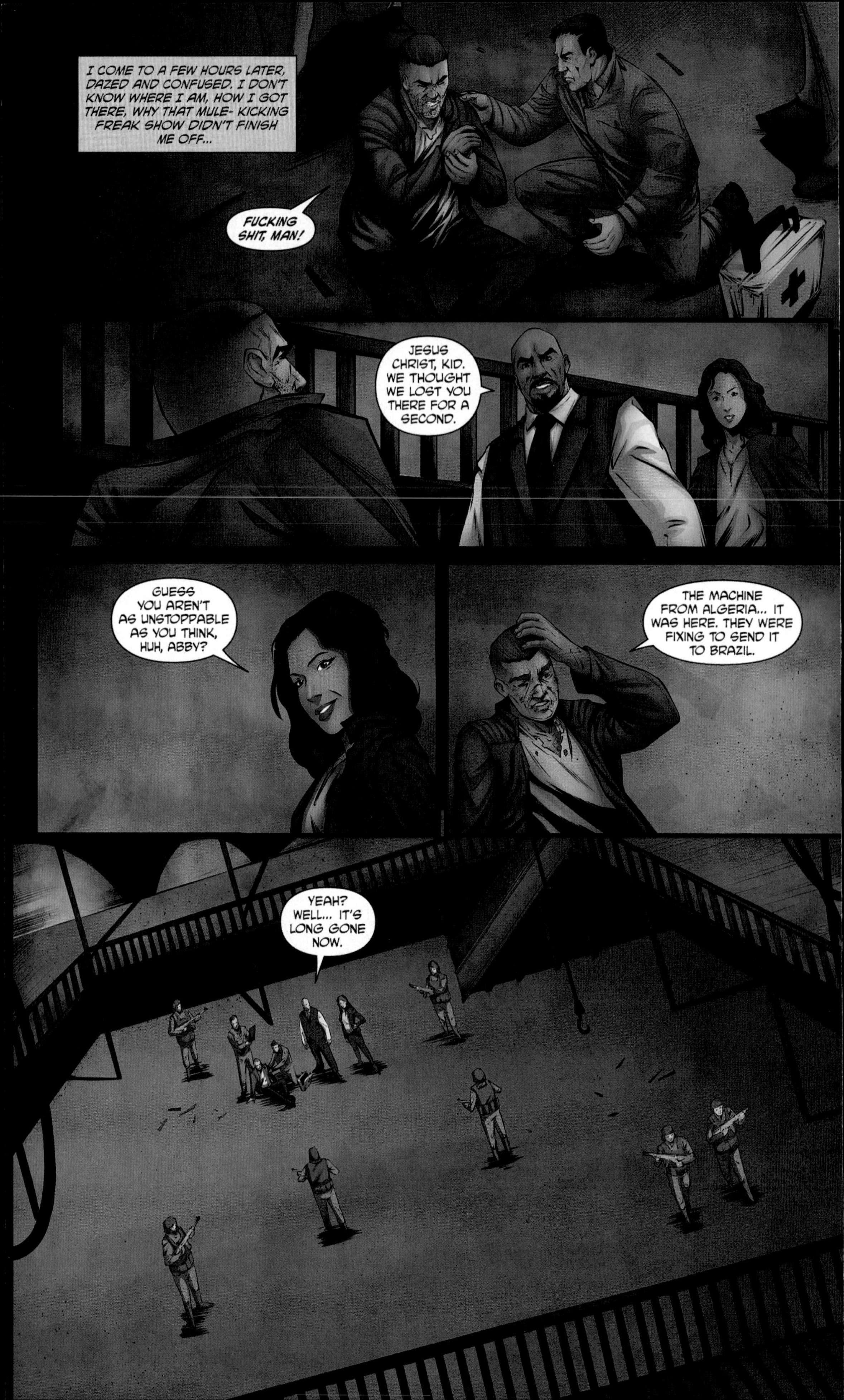
I COME TO A FEW HOURS LATER, DAZED AND CONFUSED. I DON'T KNOW WHERE I AM, HOW I GOT THERE, WHY THAT MULE- KICKING FREAK SHOW DIDN'T FINISH ME OFF...
FUCKING SHIT, MAN!
JESUS CHRIST, KID. WE THOUGHT WE LOST YOU THERE FOR A SECOND.
GUESS YOU AREN'T AS UNSTOPPABLE AS YOU THINK, HUH, ABBY?
THE MACHINE FROM ALGERIA... IT WAS HERE. THEY WERE FIXING TO SEND IT TO BRAZIL.
YEAH? WELL... IT'S LONG GONE NOW.

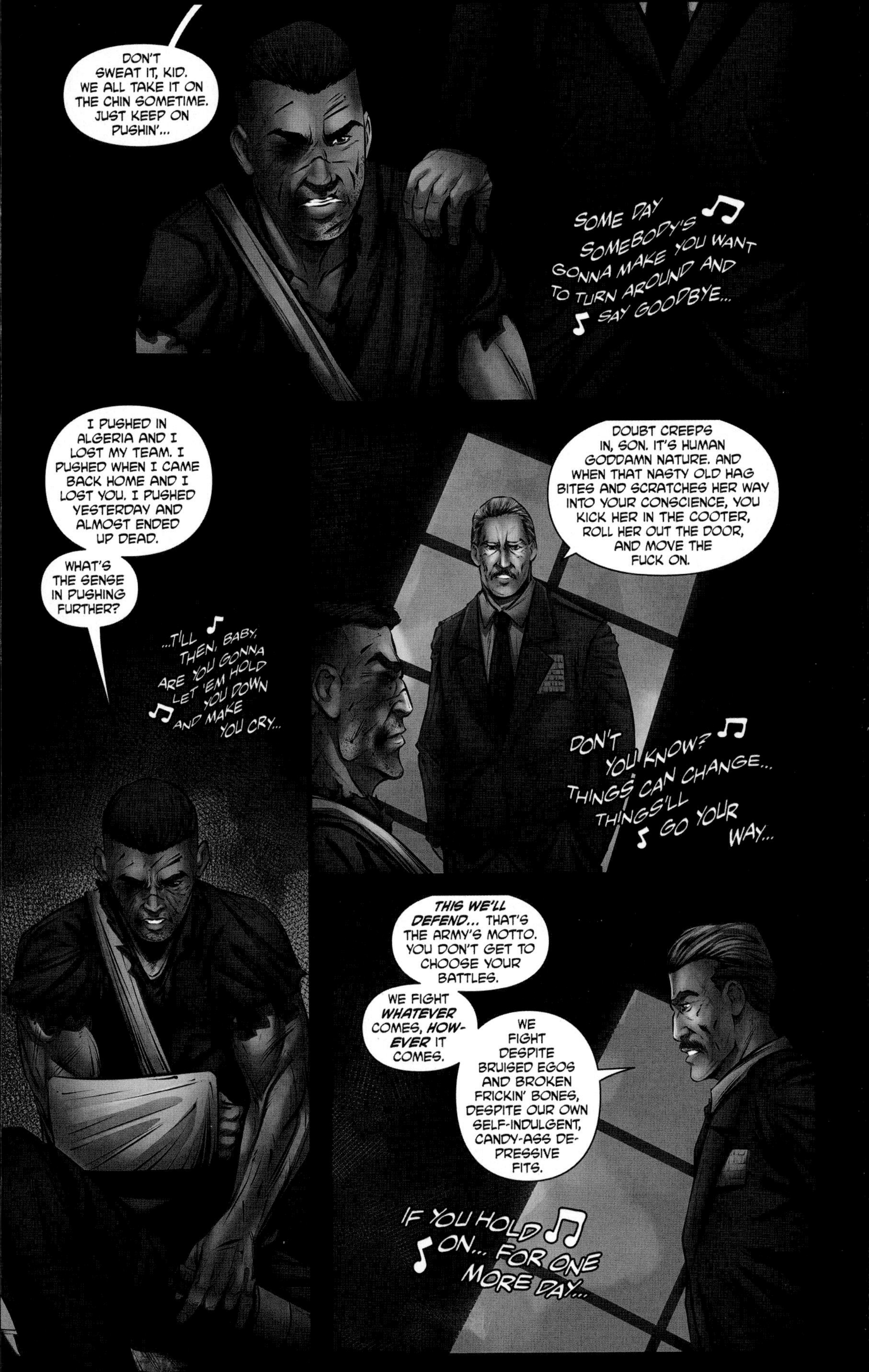

DON'T SWEAT IT, KID. WE ALL TAKE IT ON THE CHIN SOMETIME. JUST KEEP ON PUSHIN'...
SOME DAY SOMEBODY'S GONNA MAKE YOU WANT TO TURN AROUND AND SAY GOODBYE...
I PUSHED IN ALGERIA AND I LOST MY TEAM. I PUSHED WHEN I CAME BACK HOME AND I LOST YOU. I PUSHED YESTERDAY AND ALMOST ENDED UP DEAD.
WHAT'S THE SENSE IN PUSHING FURTHER?
...TILL THEN, BABY, ARE YOU GONNA LET 'EM HOLD YOU DOWN AND MAKE YOU CRY...
DOUBT CREEPS IN, SON. IT'S HUMAN GODDAMN NATURE. AND WHEN THAT NASTY OLD HAG BITES AND SCRATCHES HER WAY INTO YOUR CONSCIENCE, YOU KICK HER IN THE COOTER, ROLL HER OUT THE DOOR, AND MOVE THE FUCK ON.
DON'T YOU KNOW? THINGS CAN CHANGE... THINGS'LL GO YOUR WAY...
THIS WE'LL DEFEND... THAT'S THE ARMY'S MOTTO. YOU DON'T GET TO CHOOSE YOUR BATTLES.
WE FIGHT WHATEVER COMES, HOWEVER IT COMES.
WE FIGHT DESPITE BRUISED EGOS AND BROKEN FRICKIN' BONES, DESPITE OUR OWN SELF-INDULGENT, CANDY-ASS DEPRESSIVE FITS.
IF YOU HOLD ON... FOR ONE MORE DAY...

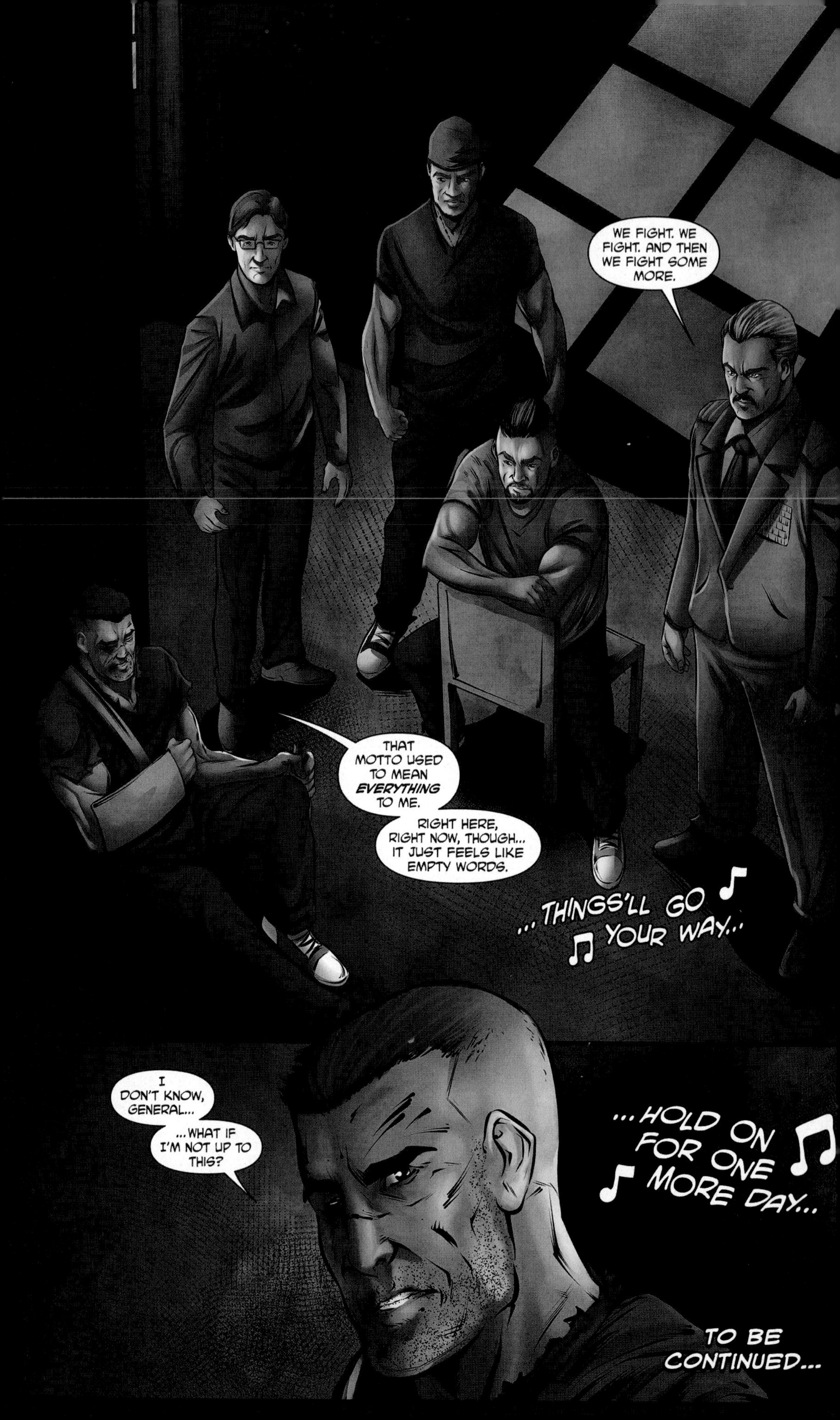
WE FIGHT. WE FIGHT. AND THEN WE FIGHT SOME MORE.
THAT MOTTO USED TO MEAN *EVERYTHING* TO ME.
RIGHT HERE, RIGHT NOW, THOUGH... IT JUST FEELS LIKE EMPTY WORDS.
...THINGS'LL GO YOUR WAY...
I DON'T KNOW, GENERAL...
...WHAT IF I'M NOT UP TO THIS?
...HOLD ON FOR ONE MORE DAY...
TO BE CONTINUED...

Aberrant

GOT ABERRANT-RELATED RANTS, RAVES, FULMINATIONS, VOCIFERATIONS, INVECTIVES, OR OBLOQUIES? GOT FAN ART? NEED TO BE SCREAMED AT? WANT A STIFF KICK IN THE JIMMY?

SEND ALL BUSINESS FIT TO PRINT TO: HALFEVILCOMICS@GMAIL.COM

WWW.HALFEVILCOMICS.COM

f FACEBOOK.COM/HALFEVILCOMICS

🐦 @HALFEVILCOMICS.COM

RISING SPIRIT
ENTERTAINMENT

WWW.RISINGSPIRITFILMS.COM

f FACEBOOK.COM/RISINGSPIRITFILMS

This Month's Music:

Hold On
Words and Music by Carnie Wilson, Chynna
Phillips and Glen Ballard
Copyright © 1990 EMI Blackwood Music Inc.,
Smooshie Music, Universal Music Corp.
and Aerostation Corporation. All Rights on
behalf of EMI Blackwood Music Inc. and
Smooshie Music
Administered by Sony/ATV Music
Publishing LLC, 8 Music Square West,
Nashville, TN 37203
All Rights on behalf of Aerostation Corporation
Administered by Universal Music Corp.
International Copyright Secured
All Rights Reserved
Reprinted by Permission of Hal Leonard LLC

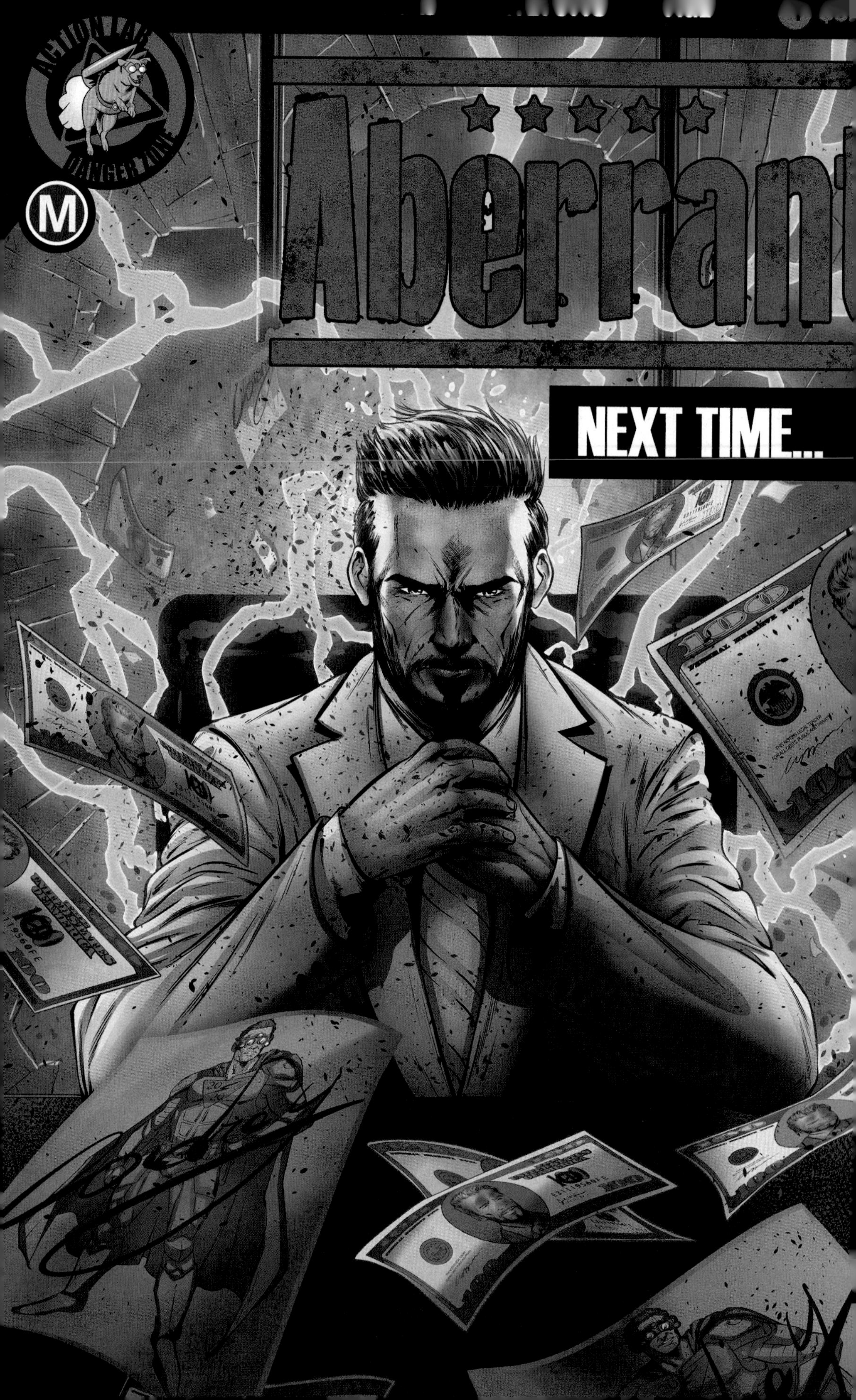
ACTION LAB
DANGER ZONE
M
Aberrant
NEXT TIME...

Aberrant

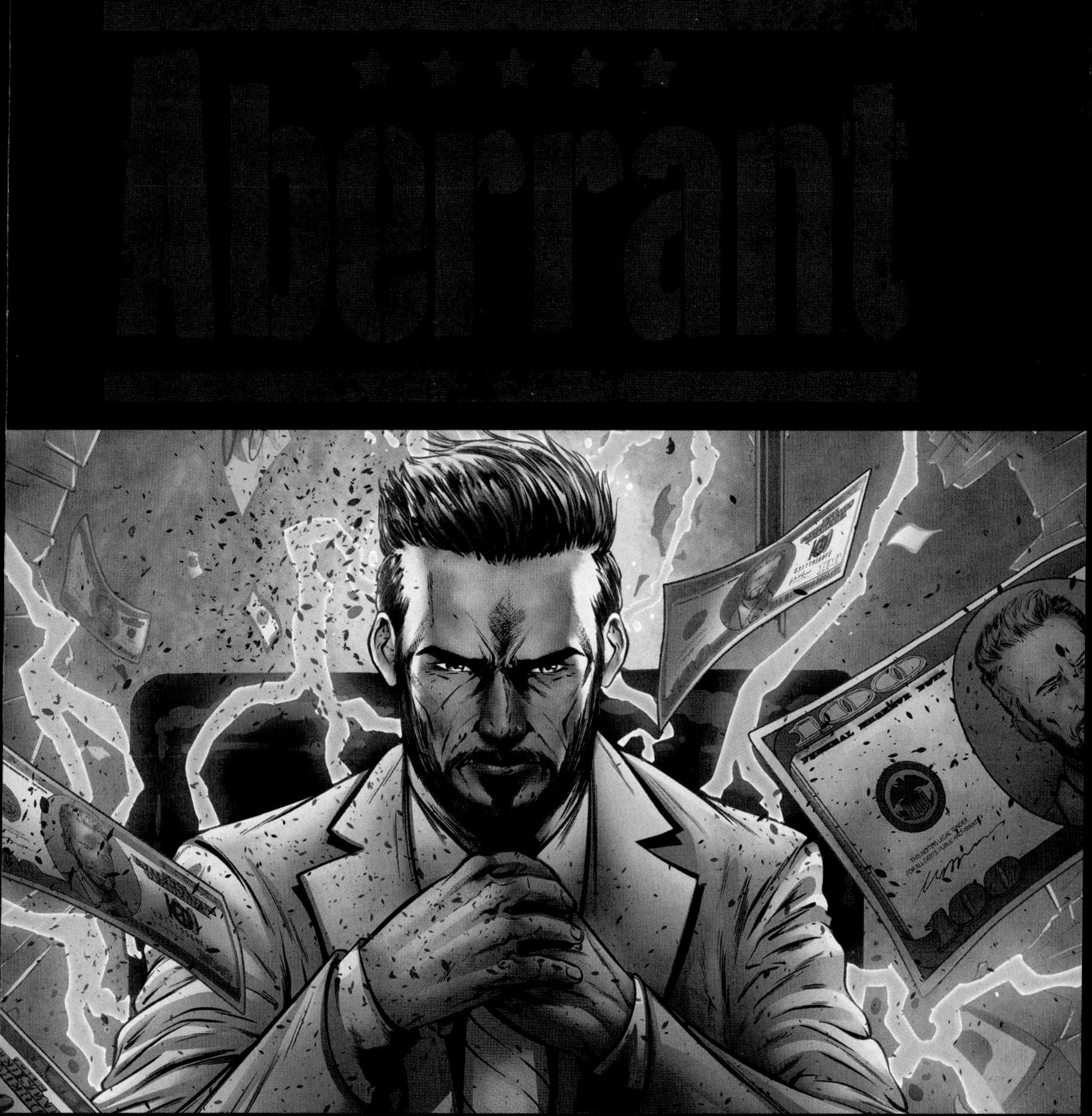

Chapter 4: I Believe I Can Fly

Rylend Grant
Writer/Director
@rylendgrant

Davi Leon Dias
Artist
@davileon

Iwan Joko Triyono
Colorist

HdE
Letterer

R.J. Hendricks
Executive Producer

Executive Producer: Ryan Colucci
Graphic Designer: Jessie Weinberg @jeweinbe

Jason Martin: Publisher • Shawn Gabborin: Editor in Chief • Nicole D'Andria: Marketing Director/Editor
Danielle Davison: Executive Administrator • Bryan Seaton: CEO • Shawn Pryor: President of Creator Relations

Special thanks to Karla Nappi, Jeff Leeds, Steven Prince, Karol Wisniewski, Jim Higgins
and everyone at Meltdown Comics

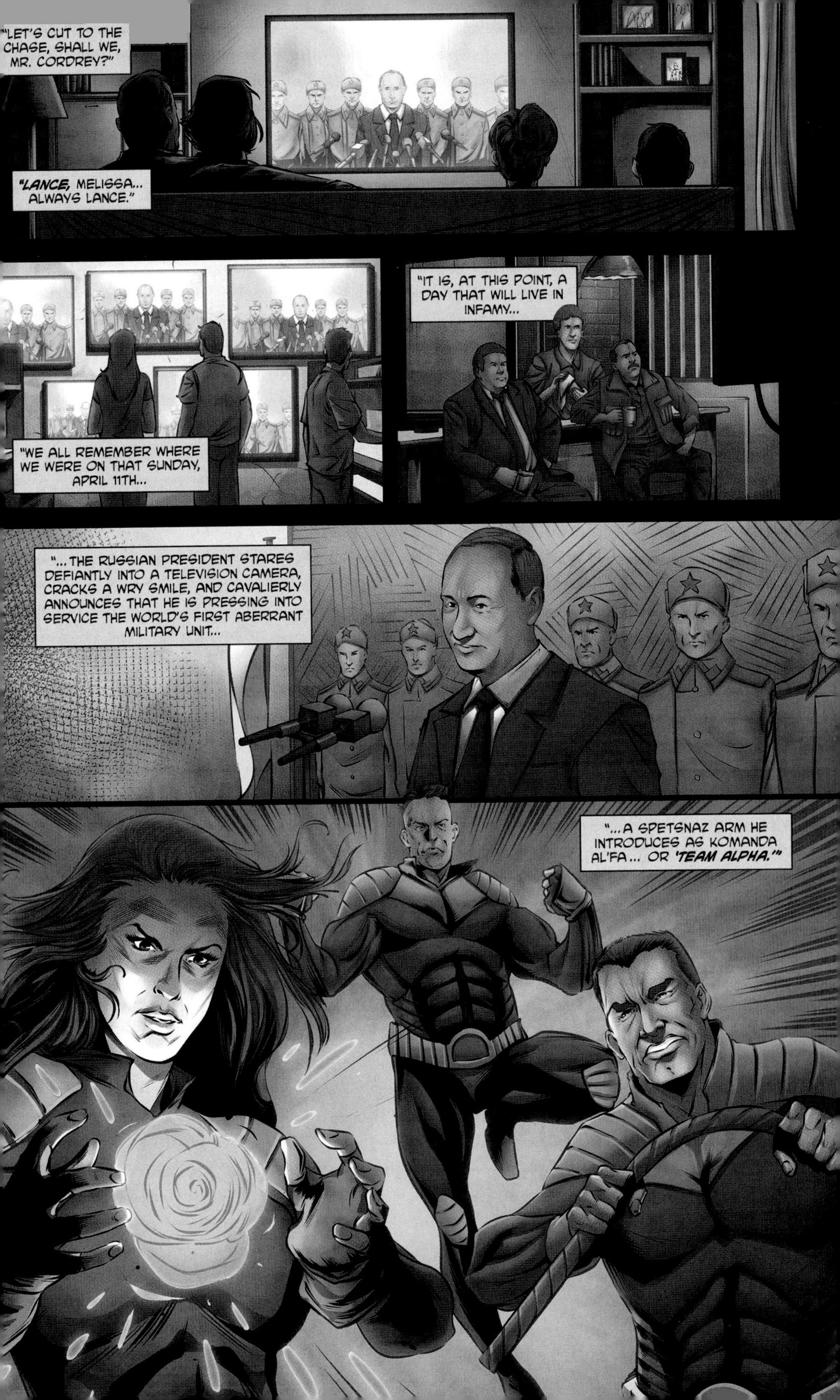
"LET'S CUT TO THE CHASE, SHALL WE, MR. CORDREY?"
"*LANCE,* MELISSA... ALWAYS LANCE."
"WE ALL REMEMBER WHERE WE WERE ON THAT SUNDAY, APRIL 11TH...
"IT IS, AT THIS POINT, A DAY THAT WILL LIVE IN INFAMY...
"...THE RUSSIAN PRESIDENT STARES DEFIANTLY INTO A TELEVISION CAMERA, CRACKS A WRY SMILE, AND CAVALIERLY ANNOUNCES THAT HE IS PRESSING INTO SERVICE THE WORLD'S FIRST ABERRANT MILITARY UNIT...
"...A SPETSNAZ ARM HE INTRODUCES AS KOMANDA AL'FA... OR *'TEAM ALPHA.'*"

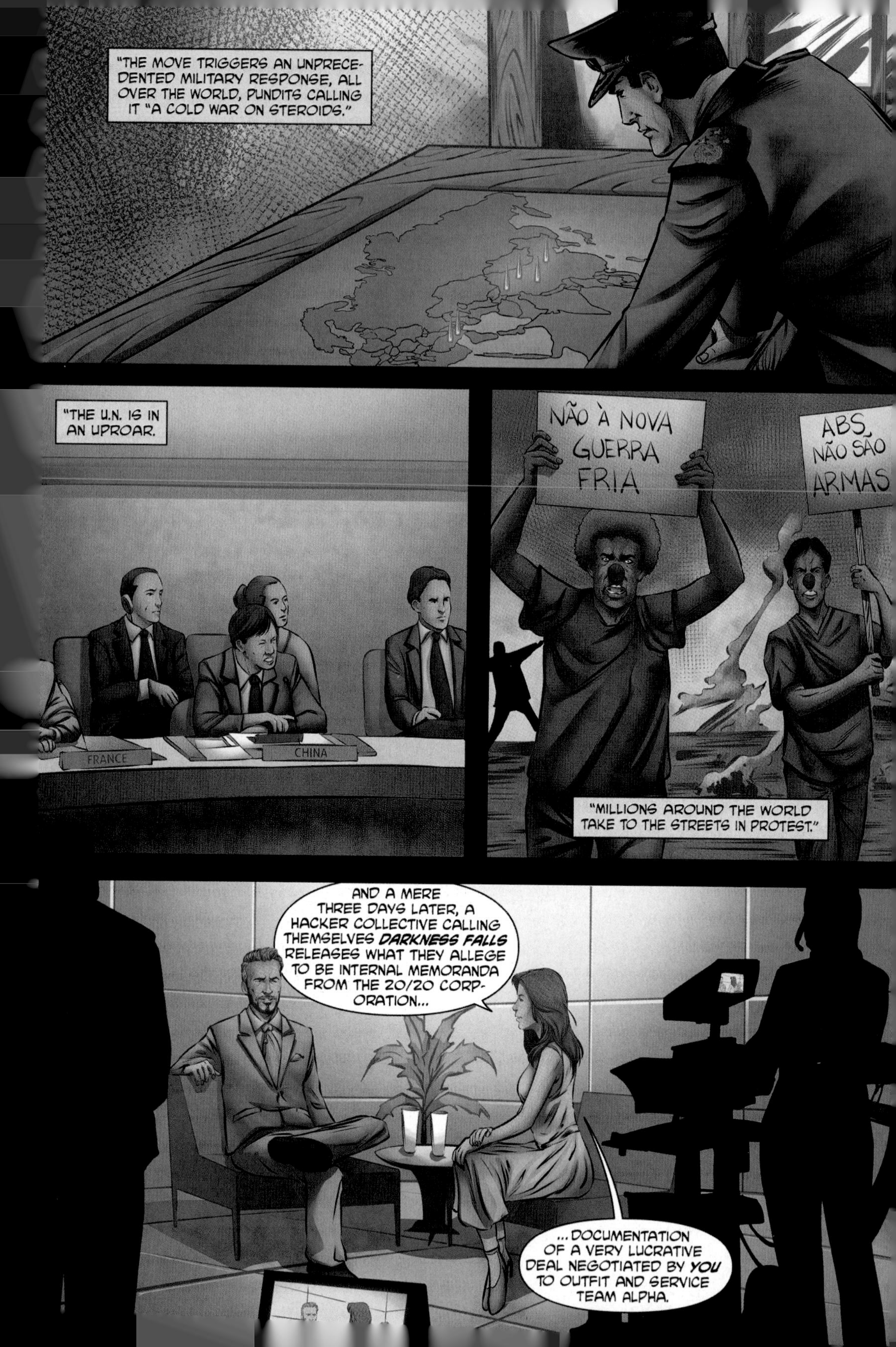
"THE MOVE TRIGGERS AN UNPRECEDENTED MILITARY RESPONSE, ALL OVER THE WORLD, PUNDITS CALLING IT "A COLD WAR ON STEROIDS."
"THE U.N. IS IN AN UPROAR.
FRANCE
CHINA
NÃO À NOVA GUERRA FRIA
ABS, NÃO SÃO ARMAS
"MILLIONS AROUND THE WORLD TAKE TO THE STREETS IN PROTEST."
AND A MERE THREE DAYS LATER, A HACKER COLLECTIVE CALLING THEMSELVES *DARKNESS FALLS* RELEASES WHAT THEY ALLEGE TO BE INTERNAL MEMORANDA FROM THE 20/20 CORPORATION...
...DOCUMENTATION OF A VERY LUCRATIVE DEAL NEGOTIATED BY *YOU* TO OUTFIT AND SERVICE TEAM ALPHA.

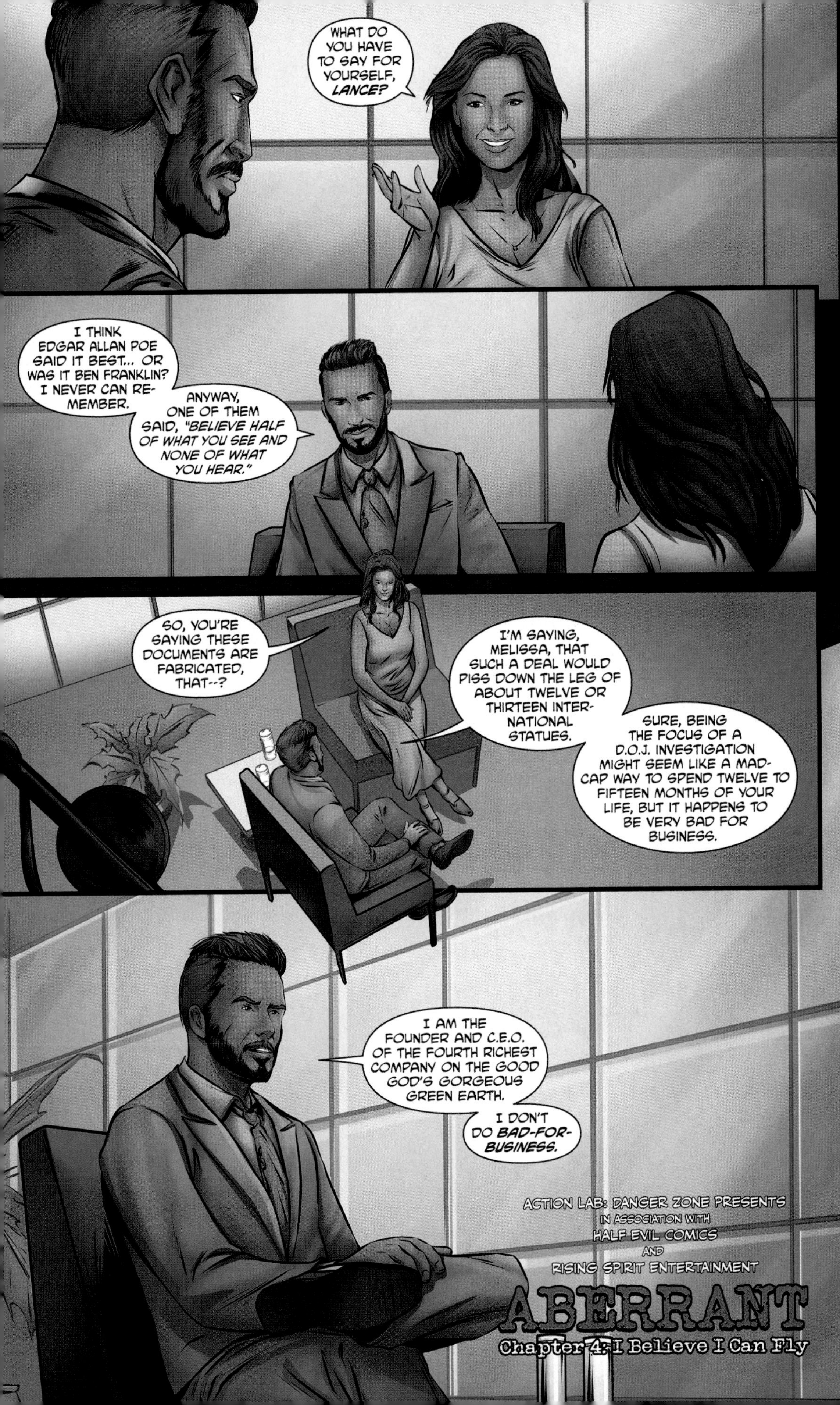

WHAT DO YOU HAVE TO SAY FOR YOURSELF, *LANCE?*
I THINK EDGAR ALLAN POE SAID IT BEST... OR WAS IT BEN FRANKLIN? I NEVER CAN REMEMBER.
ANYWAY, ONE OF THEM SAID, *"BELIEVE HALF OF WHAT YOU SEE AND NONE OF WHAT YOU HEAR."*
SO, YOU'RE SAYING THESE DOCUMENTS ARE FABRICATED, THAT--?
I'M SAYING, MELISSA, THAT SUCH A DEAL WOULD PISS DOWN THE LEG OF ABOUT TWELVE OR THIRTEEN INTERNATIONAL STATUES.
SURE, BEING THE FOCUS OF A D.O.J. INVESTIGATION MIGHT SEEM LIKE A MADCAP WAY TO SPEND TWELVE TO FIFTEEN MONTHS OF YOUR LIFE, BUT IT HAPPENS TO BE VERY BAD FOR BUSINESS.
I AM THE FOUNDER AND C.E.O. OF THE FOURTH RICHEST COMPANY ON THE GOOD GOD'S GORGEOUS GREEN EARTH.
I DON'T DO *BAD-FOR-BUSINESS.*
ACTION LAB: DANGER ZONE PRESENTS
IN ASSOCIATION WITH
HALF EVIL COMICS
AND
RISING SPIRIT ENTERTAINMENT
ABERRANT
Chapter 4: I Believe I Can Fly

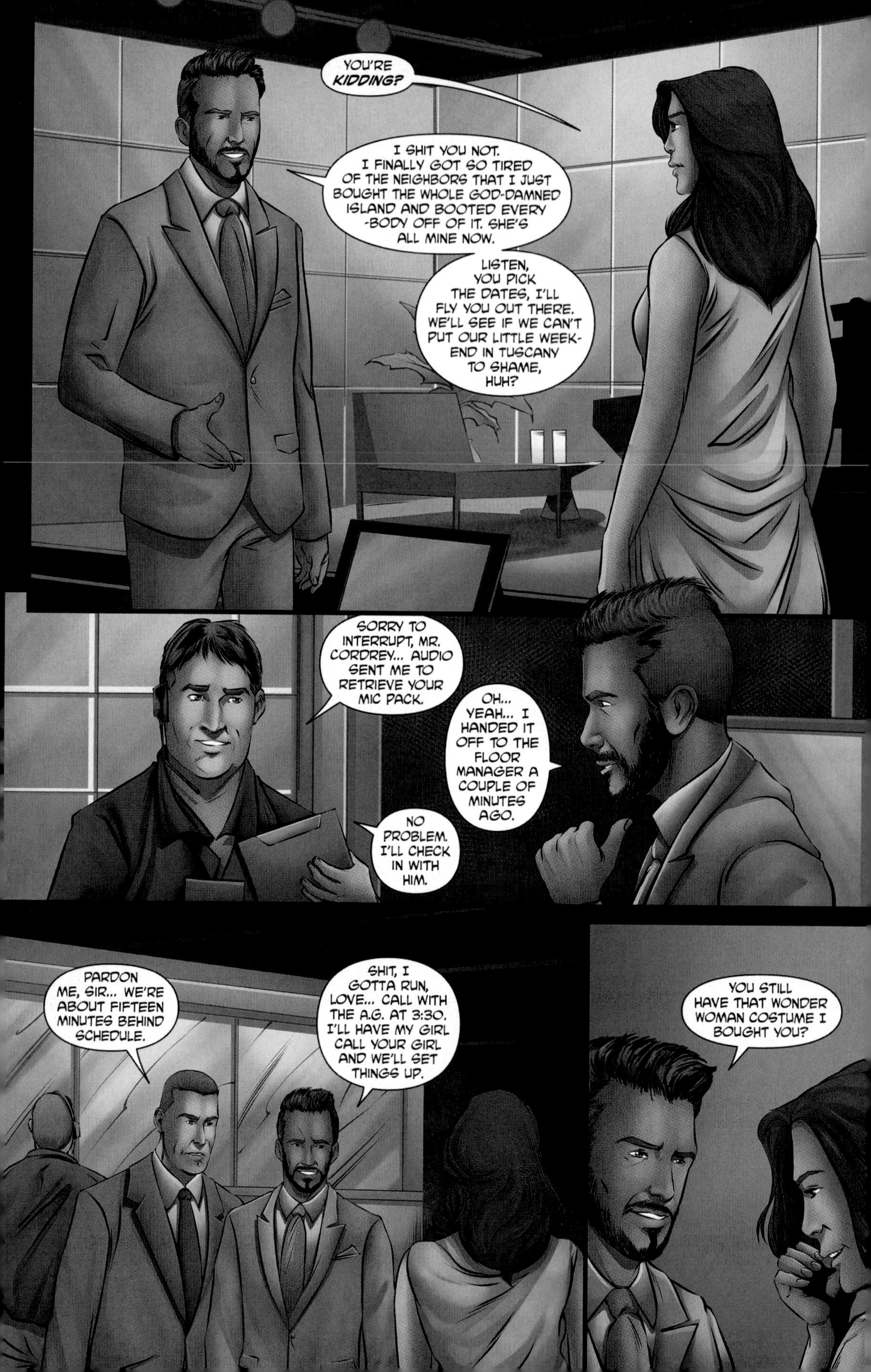
YOU'RE *KIDDING?*
I SHIT YOU NOT. I FINALLY GOT SO TIRED OF THE NEIGHBORS THAT I JUST BOUGHT THE WHOLE GOD-DAMNED ISLAND AND BOOTED EVERY -BODY OFF OF IT. SHE'S ALL MINE NOW.
LISTEN, YOU PICK THE DATES, I'LL FLY YOU OUT THERE. WE'LL SEE IF WE CAN'T PUT OUR LITTLE WEEK-END IN TUSCANY TO SHAME, HUH?
SORRY TO INTERRUPT, MR. CORDREY... AUDIO SENT ME TO RETRIEVE YOUR MIC PACK.
OH... YEAH... I HANDED IT OFF TO THE FLOOR MANAGER A COUPLE OF MINUTES AGO.
NO PROBLEM. I'LL CHECK IN WITH HIM.
PARDON ME, SIR... WE'RE ABOUT FIFTEEN MINUTES BEHIND SCHEDULE.
SHIT, I GOTTA RUN, LOVE... CALL WITH THE A.G. AT 3:30. I'LL HAVE MY GIRL CALL YOUR GIRL AND WE'LL SET THINGS UP.
YOU STILL HAVE THAT WONDER WOMAN COSTUME I BOUGHT YOU?

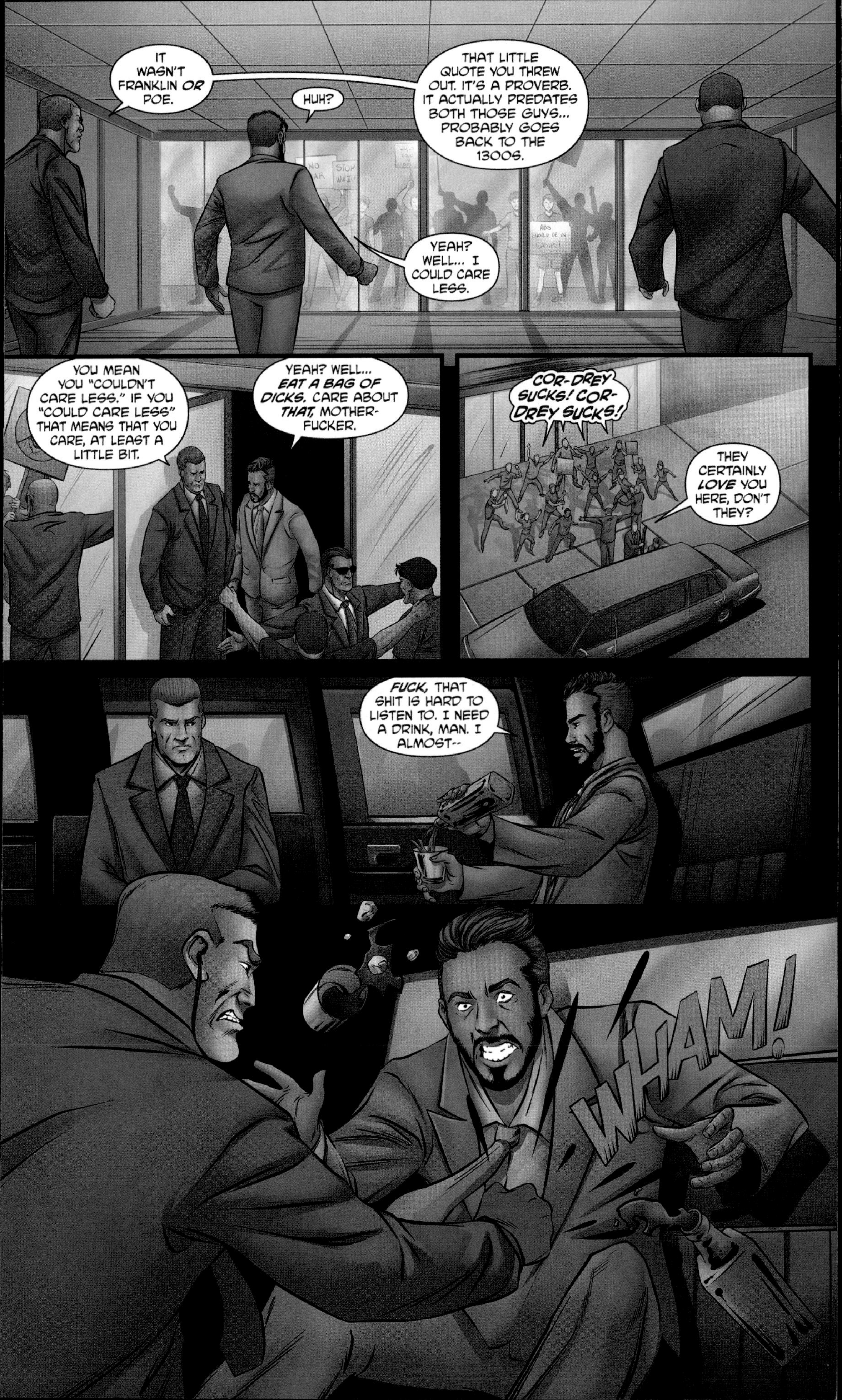

IT WASN'T FRANKLIN *OR* POE.
HUH?
THAT LITTLE QUOTE YOU THREW OUT. IT'S A PROVERB. IT ACTUALLY PREDATES BOTH THOSE GUYS... PROBABLY GOES BACK TO THE 1300S.
YEAH? WELL... I COULD CARE LESS.
YOU MEAN YOU "COULDN'T CARE LESS." IF YOU "COULD CARE LESS" THAT MEANS THAT YOU CARE, AT LEAST A LITTLE BIT.
YEAH? WELL... ***EAT A BAG OF DICKS.*** CARE ABOUT ***THAT,*** MOTHER-FUCKER.
COR-DREY SUCKS! COR-DREY SUCKS!
THEY CERTAINLY ***LOVE*** YOU HERE, DON'T THEY?
FUCK, THAT SHIT IS HARD TO LISTEN TO. I NEED A DRINK, MAN. I ALMOST--
WHAM!

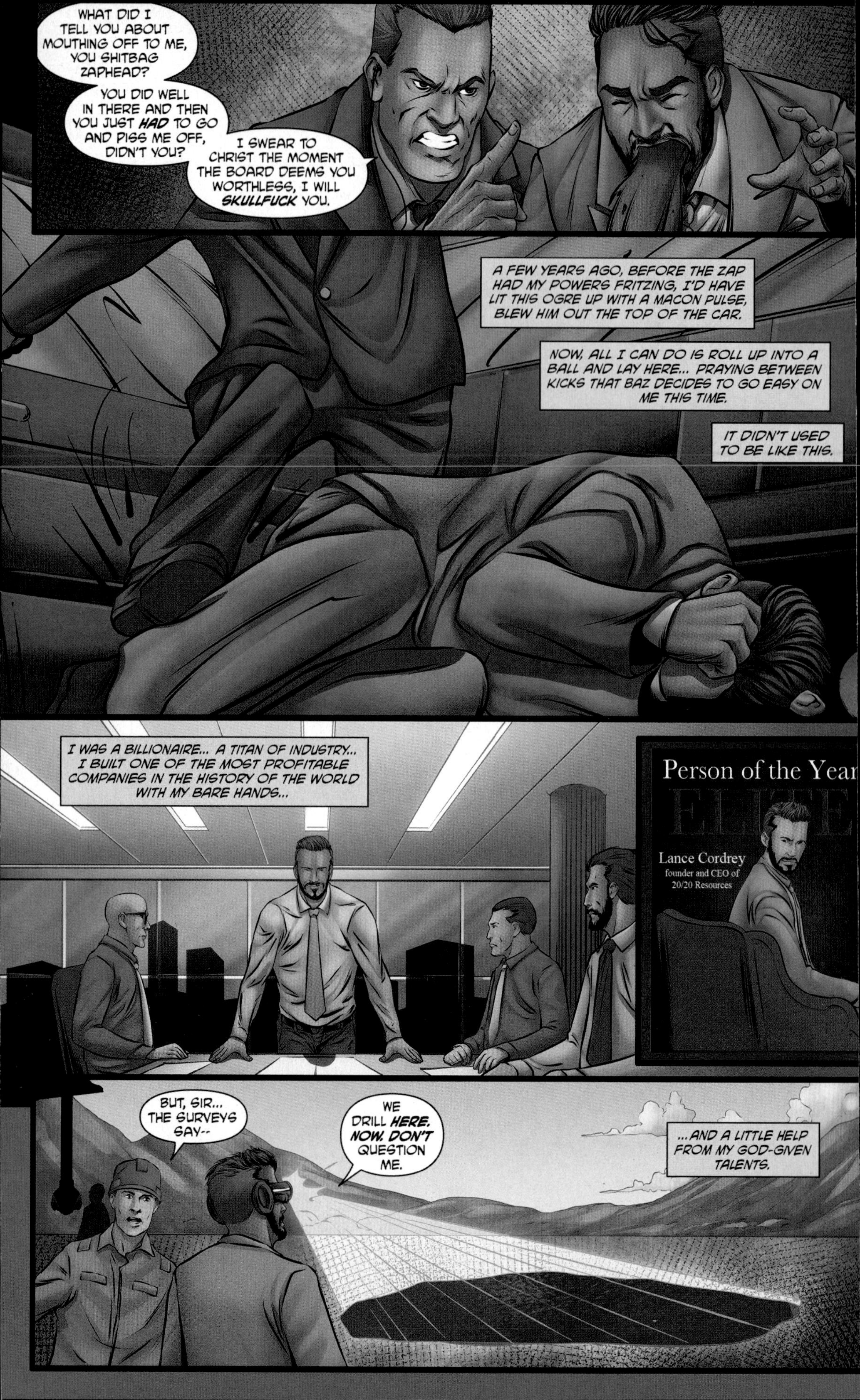
WHAT DID I TELL YOU ABOUT MOUTHING OFF TO ME, YOU SHITBAG ZAPHEAD?
YOU DID WELL IN THERE AND THEN YOU JUST HAD TO GO AND PISS ME OFF, DIDN'T YOU?
I SWEAR TO CHRIST THE MOMENT THE BOARD DEEMS YOU WORTHLESS, I WILL SKULLFUCK YOU.
A FEW YEARS AGO, BEFORE THE ZAP HAD MY POWERS FRITZING, I'D HAVE LIT THIS OGRE UP WITH A MACON PULSE, BLEW HIM OUT THE TOP OF THE CAR.
NOW, ALL I CAN DO IS ROLL UP INTO A BALL AND LAY HERE... PRAYING BETWEEN KICKS THAT BAZ DECIDES TO GO EASY ON ME THIS TIME.
IT DIDN'T USED TO BE LIKE THIS.
I WAS A BILLIONAIRE... A TITAN OF INDUSTRY... I BUILT ONE OF THE MOST PROFITABLE COMPANIES IN THE HISTORY OF THE WORLD WITH MY BARE HANDS...
Person of the Year
ELITE
Lance Cordrey
founder and CEO of
20/20 Resources
BUT, SIR... THE SURVEYS SAY--
WE DRILL HERE. NOW. DON'T QUESTION ME.
...AND A LITTLE HELP FROM MY GOD-GIVEN TALENTS.

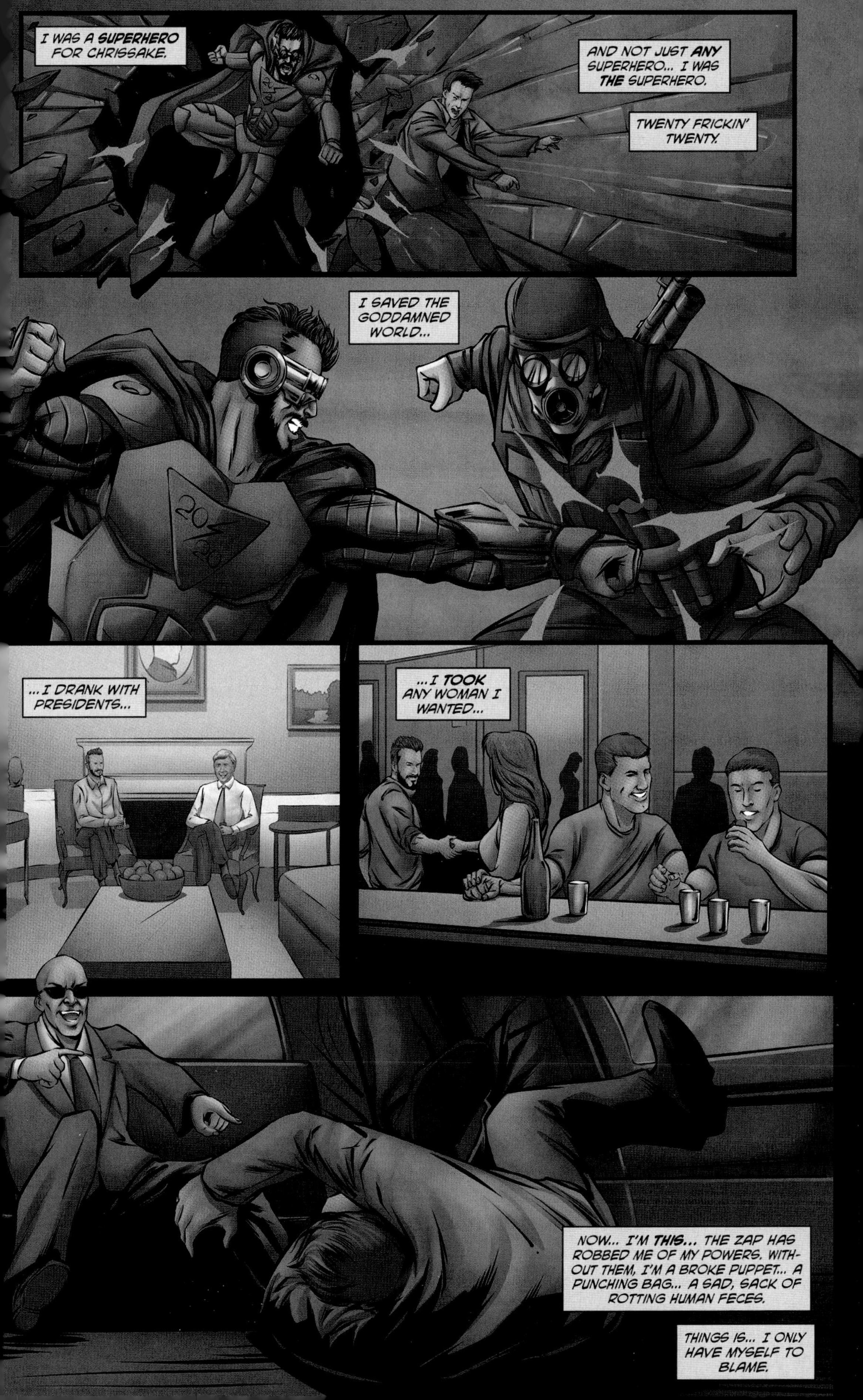
I WAS A SUPERHERO FOR CHRISSAKE.
AND NOT JUST ANY SUPERHERO... I WAS THE SUPERHERO.
TWENTY FRICKIN' TWENTY.
I SAVED THE GODDAMNED WORLD...
...I DRANK WITH PRESIDENTS...
...I TOOK ANY WOMAN I WANTED...
NOW... I'M THIS... THE ZAP HAS ROBBED ME OF MY POWERS. WITH-OUT THEM, I'M A BROKE PUPPET... A PUNCHING BAG... A SAD, SACK OF ROTTING HUMAN FECES.
THINGS IS... I ONLY HAVE MYSELF TO BLAME.

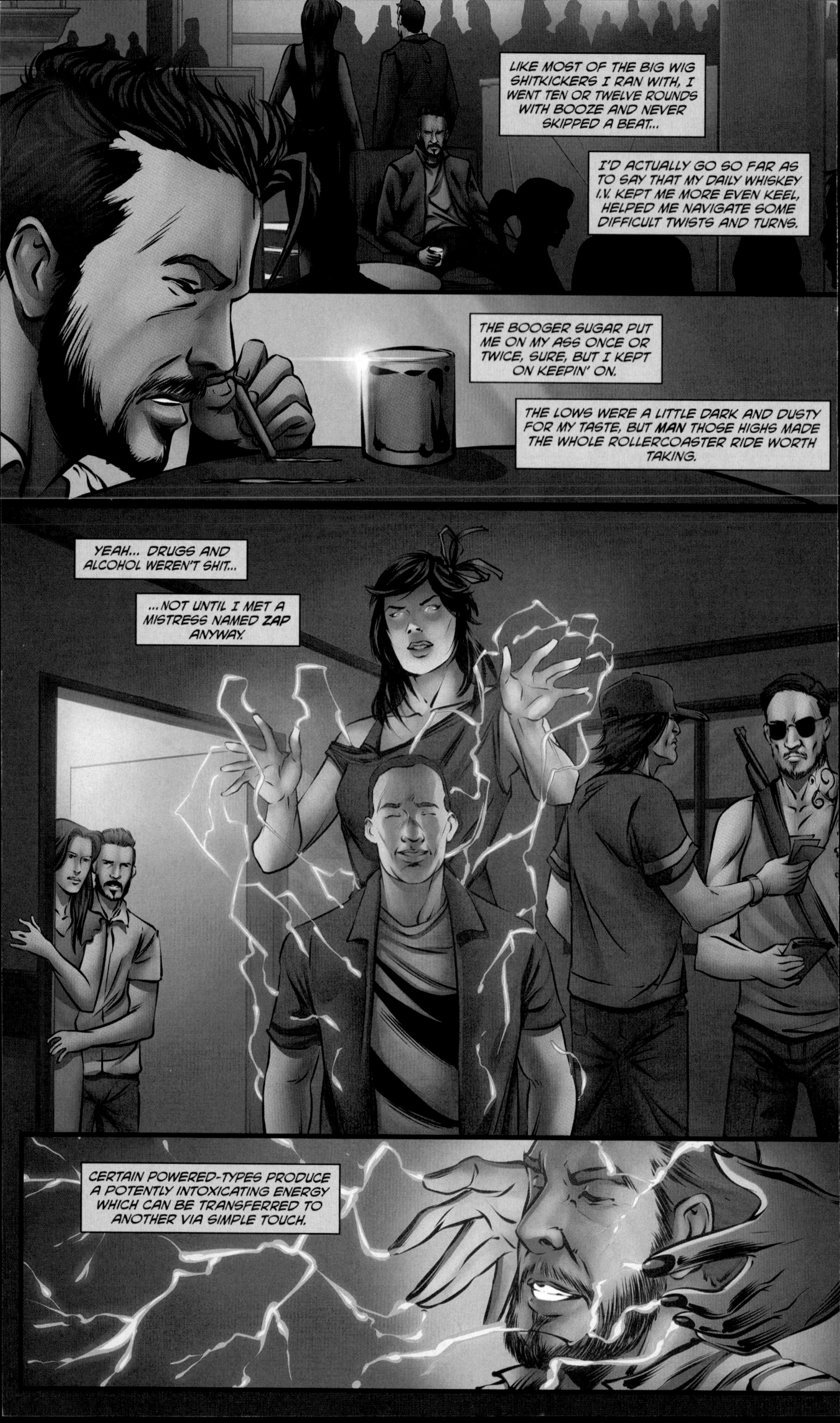
LIKE MOST OF THE BIG WIG SHITKICKERS I RAN WITH, I WENT TEN OR TWELVE ROUNDS WITH BOOZE AND NEVER SKIPPED A BEAT...
I'D ACTUALLY GO SO FAR AS TO SAY THAT MY DAILY WHISKEY I.V. KEPT ME MORE EVEN KEEL, HELPED ME NAVIGATE SOME DIFFICULT TWISTS AND TURNS.
THE BOOGER SUGAR PUT ME ON MY ASS ONCE OR TWICE, SURE, BUT I KEPT ON KEEPIN' ON.
THE LOWS WERE A LITTLE DARK AND DUSTY FOR MY TASTE, BUT MAN THOSE HIGHS MADE THE WHOLE ROLLERCOASTER RIDE WORTH TAKING.
YEAH... DRUGS AND ALCOHOL WEREN'T SHIT...
...NOT UNTIL I MET A MISTRESS NAMED ZAP ANYWAY.
CERTAIN POWERED-TYPES PRODUCE A POTENTLY INTOXICATING ENERGY WHICH CAN BE TRANSFERRED TO ANOTHER VIA SIMPLE TOUCH.

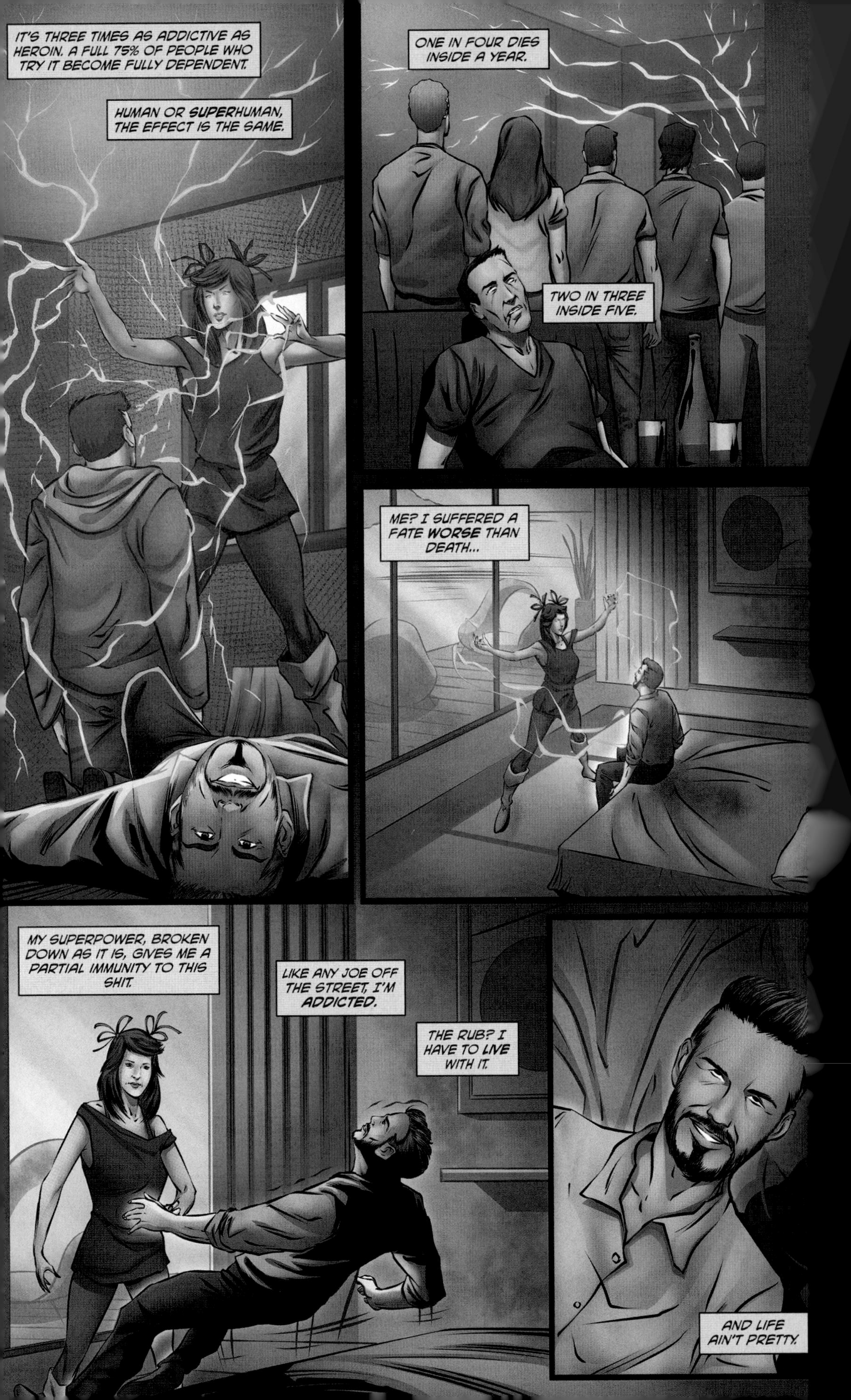
IT'S THREE TIMES AS ADDICTIVE AS HEROIN. A FULL 75% OF PEOPLE WHO TRY IT BECOME FULLY DEPENDENT.
HUMAN OR SUPERHUMAN, THE EFFECT IS THE SAME.
ONE IN FOUR DIES INSIDE A YEAR.
TWO IN THREE INSIDE FIVE.
ME? I SUFFERED A FATE WORSE THAN DEATH...
MY SUPERPOWER, BROKEN DOWN AS IT IS, GIVES ME A PARTIAL IMMUNITY TO THIS SHIT.
LIKE ANY JOE OFF THE STREET, I'M ADDICTED.
THE RUB? I HAVE TO LIVE WITH IT.
AND LIFE AIN'T PRETTY.

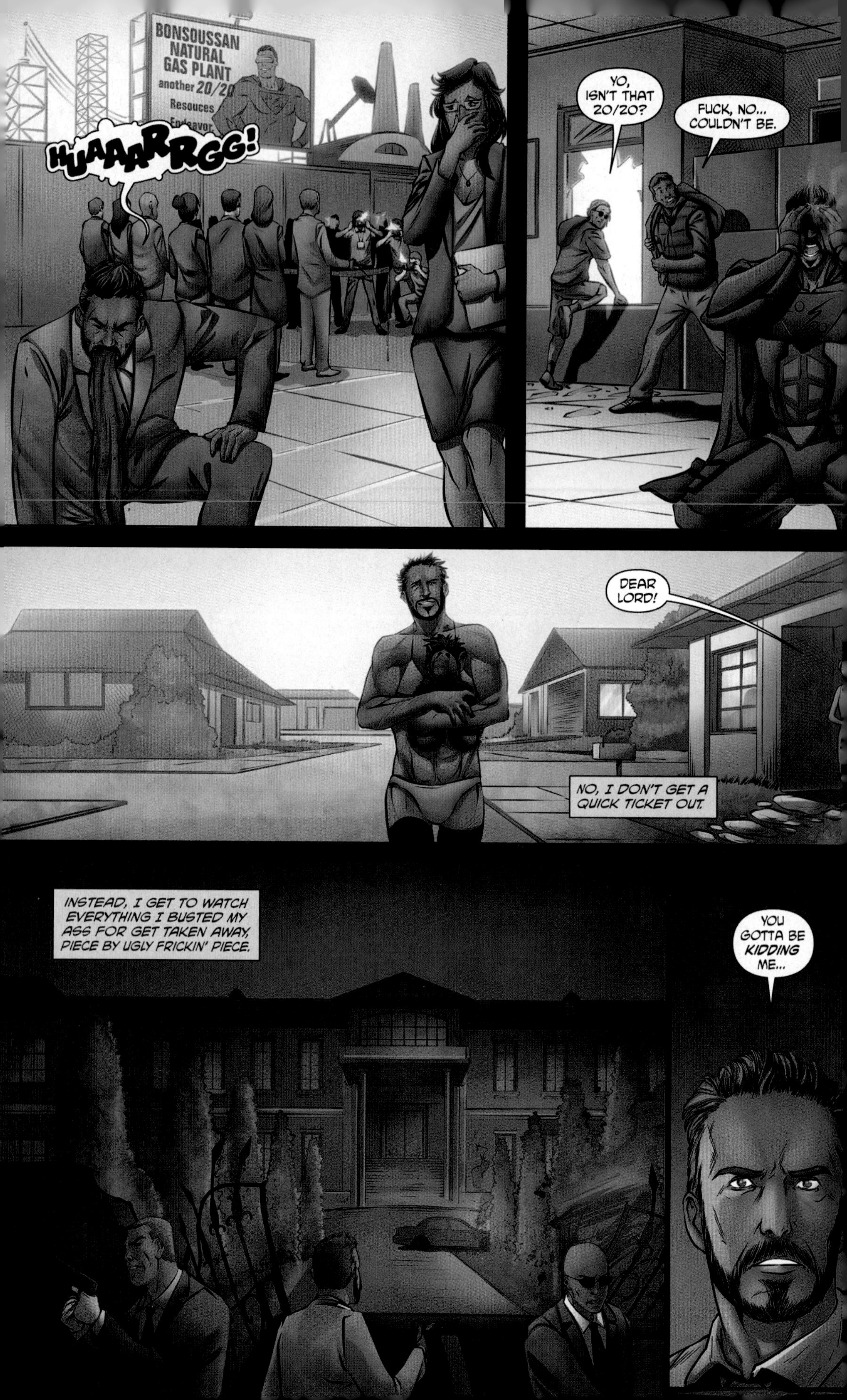

BONSOUSSAN NATURAL GAS PLANT
another 20/20
Resouces
Endeavor
HUAAARRGG!
YO, ISN'T THAT 20/20?
FUCK, NO... COULDN'T BE.
DEAR LORD!
NO, I DON'T GET A QUICK TICKET OUT.
INSTEAD, I GET TO WATCH EVERYTHING I BUSTED MY ASS FOR GET TAKEN AWAY, PIECE BY UGLY FRICKIN' PIECE.
YOU GOTTA BE *KIDDING* ME...

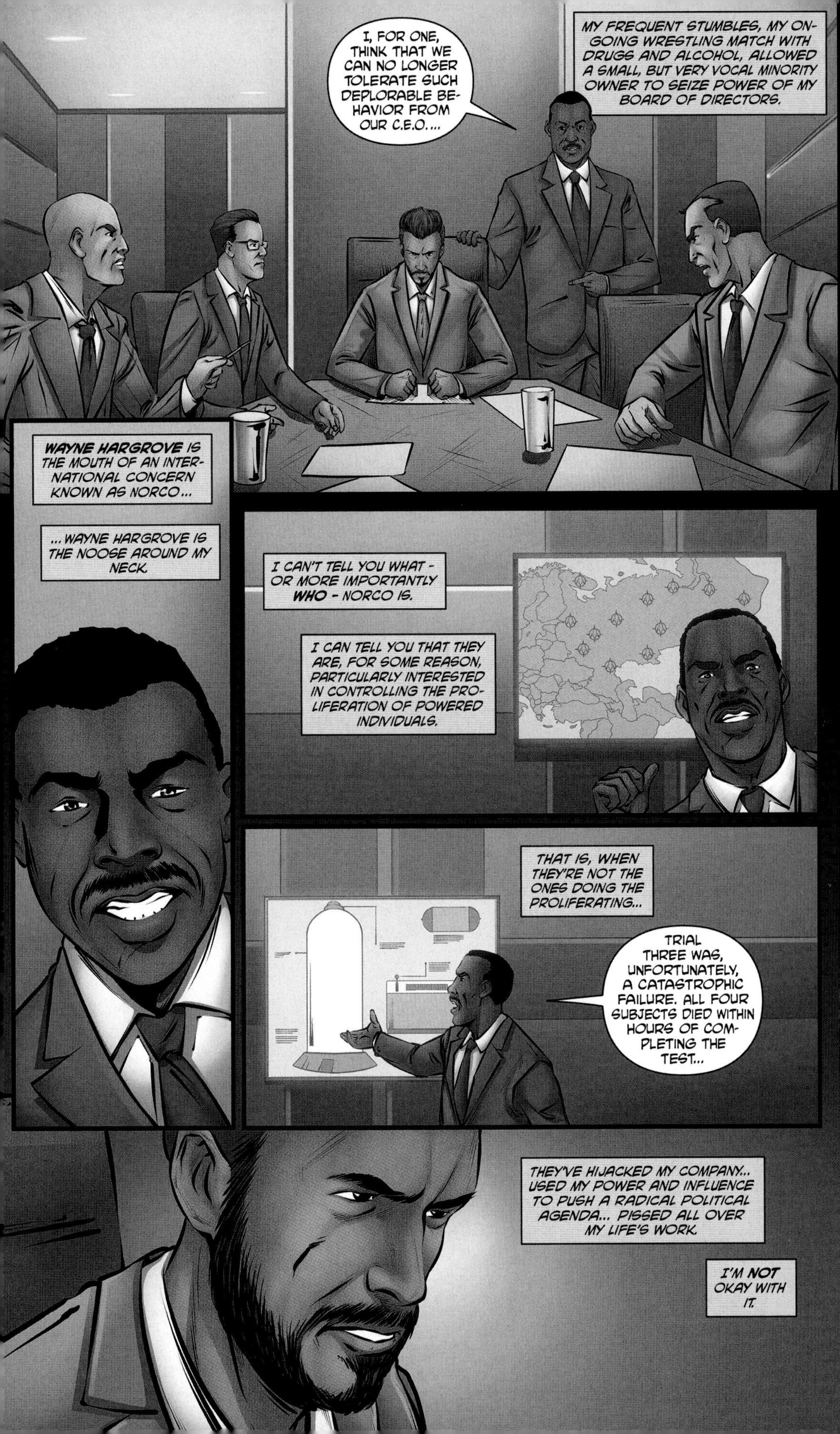
I, FOR ONE, THINK THAT WE CAN NO LONGER TOLERATE SUCH DEPLORABLE BEHAVIOR FROM OUR C.E.O....
MY FREQUENT STUMBLES, MY ONGOING WRESTLING MATCH WITH DRUGS AND ALCOHOL, ALLOWED A SMALL, BUT VERY VOCAL MINORITY OWNER TO SEIZE POWER OF MY BOARD OF DIRECTORS.
WAYNE HARGROVE IS THE MOUTH OF AN INTERNATIONAL CONCERN KNOWN AS NORCO...
...WAYNE HARGROVE IS THE NOOSE AROUND MY NECK.
I CAN'T TELL YOU WHAT - OR MORE IMPORTANTLY WHO - NORCO IS.
I CAN TELL YOU THAT THEY ARE, FOR SOME REASON, PARTICULARLY INTERESTED IN CONTROLLING THE PROLIFERATION OF POWERED INDIVIDUALS.
THAT IS, WHEN THEY'RE NOT THE ONES DOING THE PROLIFERATING...
TRIAL THREE WAS, UNFORTUNATELY, A CATASTROPHIC FAILURE. ALL FOUR SUBJECTS DIED WITHIN HOURS OF COMPLETING THE TEST...
THEY'VE HIJACKED MY COMPANY... USED MY POWER AND INFLUENCE TO PUSH A RADICAL POLITICAL AGENDA... PISSED ALL OVER MY LIFE'S WORK.
I'M NOT OKAY WITH IT.

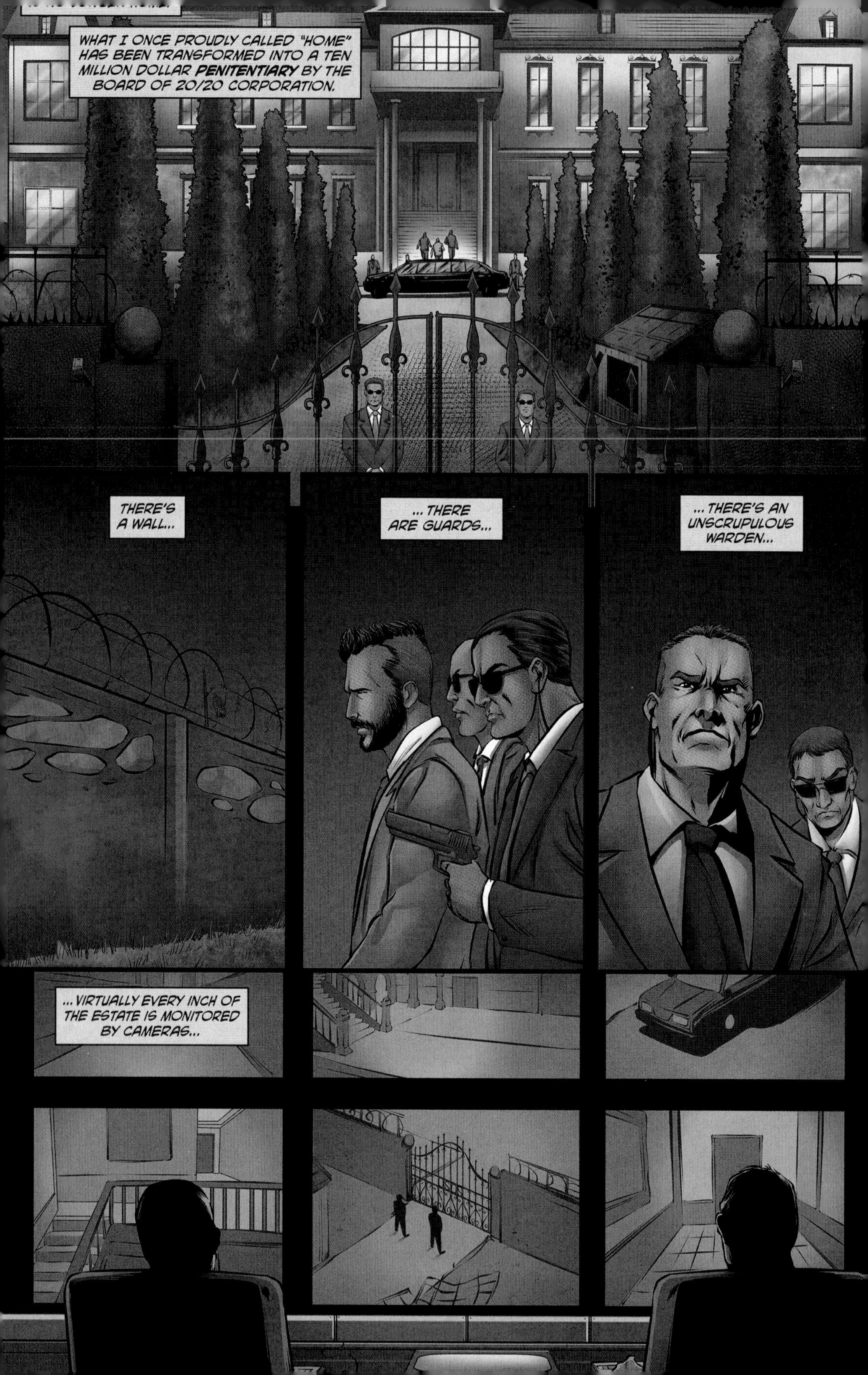
WHAT I ONCE PROUDLY CALLED "HOME" HAS BEEN TRANSFORMED INTO A TEN MILLION DOLLAR PENITENTIARY BY THE BOARD OF 20/20 CORPORATION.
THERE'S A WALL...
...THERE ARE GUARDS...
...THERE'S AN UNSCRUPULOUS WARDEN...
...VIRTUALLY EVERY INCH OF THE ESTATE IS MONITORED BY CAMERAS...

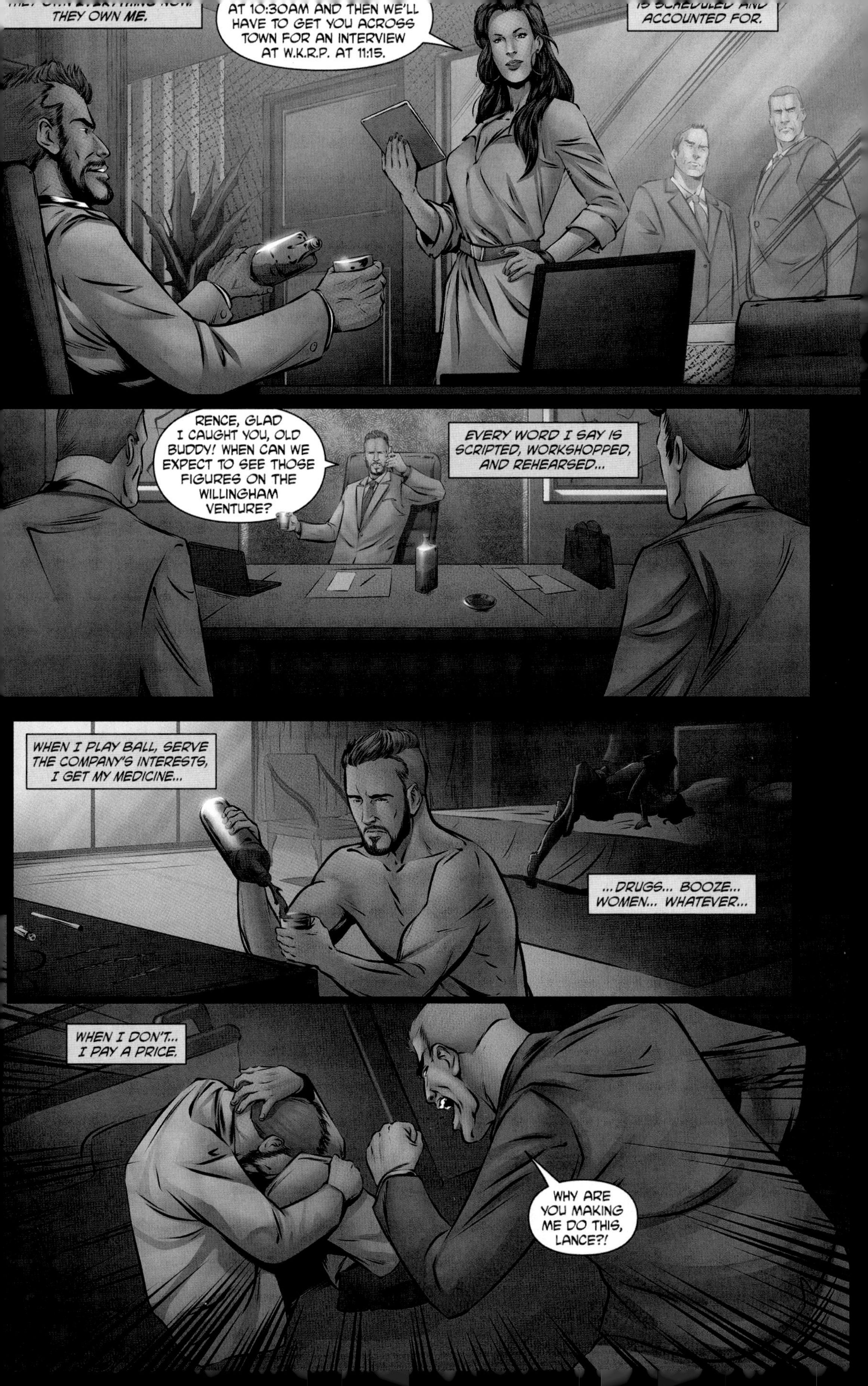
THEY OWN ME.
AT 10:30AM AND THEN WE'LL HAVE TO GET YOU ACROSS TOWN FOR AN INTERVIEW AT W.K.R.P. AT 11:15.
ACCOUNTED FOR.
RENCE, GLAD I CAUGHT YOU, OLD BUDDY! WHEN CAN WE EXPECT TO SEE THOSE FIGURES ON THE WILLINGHAM VENTURE?
EVERY WORD I SAY IS SCRIPTED, WORKSHOPPED, AND REHEARSED...
WHEN I PLAY BALL, SERVE THE COMPANY'S INTERESTS, I GET MY MEDICINE...
...DRUGS... BOOZE... WOMEN... WHATEVER...
WHEN I DON'T... I PAY A PRICE.
WHY ARE YOU MAKING ME DO THIS, LANCE?!

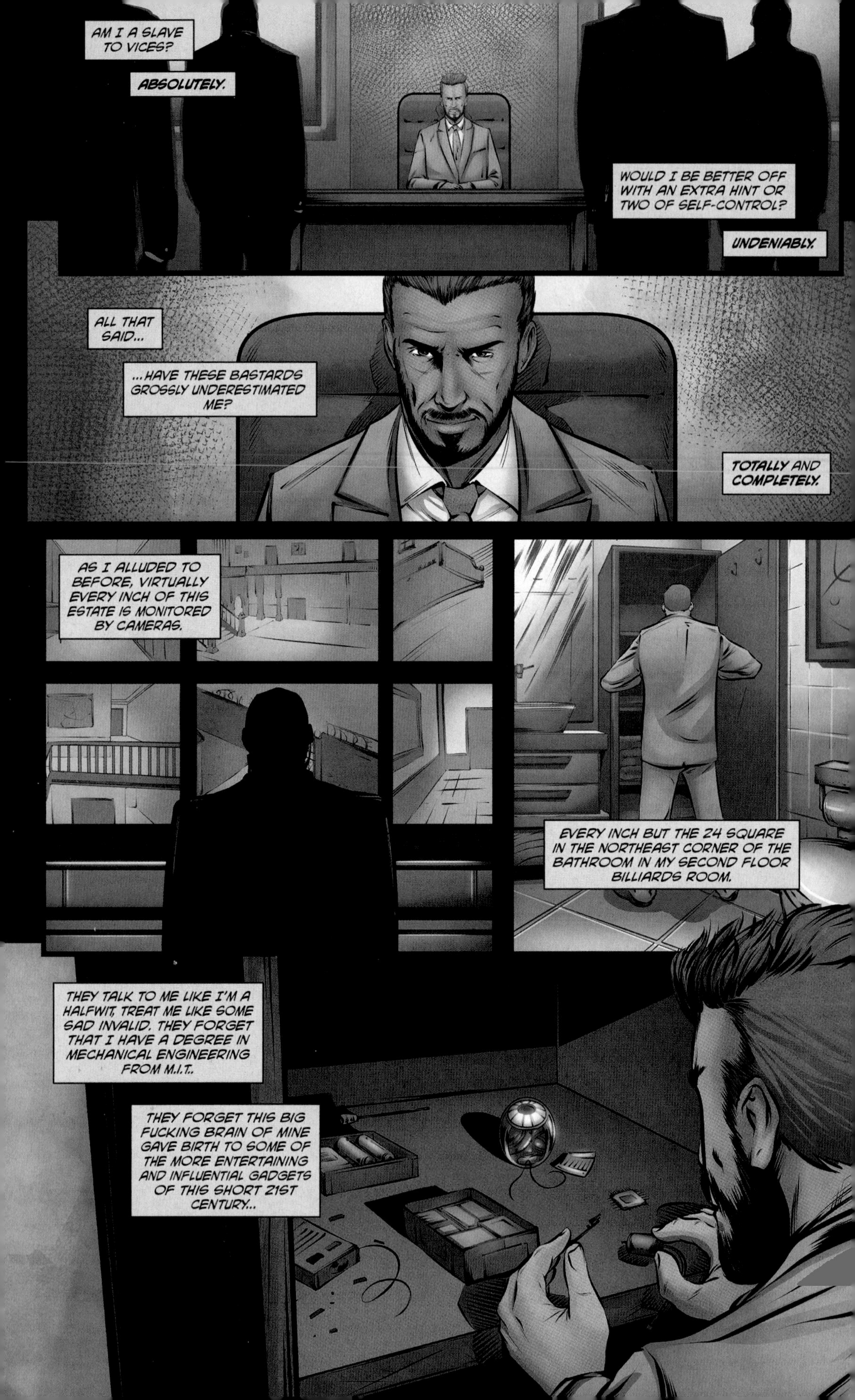
AM I A SLAVE TO VICES?
ABSOLUTELY.
WOULD I BE BETTER OFF WITH AN EXTRA HINT OR TWO OF SELF-CONTROL?
UNDENIABLY.
ALL THAT SAID...
...HAVE THESE BASTARDS GROSSLY UNDERESTIMATED ME?
TOTALLY AND COMPLETELY.
AS I ALLUDED TO BEFORE, VIRTUALLY EVERY INCH OF THIS ESTATE IS MONITORED BY CAMERAS.
EVERY INCH BUT THE 24 SQUARE IN THE NORTHEAST CORNER OF THE BATHROOM IN MY SECOND FLOOR BILLIARDS ROOM.
THEY TALK TO ME LIKE I'M A HALFWIT, TREAT ME LIKE SOME SAD INVALID. THEY FORGET THAT I HAVE A DEGREE IN MECHANICAL ENGINEERING FROM M.I.T..
THEY FORGET THIS BIG FUCKING BRAIN OF MINE GAVE BIRTH TO SOME OF THE MORE ENTERTAINING AND INFLUENTIAL GADGETS OF THIS SHORT 21ST CENTURY...

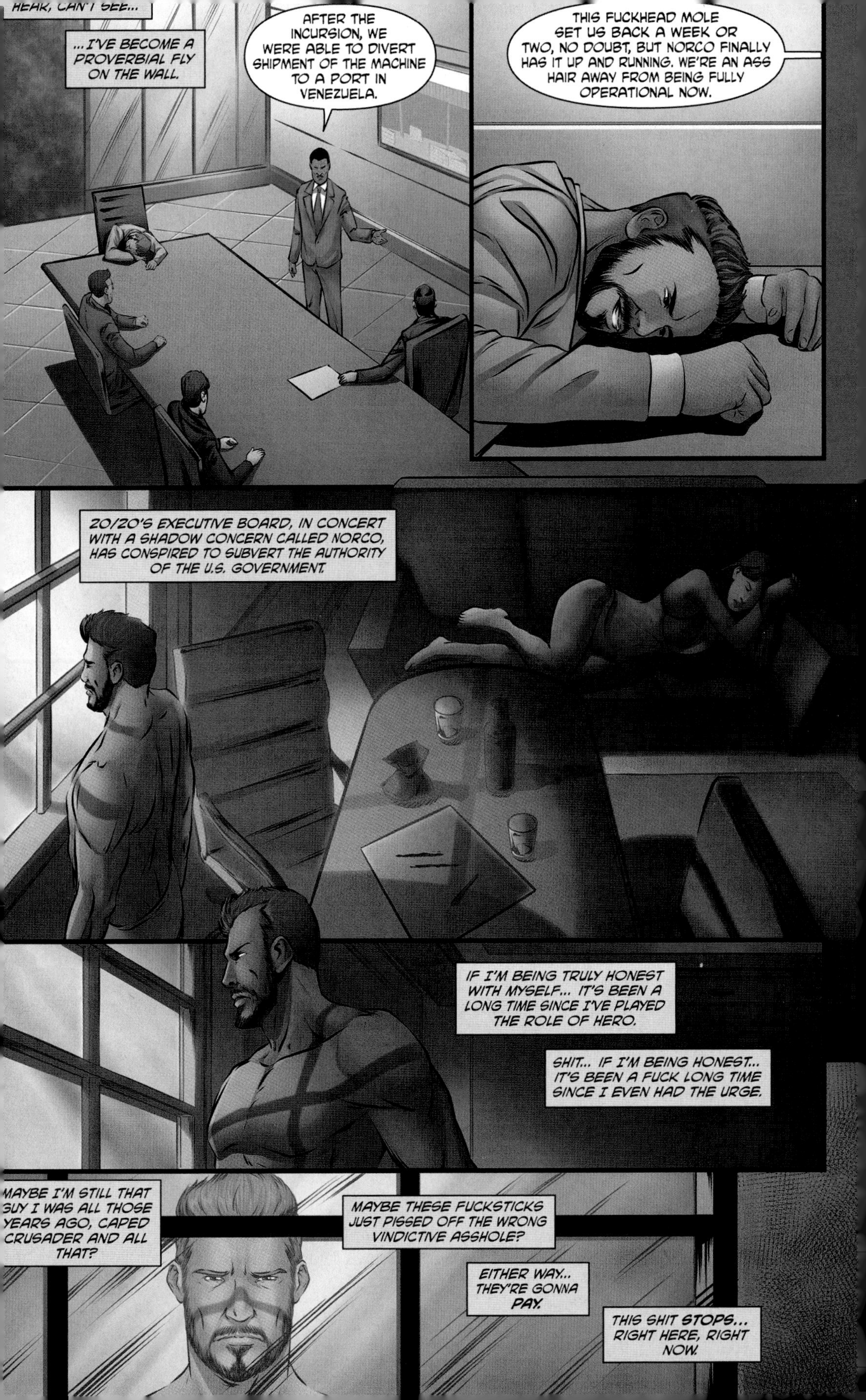
HEAR, CAN'T SEE...
...I'VE BECOME A PROVERBIAL FLY ON THE WALL.
AFTER THE INCURSION, WE WERE ABLE TO DIVERT SHIPMENT OF THE MACHINE TO A PORT IN VENEZUELA.
THIS FUCKHEAD MOLE SET US BACK A WEEK OR TWO, NO DOUBT, BUT NORCO FINALLY HAS IT UP AND RUNNING. WE'RE AN ASS HAIR AWAY FROM BEING FULLY OPERATIONAL NOW.
20/20'S EXECUTIVE BOARD, IN CONCERT WITH A SHADOW CONCERN CALLED NORCO, HAS CONSPIRED TO SUBVERT THE AUTHORITY OF THE U.S. GOVERNMENT.
IF I'M BEING TRULY HONEST WITH MYSELF... IT'S BEEN A LONG TIME SINCE I'VE PLAYED THE ROLE OF HERO.
SHIT... IF I'M BEING HONEST... IT'S BEEN A FUCK LONG TIME SINCE I EVEN HAD THE URGE.
MAYBE I'M STILL THAT GUY I WAS ALL THOSE YEARS AGO, CAPED CRUSADER AND ALL THAT?
MAYBE THESE FUCKSTICKS JUST PISSED OFF THE WRONG VINDICTIVE ASSHOLE?
EITHER WAY... THEY'RE GONNA PAY.
THIS SHIT STOPS... RIGHT HERE, RIGHT NOW.

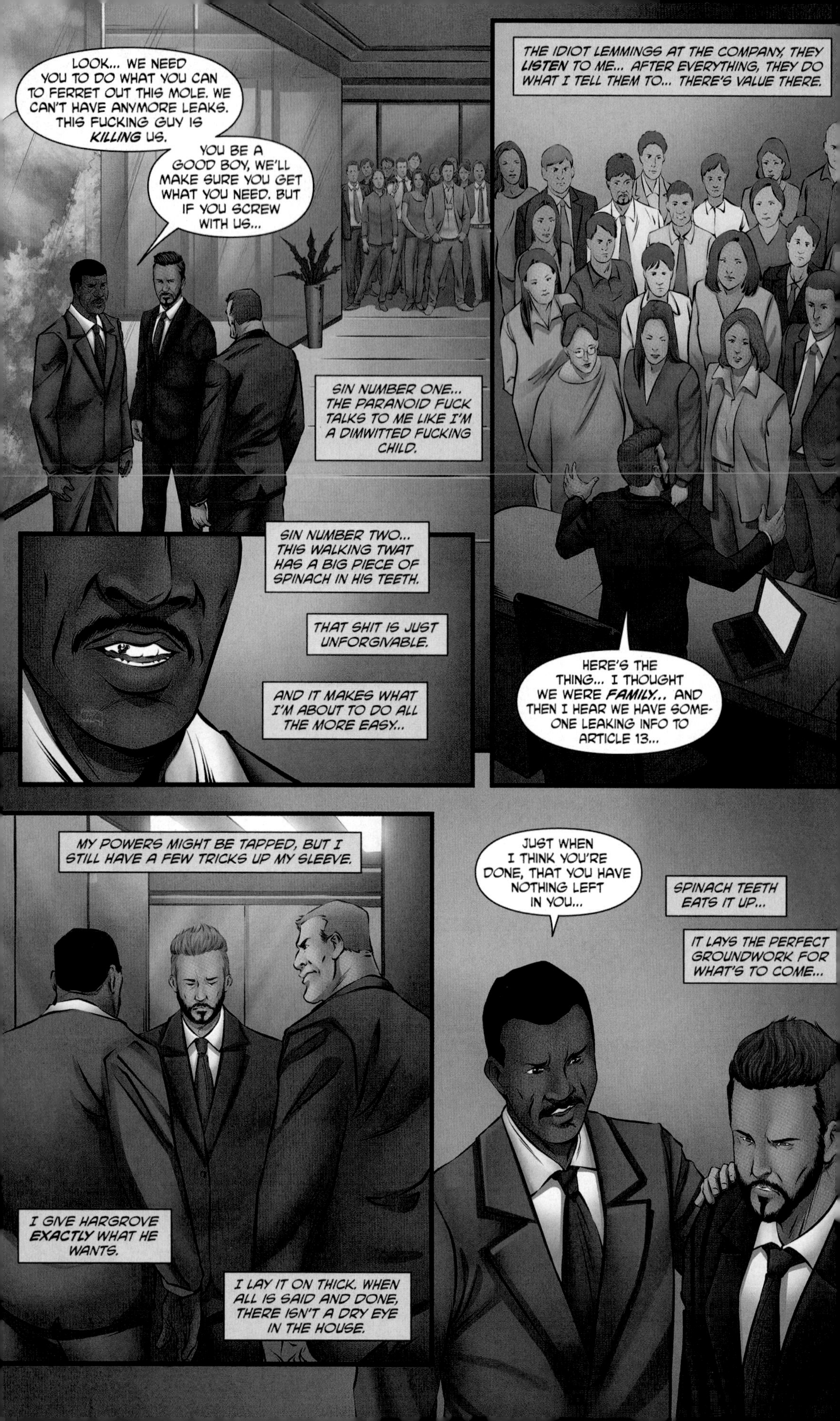

LOOK... WE NEED YOU TO DO WHAT YOU CAN TO FERRET OUT THIS MOLE. WE CAN'T HAVE ANYMORE LEAKS. THIS FUCKING GUY IS KILLING US.
YOU BE A GOOD BOY, WE'LL MAKE SURE YOU GET WHAT YOU NEED. BUT IF YOU SCREW WITH US...
SIN NUMBER ONE... THE PARANOID FUCK TALKS TO ME LIKE I'M A DIMWITTED FUCKING CHILD.
SIN NUMBER TWO... THIS WALKING TWAT HAS A BIG PIECE OF SPINACH IN HIS TEETH.
THAT SHIT IS JUST UNFORGIVABLE.
AND IT MAKES WHAT I'M ABOUT TO DO ALL THE MORE EASY...
THE IDIOT LEMMINGS AT THE COMPANY, THEY LISTEN TO ME... AFTER EVERYTHING, THEY DO WHAT I TELL THEM TO... THERE'S VALUE THERE.
HERE'S THE THING... I THOUGHT WE WERE FAMILY... AND THEN I HEAR WE HAVE SOME-ONE LEAKING INFO TO ARTICLE 13...
MY POWERS MIGHT BE TAPPED, BUT I STILL HAVE A FEW TRICKS UP MY SLEEVE.
I GIVE HARGROVE EXACTLY WHAT HE WANTS.
I LAY IT ON THICK. WHEN ALL IS SAID AND DONE, THERE ISN'T A DRY EYE IN THE HOUSE.
JUST WHEN I THINK YOU'RE DONE, THAT YOU HAVE NOTHING LEFT IN YOU...
SPINACH TEETH EATS IT UP...
IT LAYS THE PERFECT GROUNDWORK FOR WHAT'S TO COME...

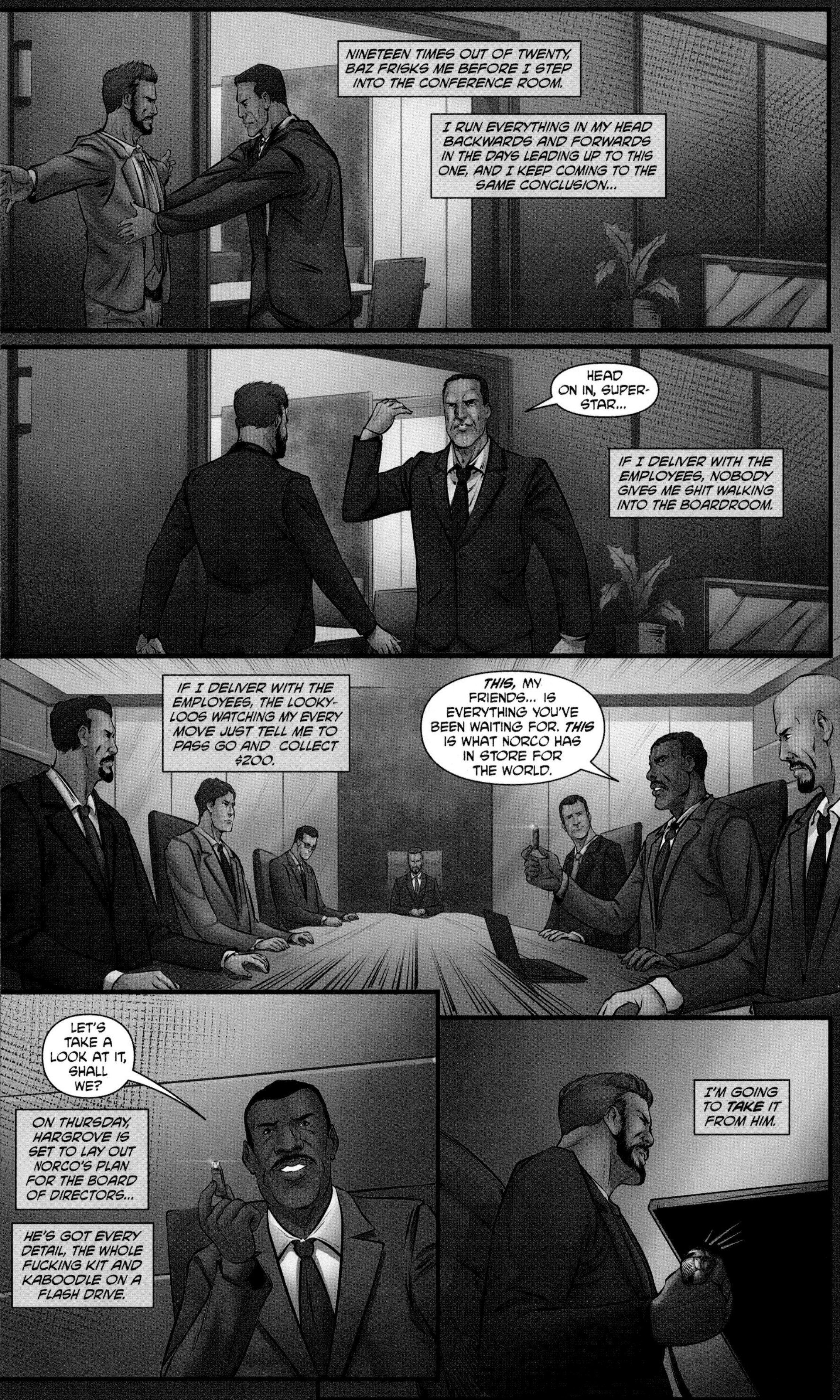
NINETEEN TIMES OUT OF TWENTY, BAZ FRISKS ME BEFORE I STEP INTO THE CONFERENCE ROOM.
I RUN EVERYTHING IN MY HEAD BACKWARDS AND FORWARDS IN THE DAYS LEADING UP TO THIS ONE, AND I KEEP COMING TO THE SAME CONCLUSION...
HEAD ON IN, SUPER-STAR...
IF I DELIVER WITH THE EMPLOYEES, NOBODY GIVES ME SHIT WALKING INTO THE BOARDROOM.
IF I DELIVER WITH THE EMPLOYEES, THE LOOKY-LOOS WATCHING MY EVERY MOVE JUST TELL ME TO PASS GO AND COLLECT $200.
THIS, MY FRIENDS... IS EVERYTHING YOU'VE BEEN WAITING FOR. THIS IS WHAT NORCO HAS IN STORE FOR THE WORLD.
LET'S TAKE A LOOK AT IT, SHALL WE?
ON THURSDAY, HARGROVE IS SET TO LAY OUT NORCO'S PLAN FOR THE BOARD OF DIRECTORS...
HE'S GOT EVERY DETAIL, THE WHOLE FUCKING KIT AND KABOODLE ON A FLASH DRIVE.
I'M GOING TO TAKE IT FROM HIM.

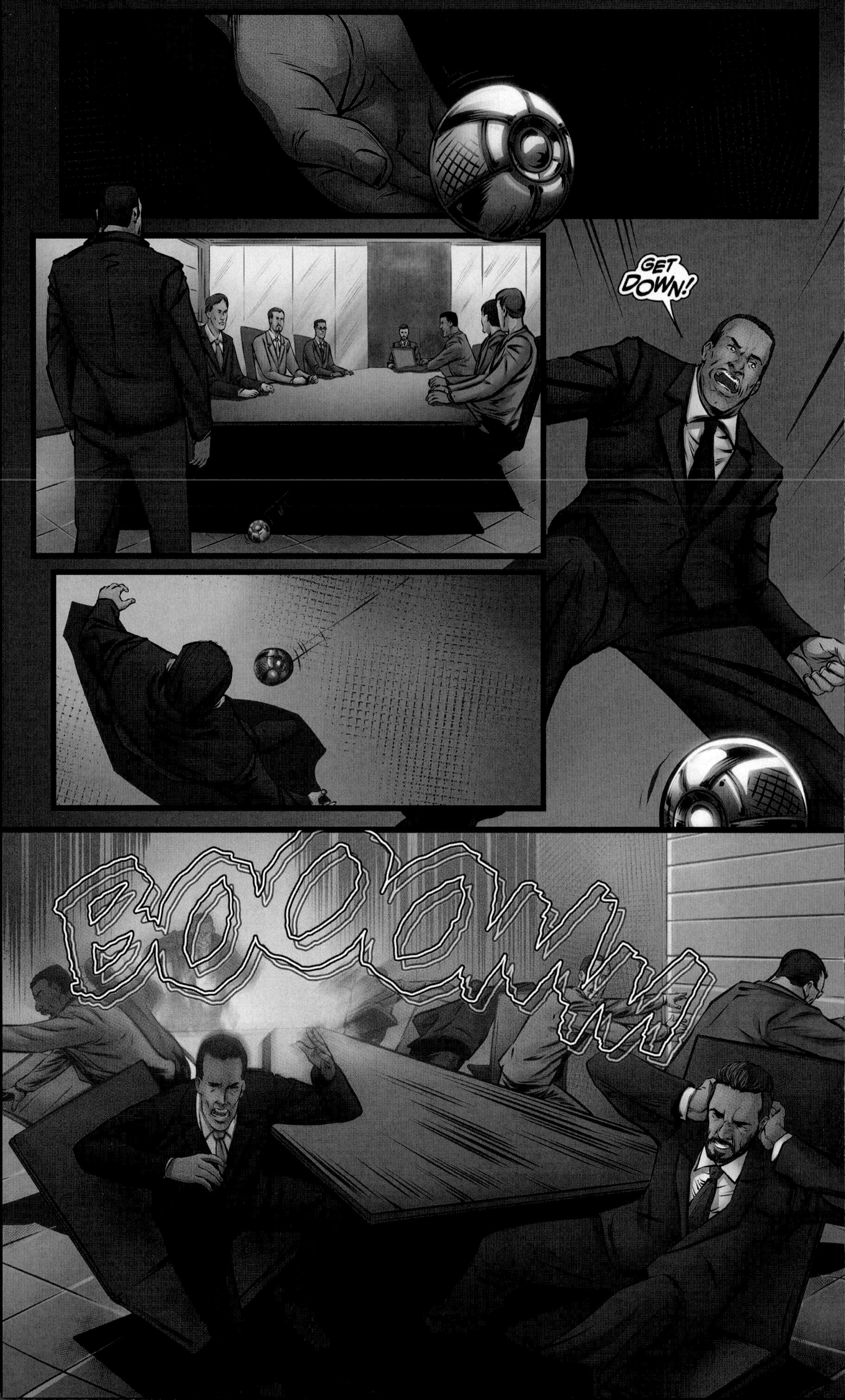
GET DOWN!
BOOOM

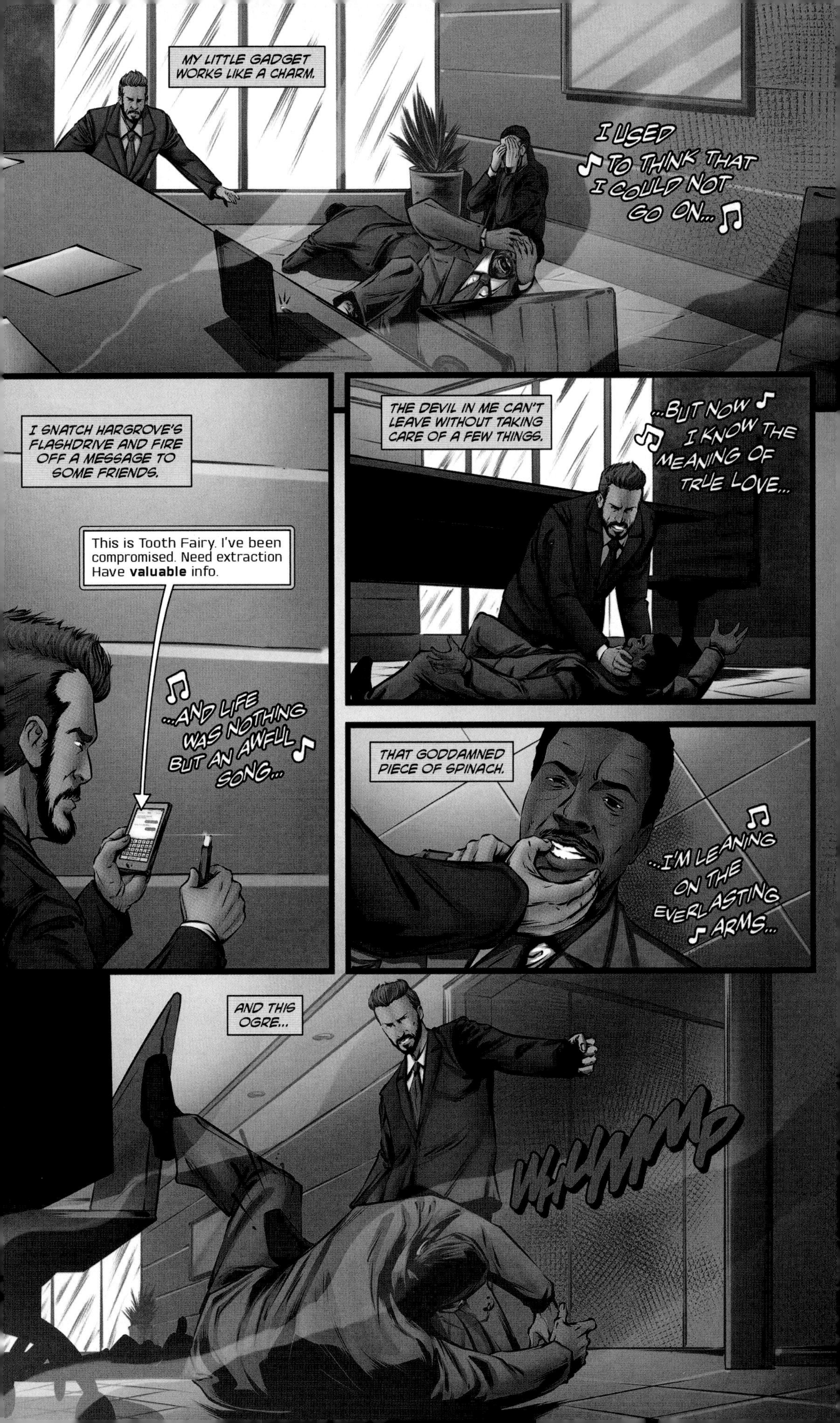
MY LITTLE GADGET WORKS LIKE A CHARM.
I USED TO THINK THAT I COULD NOT GO ON...
I SNATCH HARGROVE'S FLASHDRIVE AND FIRE OFF A MESSAGE TO SOME FRIENDS.
This is Tooth Fairy. I've been compromised. Need extraction Have **valuable** info.
...AND LIFE WAS NOTHING BUT AN AWFUL SONG...
THE DEVIL IN ME CAN'T LEAVE WITHOUT TAKING CARE OF A FEW THINGS.
...BUT NOW I KNOW THE MEANING OF TRUE LOVE...
THAT GODDAMNED PIECE OF SPINACH.
...I'M LEANING ON THE EVERLASTING ARMS...
AND THIS OGRE...
WHUMP

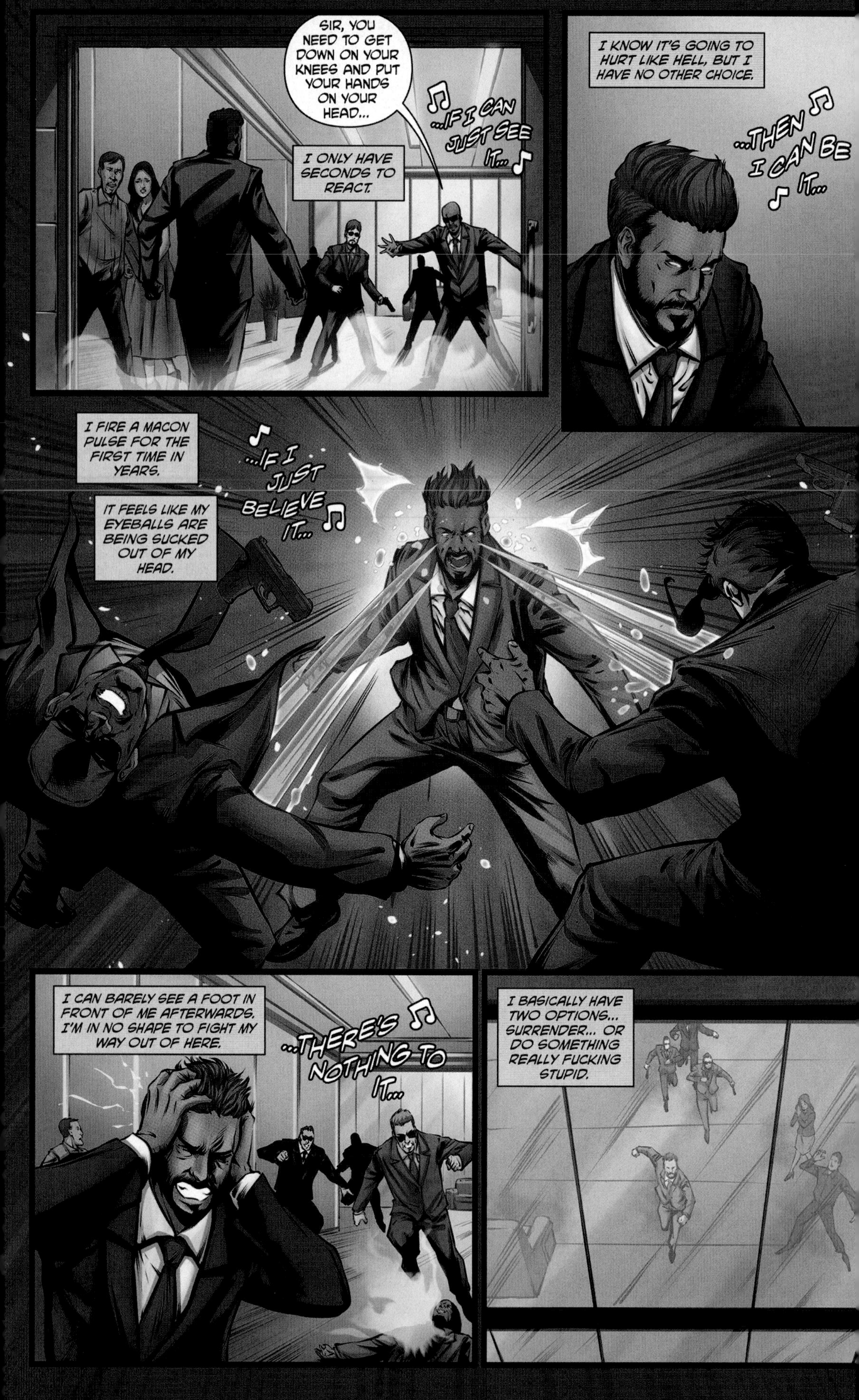
SIR, YOU NEED TO GET DOWN ON YOUR KNEES AND PUT YOUR HANDS ON YOUR HEAD...
I ONLY HAVE SECONDS TO REACT.
♫ ...IF I CAN JUST SEE IT... ♪
I KNOW IT'S GOING TO HURT LIKE HELL, BUT I HAVE NO OTHER CHOICE.
...THEN ♫ I CAN BE ♪ IT...
I FIRE A MACON PULSE FOR THE FIRST TIME IN YEARS.
IT FEELS LIKE MY EYEBALLS ARE BEING SUCKED OUT OF MY HEAD.
♪ ...IF I JUST BELIEVE IT... ♫
I CAN BARELY SEE A FOOT IN FRONT OF ME AFTERWARDS. I'M IN NO SHAPE TO FIGHT MY WAY OUT OF HERE.
...THERE'S ♫ NOTHING TO IT...
I BASICALLY HAVE TWO OPTIONS... SURRENDER... OR DO SOMETHING REALLY FUCKING STUPID.

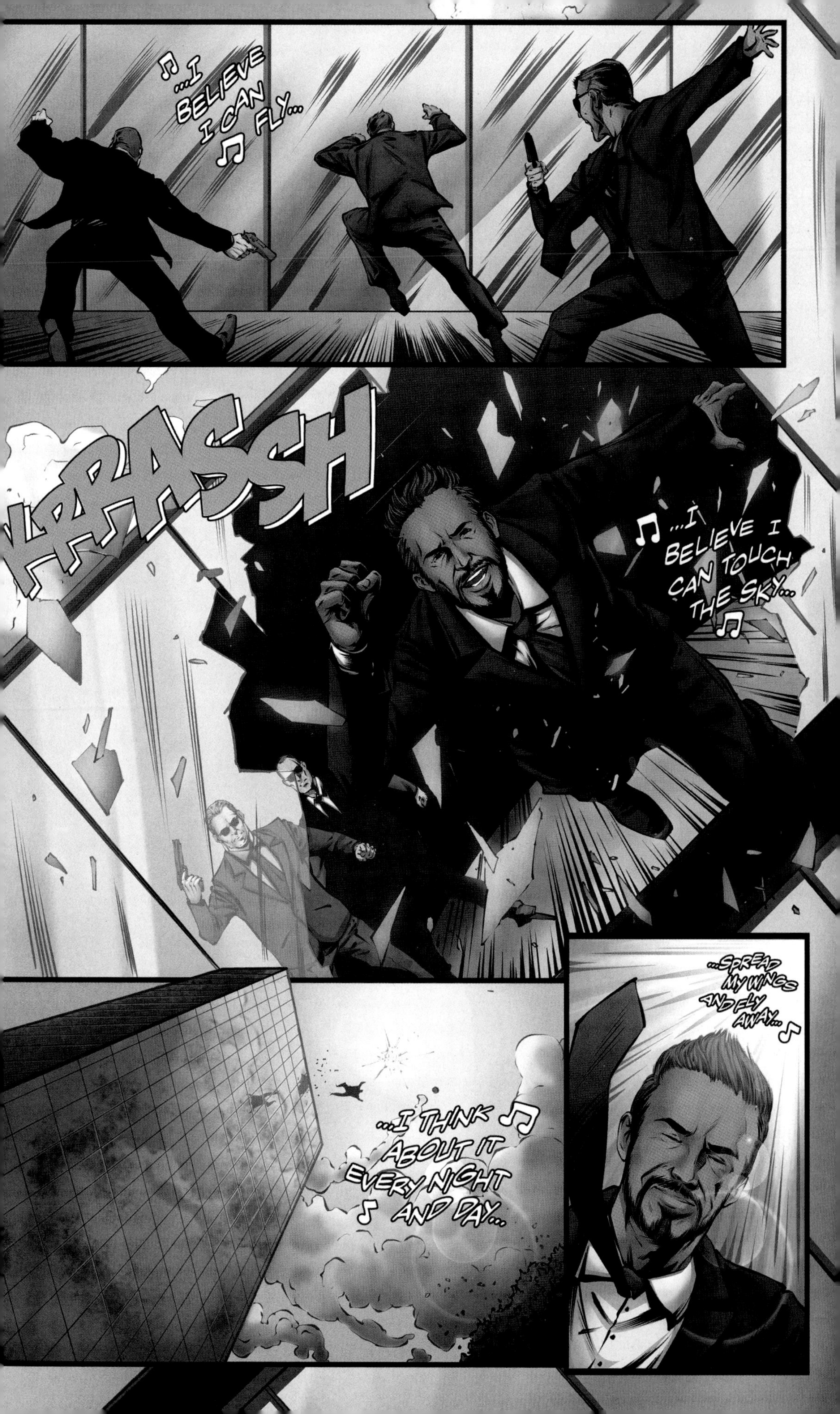
♫ ...I BELIEVE I CAN ♫ FLY...
KRASSH
♫ ...I BELIEVE I CAN TOUCH THE SKY... ♫
...I THINK ♫ ABOUT IT EVERY NIGHT ♪ AND DAY...
...SPREAD MY WINGS AND FLY AWAY... ♪

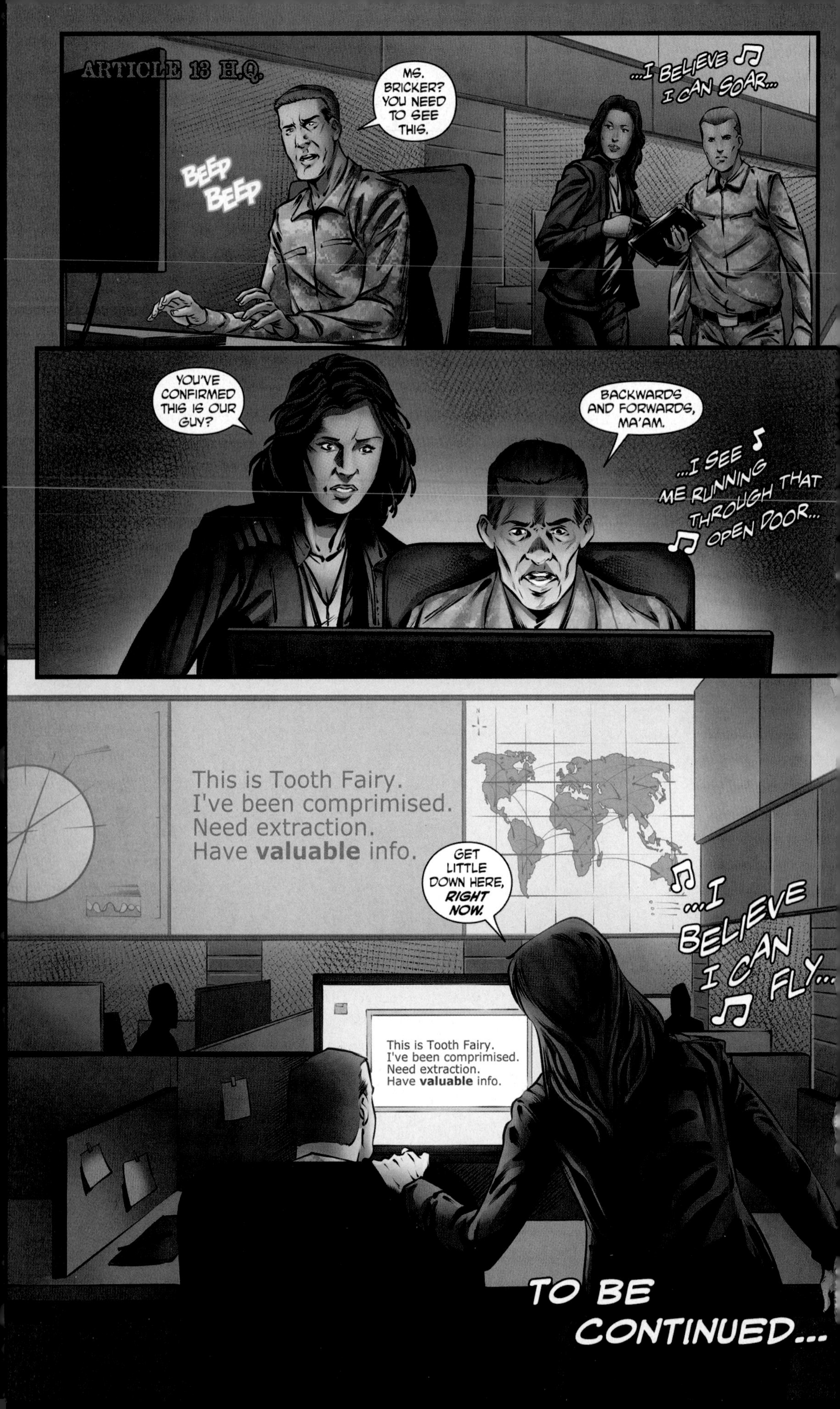

ARTICLE 13 H.Q.
MS. BRICKER? YOU NEED TO SEE THIS.
BEEP BEEP
...I BELIEVE ♫ I CAN SOAR...
YOU'VE CONFIRMED THIS IS OUR GUY?
BACKWARDS AND FORWARDS, MA'AM.
...I SEE ♪ ME RUNNING THROUGH THAT ♫ OPEN DOOR...
This is Tooth Fairy.
I've been comprimised.
Need extraction.
Have **valuable** info.
GET LITTLE DOWN HERE, ***RIGHT NOW.***
♫ ...I BELIEVE I CAN FLY... ♫
TO BE CONTINUED...

Aberrant

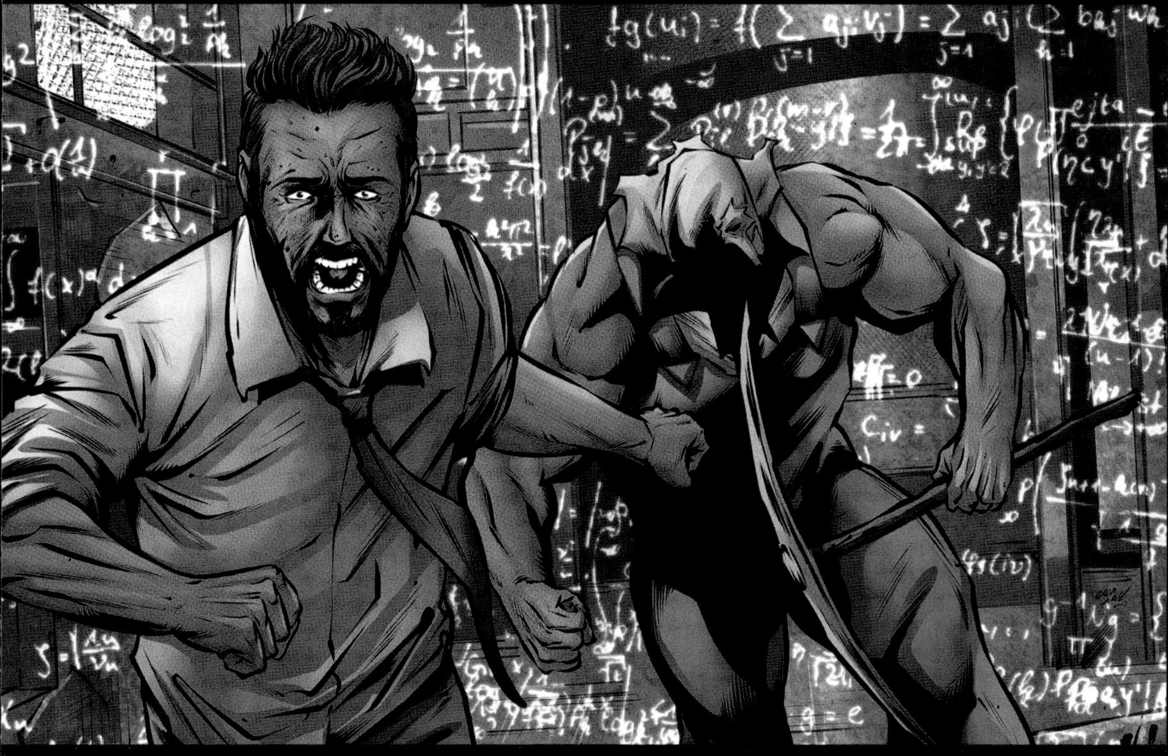

Chapter 5: God Damn It...

Rylend Grant
Writer/Director
@rylendgrant

Davi Leon Dias
Artist
@davileon

Iwan Joko Triyono
Colorist

HdE
Letterer

R.J. Hendricks
Executive Producer

Executive Producer: Ryan Colucci
Graphic Designer: Jessie Weinberg @jeweinbe

Jason Martin: Publisher • Shawn Gabborin: Editor in Chief • Nicole D'Andria: Marketing Director/Editor
Danielle Davison: Executive Administrator • Bryan Seaton: CEO • Shawn Pryor: President of Creator Relation

Special thanks to Karla Nappi, Jeff Leeds, Steven Prince, Karol Wisniewski, Jim Higgins
and everyone at Meltdown Comics

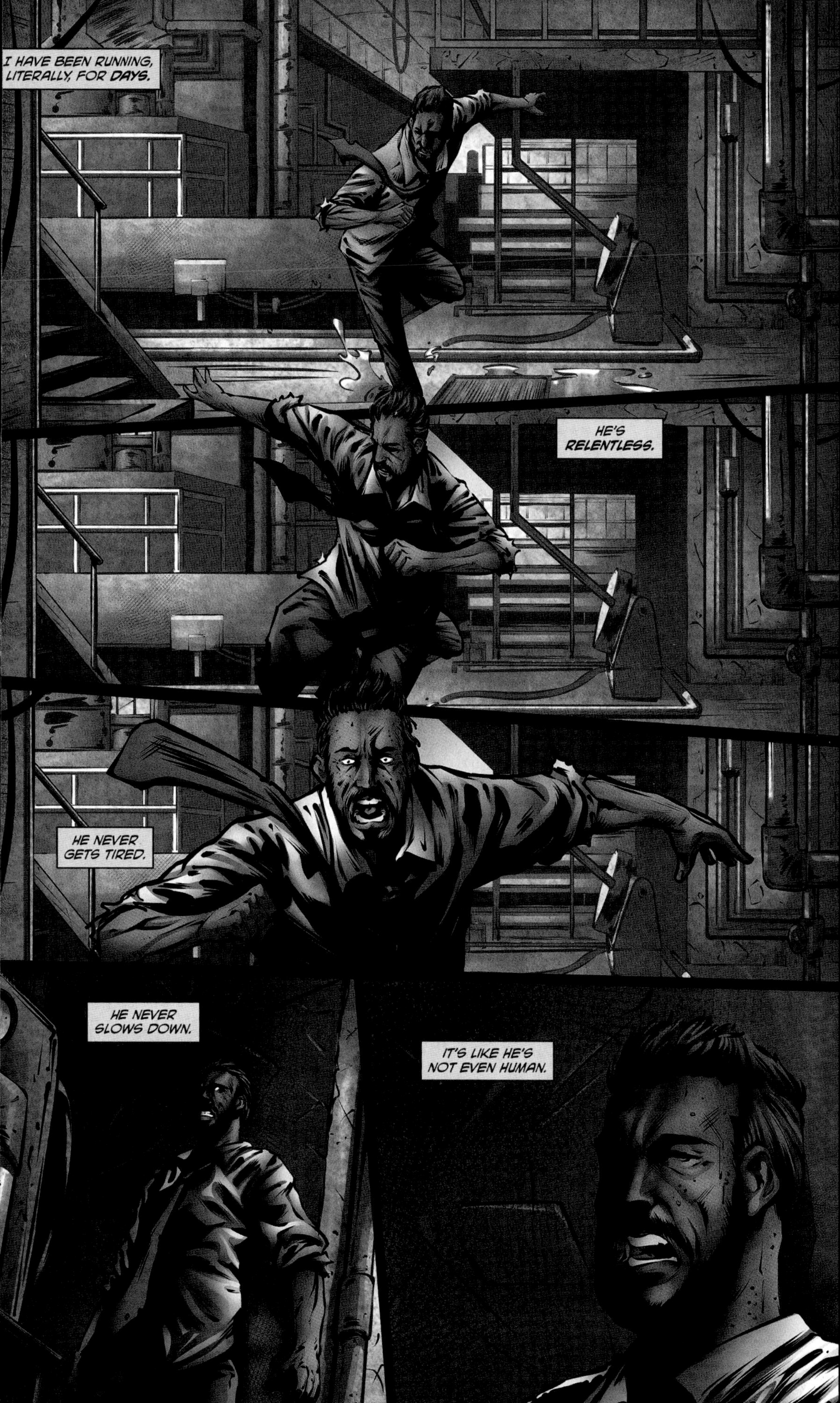
I HAVE BEEN RUNNING, LITERALLY, FOR DAYS.
HE'S RELENTLESS.
HE NEVER GETS TIRED.
HE NEVER SLOWS DOWN.
IT'S LIKE HE'S NOT EVEN HUMAN.

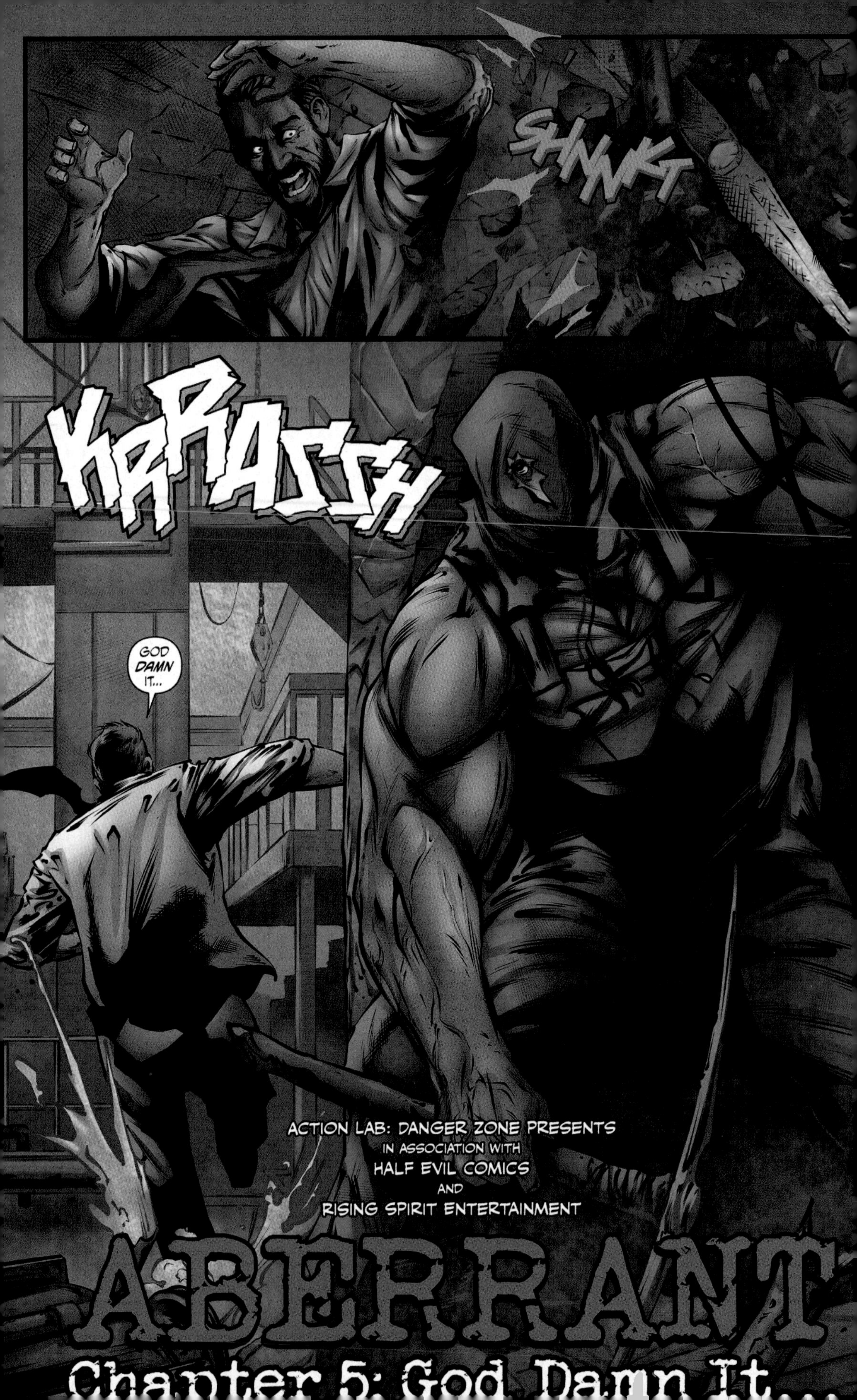

SHNNKT
KRRASSH
GOD DAMN IT...
ACTION LAB: DANGER ZONE PRESENTS
IN ASSOCIATION WITH
HALF EVIL COMICS
AND
RISING SPIRIT ENTERTAINMENT
ABERRANT
Chapter 5: God Damn It...

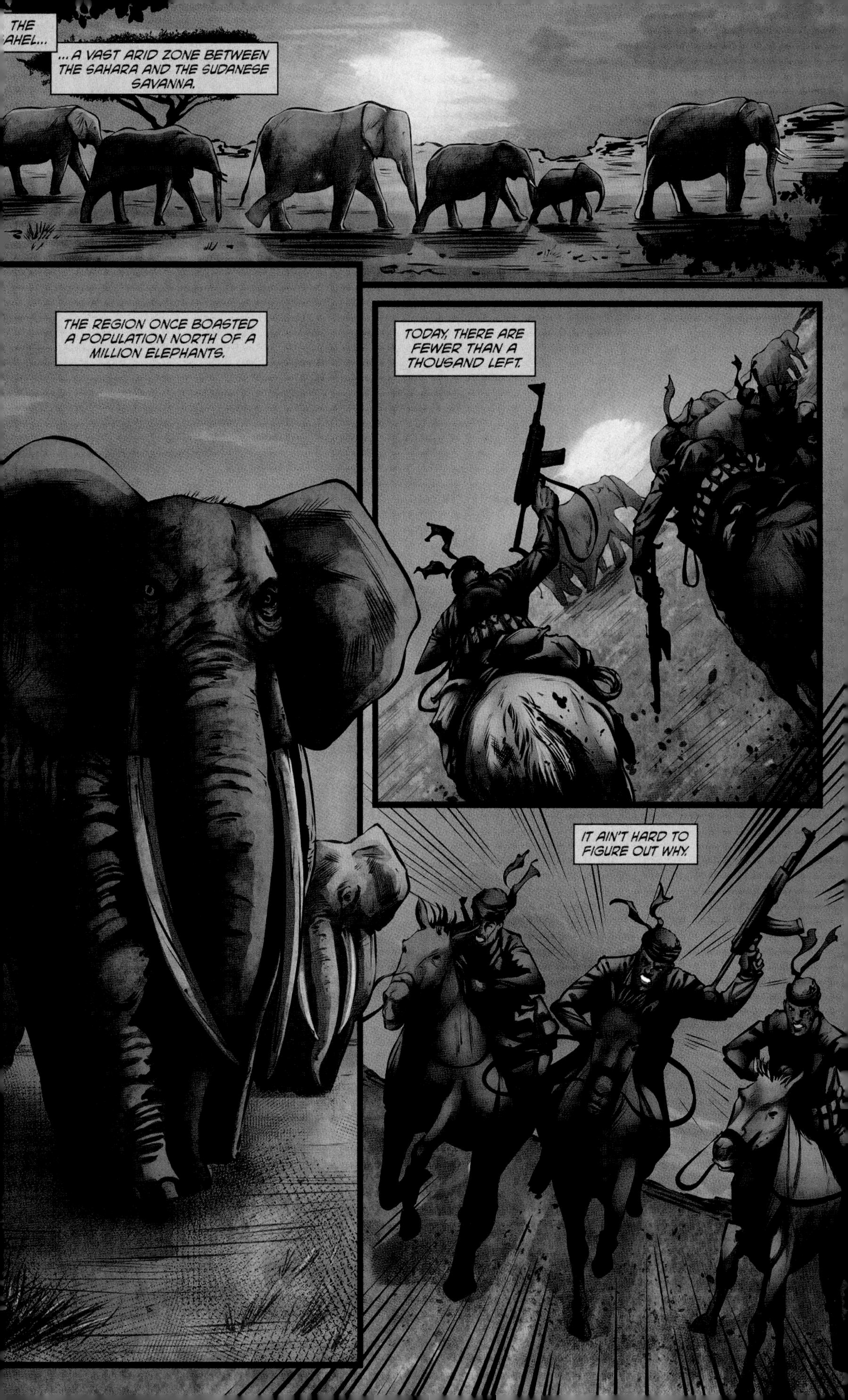
THE AHEL...
...A VAST ARID ZONE BETWEEN THE SAHARA AND THE SUDANESE SAVANNA.
THE REGION ONCE BOASTED A POPULATION NORTH OF A MILLION ELEPHANTS.
TODAY, THERE ARE FEWER THAN A THOUSAND LEFT.
IT AIN'T HARD TO FIGURE OUT WHY.

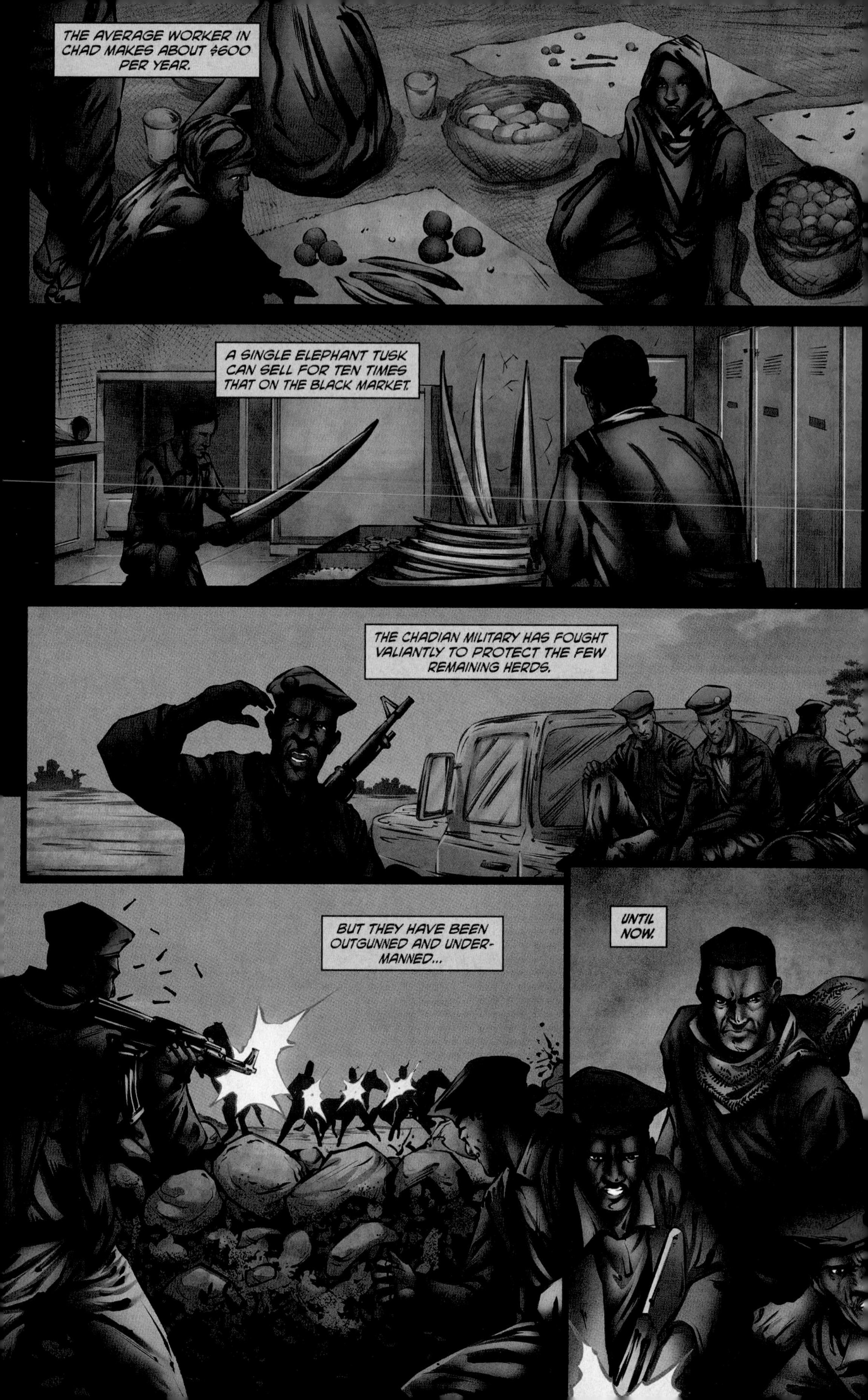
THE AVERAGE WORKER IN CHAD MAKES ABOUT $600 PER YEAR.
A SINGLE ELEPHANT TUSK CAN SELL FOR TEN TIMES THAT ON THE BLACK MARKET.
THE CHADIAN MILITARY HAS FOUGHT VALIANTLY TO PROTECT THE FEW REMAINING HERDS.
BUT THEY HAVE BEEN OUTGUNNED AND UNDER-MANNED...
UNTIL NOW.

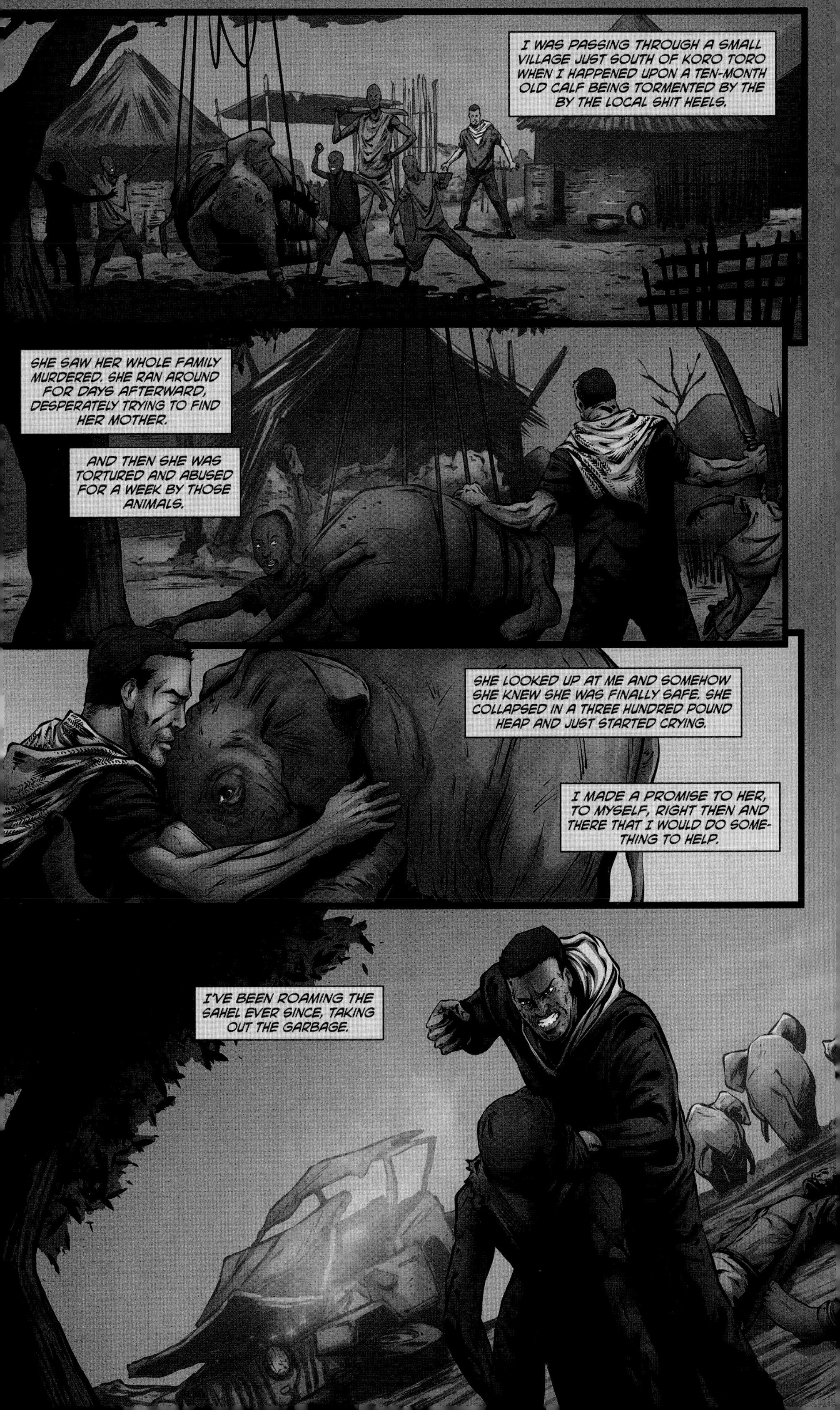
I WAS PASSING THROUGH A SMALL VILLAGE JUST SOUTH OF KORO TORO WHEN I HAPPENED UPON A TEN-MONTH OLD CALF BEING TORMENTED BY THE BY THE LOCAL SHIT HEELS.
SHE SAW HER WHOLE FAMILY MURDERED. SHE RAN AROUND FOR DAYS AFTERWARD, DESPERATELY TRYING TO FIND HER MOTHER.
AND THEN SHE WAS TORTURED AND ABUSED FOR A WEEK BY THOSE ANIMALS.
SHE LOOKED UP AT ME AND SOMEHOW SHE KNEW SHE WAS FINALLY SAFE. SHE COLLAPSED IN A THREE HUNDRED POUND HEAP AND JUST STARTED CRYING.
I MADE A PROMISE TO HER, TO MYSELF, RIGHT THEN AND THERE THAT I WOULD DO SOME-THING TO HELP.
I'VE BEEN ROAMING THE SAHEL EVER SINCE, TAKING OUT THE GARBAGE.

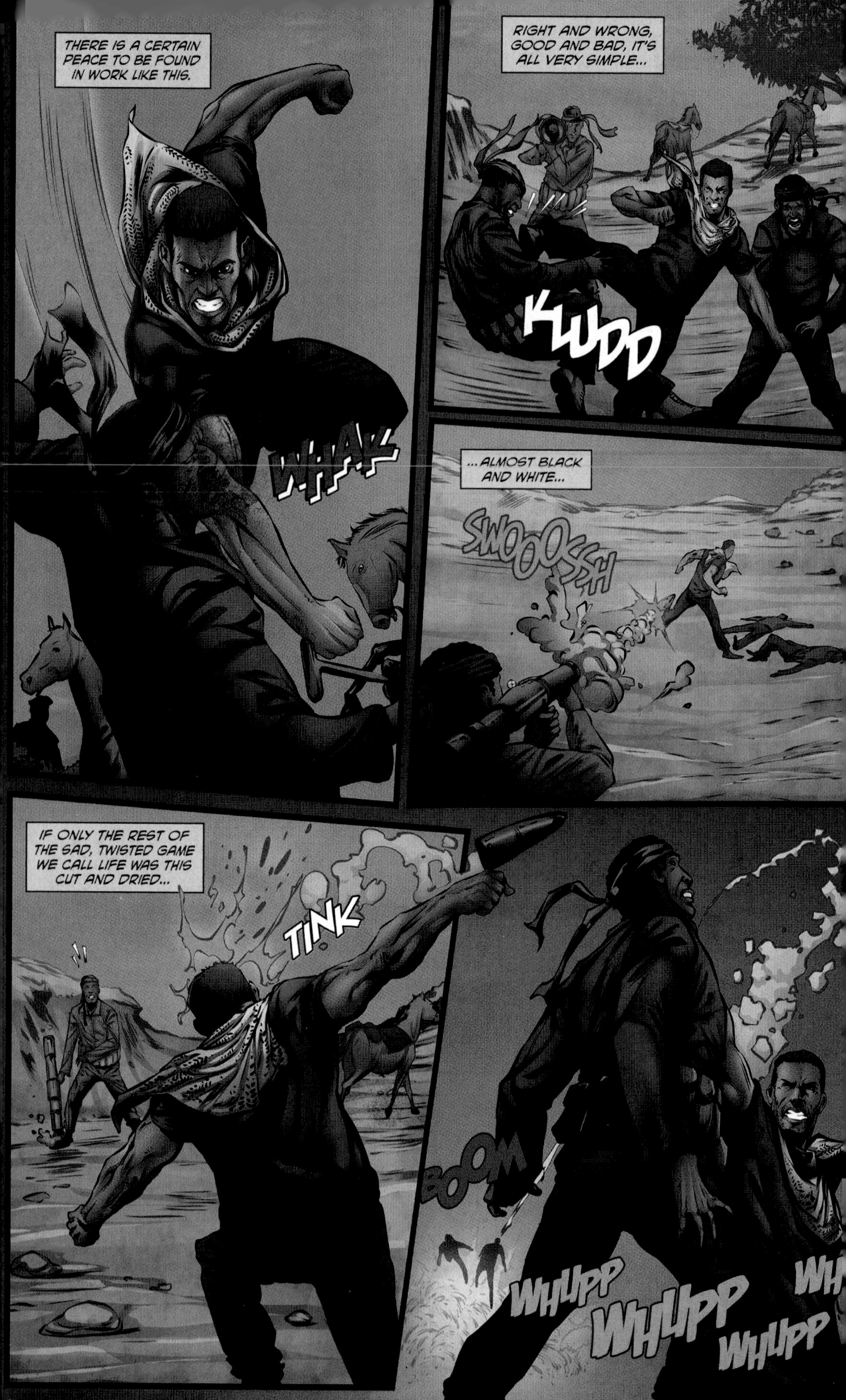
THERE IS A CERTAIN PEACE TO BE FOUND IN WORK LIKE THIS.
WHAK
RIGHT AND WRONG, GOOD AND BAD, IT'S ALL VERY SIMPLE...
KUDD
...ALMOST BLACK AND WHITE...
SWOOOSH
IF ONLY THE REST OF THE SAD, TWISTED GAME WE CALL LIFE WAS THIS CUT AND DRIED...
TINK
BOOM
WHUPP
WHUPP
WHUPP

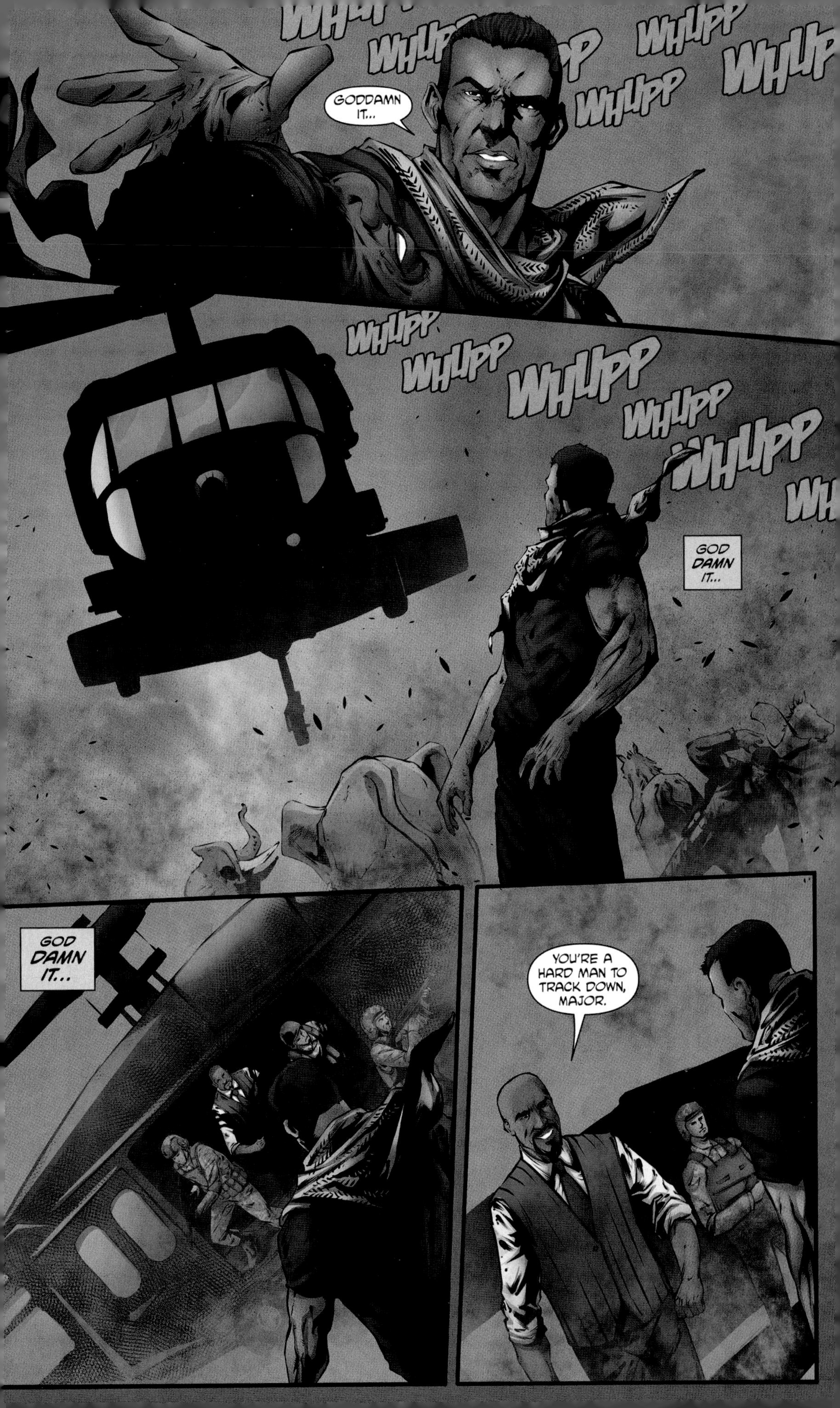
WHUPP
WHUPP
WHUPP
WHUPP
WHUPP
GODDAMN IT...
WHUPP
WHUPP
WHUPP
WHUPP
WHUPP
GOD DAMN IT...
GOD DAMN IT...
YOU'RE A HARD MAN TO TRACK DOWN, MAJOR.

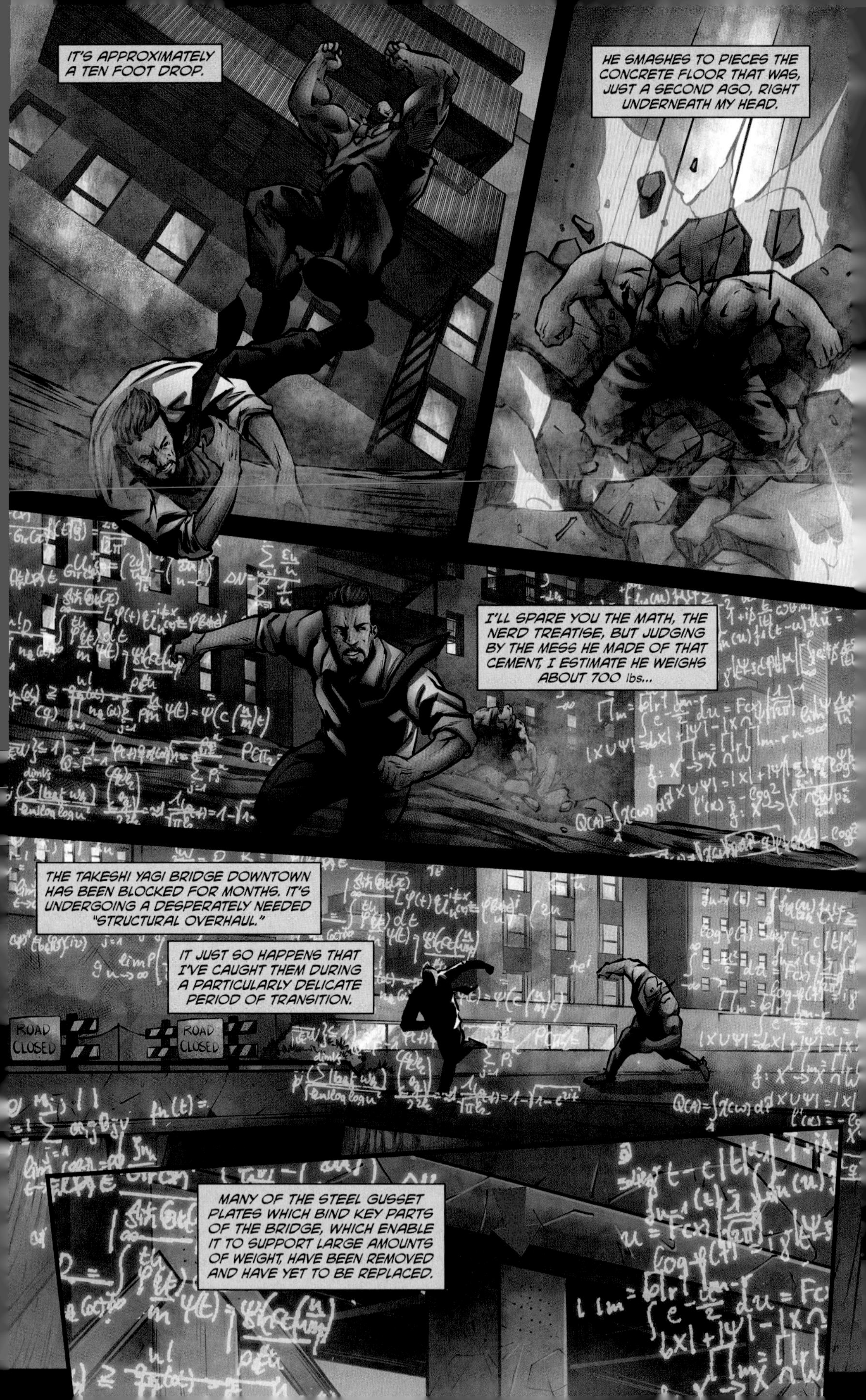
IT'S APPROXIMATELY A TEN FOOT DROP.
HE SMASHES TO PIECES THE CONCRETE FLOOR THAT WAS, JUST A SECOND AGO, RIGHT UNDERNEATH MY HEAD.
I'LL SPARE YOU THE MATH, THE NERD TREATISE, BUT JUDGING BY THE MESS HE MADE OF THAT CEMENT, I ESTIMATE HE WEIGHS ABOUT 700 lbs...
THE TAKESHI YAGI BRIDGE DOWNTOWN HAS BEEN BLOCKED FOR MONTHS. IT'S UNDERGOING A DESPERATELY NEEDED "STRUCTURAL OVERHAUL."
IT JUST SO HAPPENS THAT I'VE CAUGHT THEM DURING A PARTICULARLY DELICATE PERIOD OF TRANSITION.
ROAD CLOSED
ROAD CLOSED
MANY OF THE STEEL GUSSET PLATES WHICH BIND KEY PARTS OF THE BRIDGE, WHICH ENABLE IT TO SUPPORT LARGE AMOUNTS OF WEIGHT, HAVE BEEN REMOVED AND HAVE YET TO BE REPLACED.

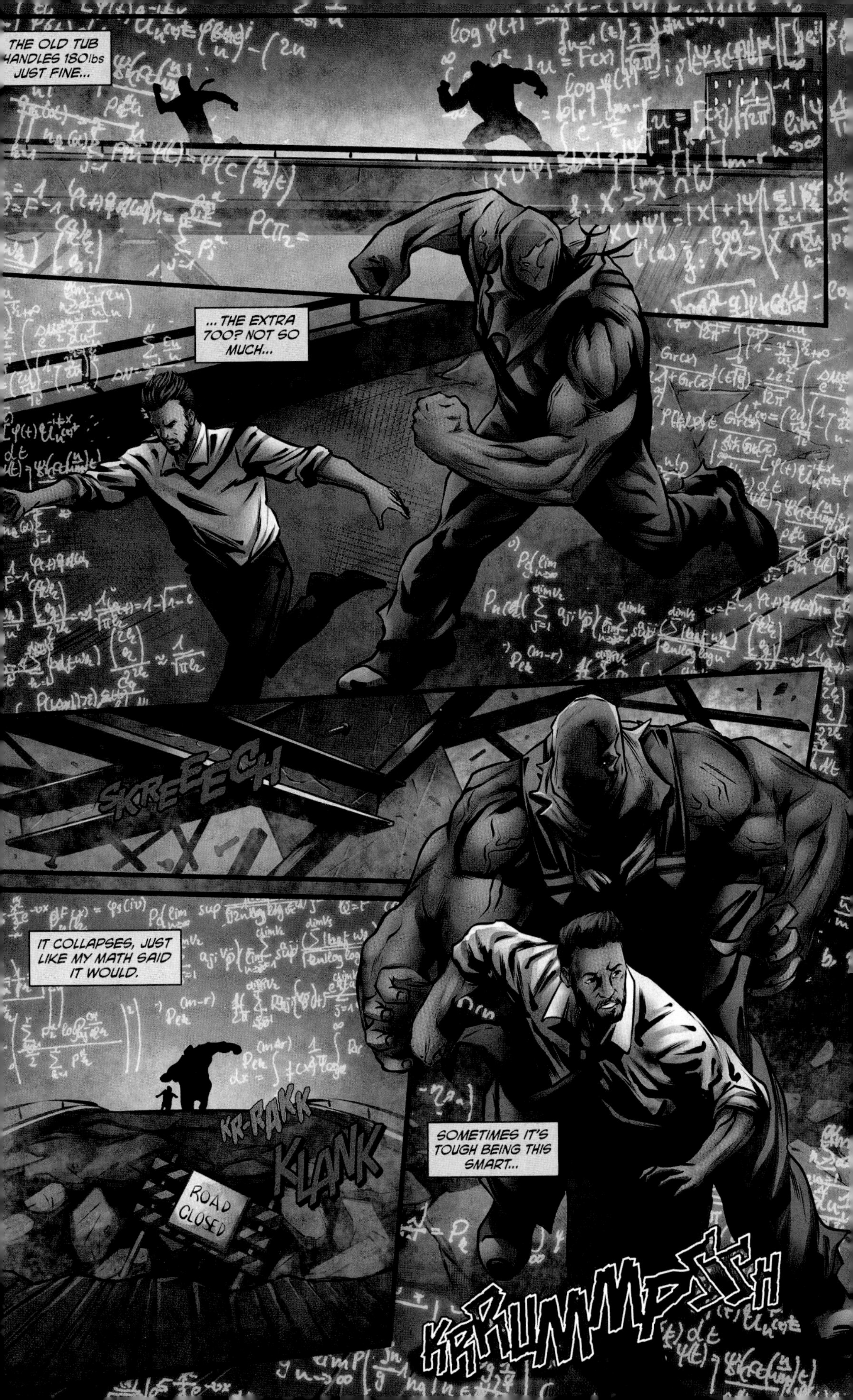
THE OLD TUB HANDLES 180lbs JUST FINE...
...THE EXTRA 700? NOT SO MUCH...
SKREEEECH
IT COLLAPSES, JUST LIKE MY MATH SAID IT WOULD.
KR-RAKK
KLANK
ROAD CLOSED
SOMETIMES IT'S TOUGH BEING THIS SMART...
KRRUMMPSSH

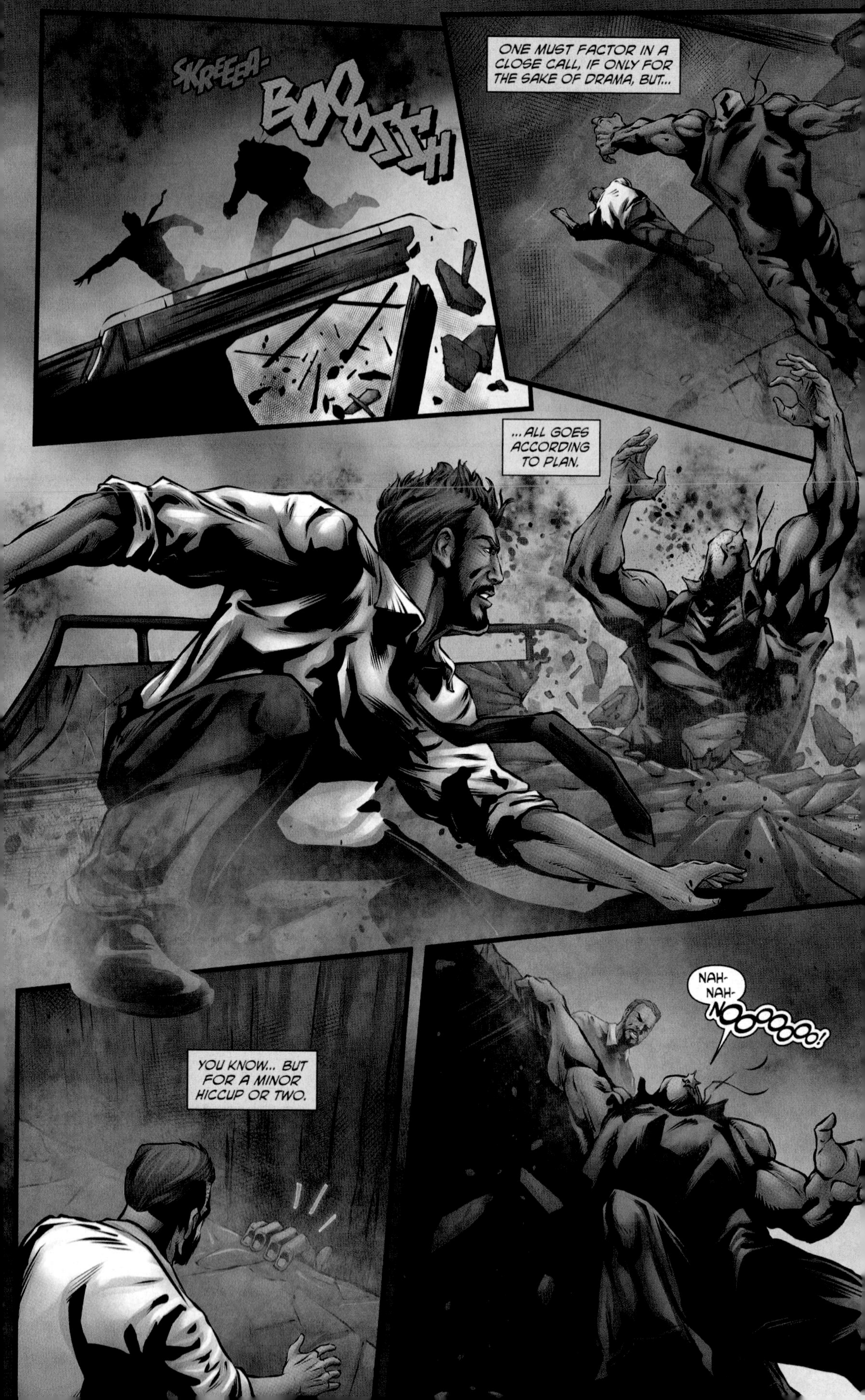
SKREEEA-
BOOOSSH
ONE MUST FACTOR IN A CLOSE CALL, IF ONLY FOR THE SAKE OF DRAMA, BUT...
...ALL GOES ACCORDING TO PLAN.
YOU KNOW... BUT FOR A MINOR HICCUP OR TWO.
NAH-NAH-NOOOOOOO!

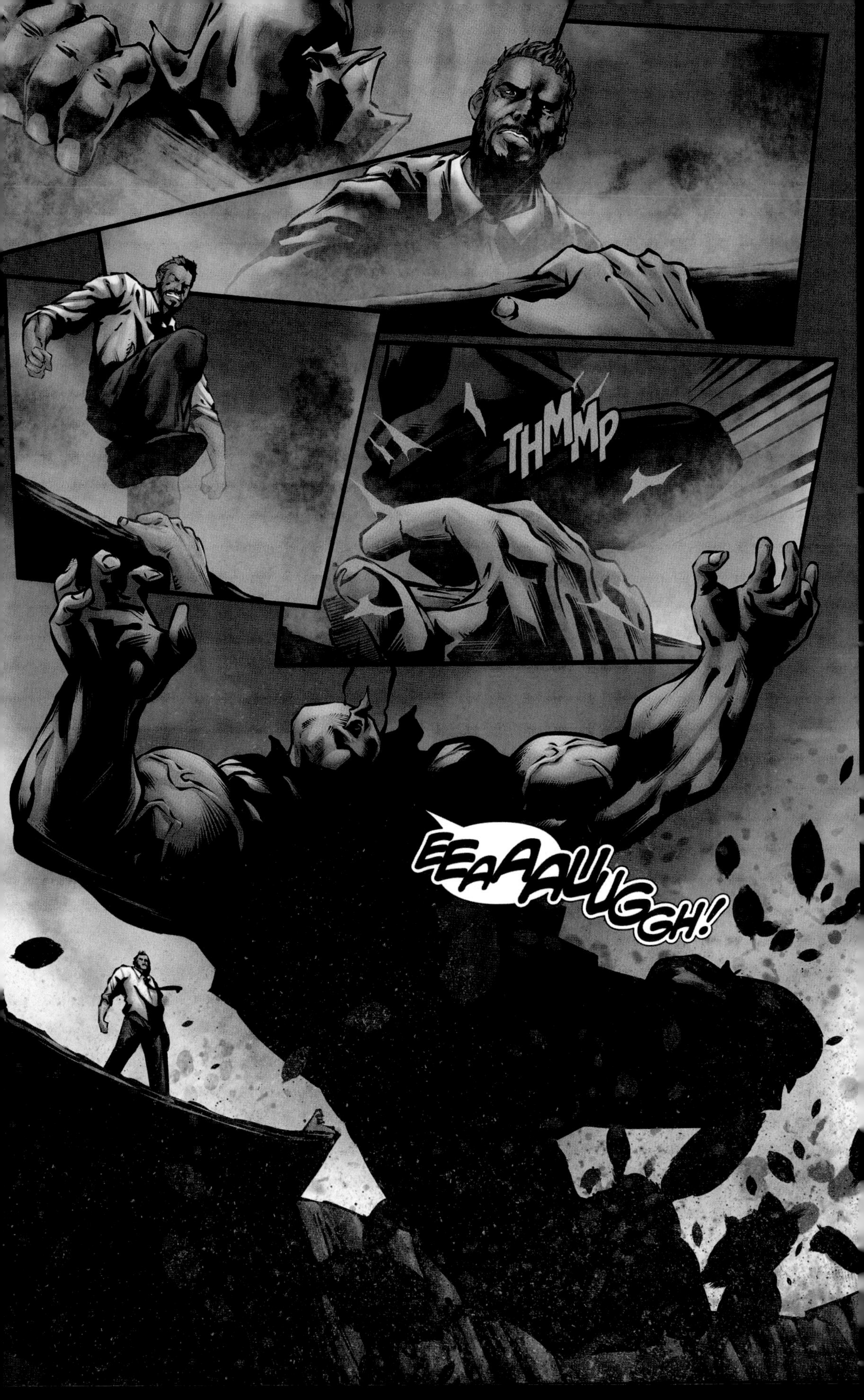
THMMP
EEAAAAUUGGH!

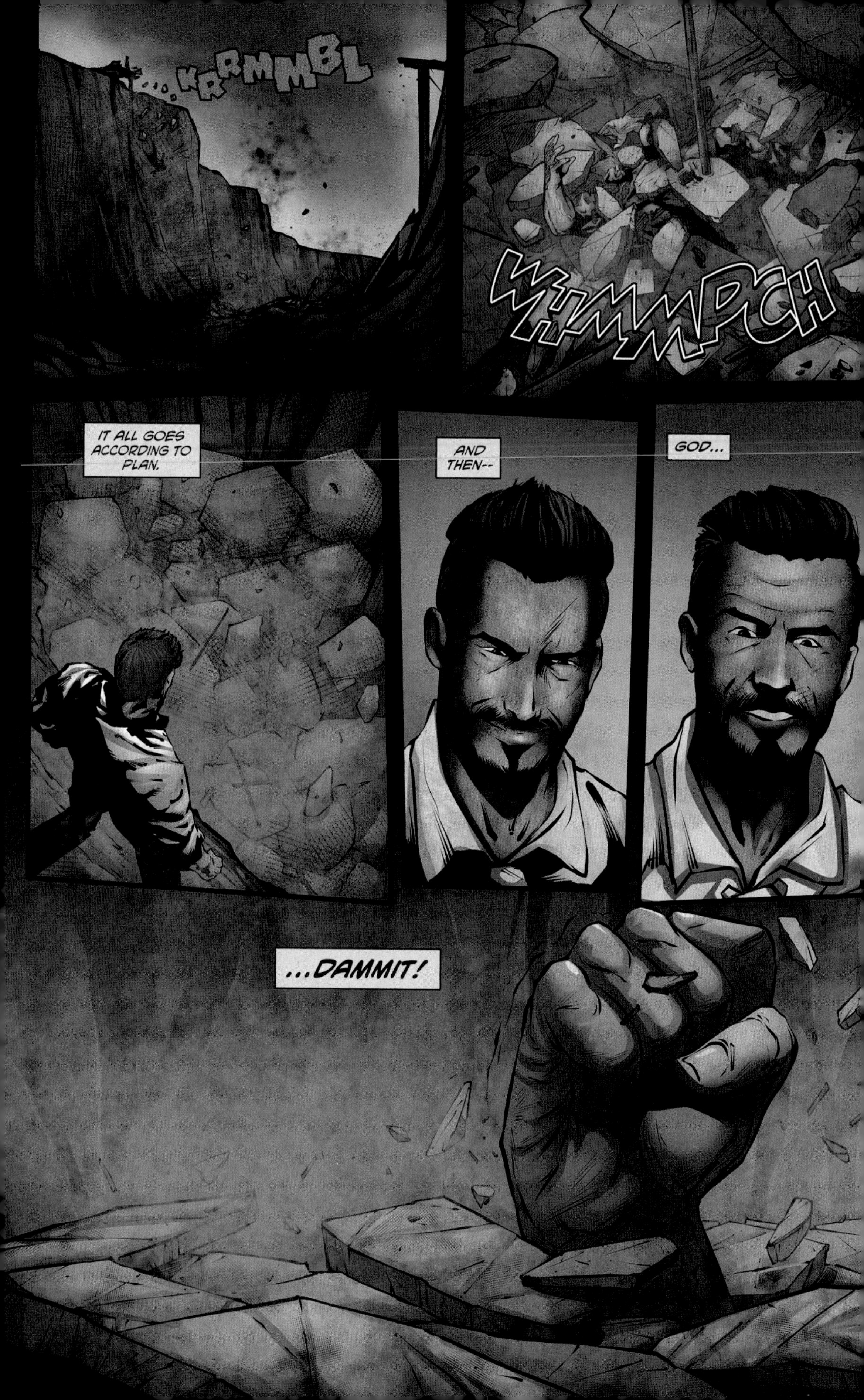
KRRMMBL
WHMMPCH
IT ALL GOES ACCORDING TO PLAN.
AND THEN--
GOD...
...DAMMIT!

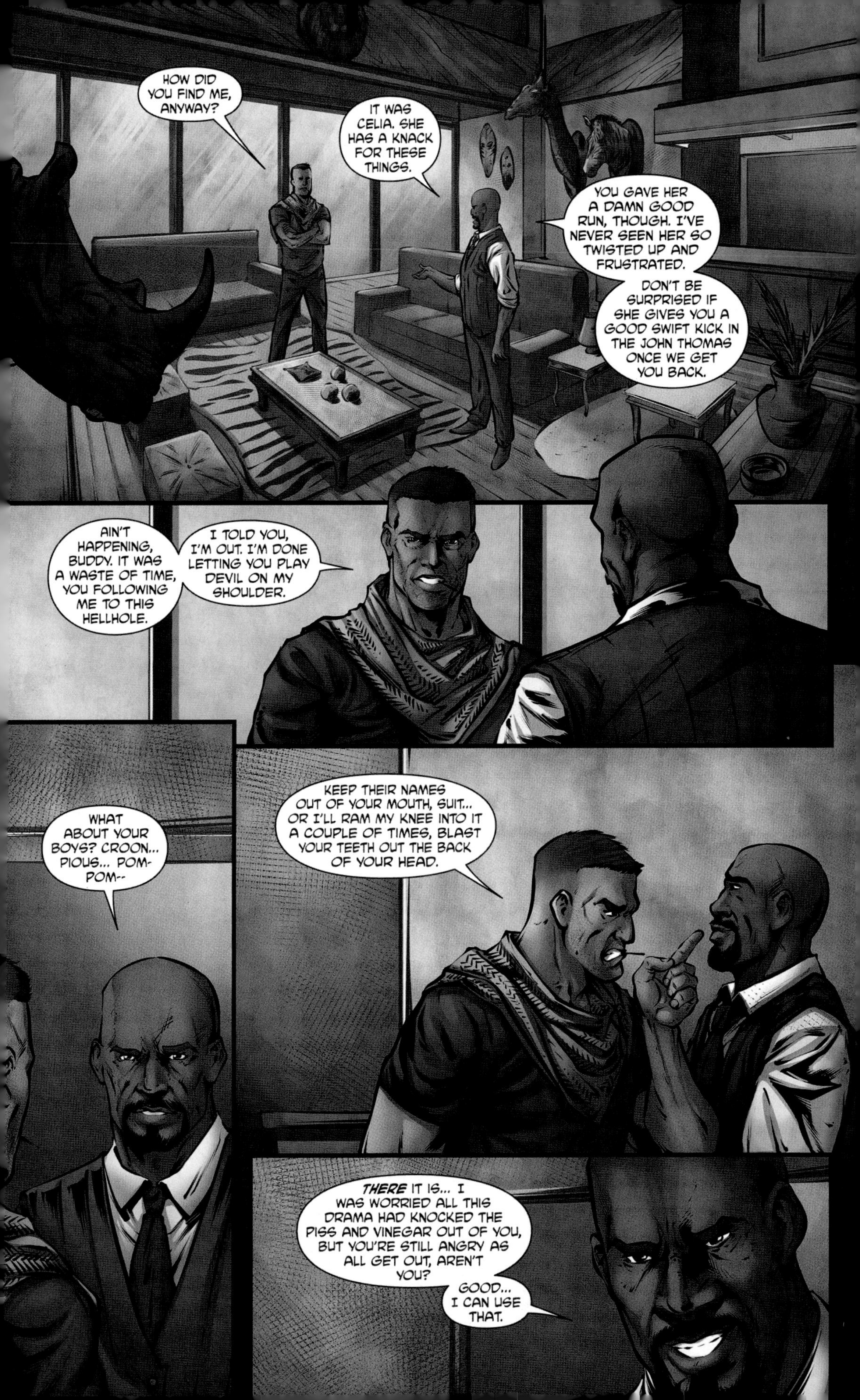
HOW DID YOU FIND ME, ANYWAY?
IT WAS CELIA. SHE HAS A KNACK FOR THESE THINGS.
YOU GAVE HER A DAMN GOOD RUN, THOUGH. I'VE NEVER SEEN HER SO TWISTED UP AND FRUSTRATED.
DON'T BE SURPRISED IF SHE GIVES YOU A GOOD SWIFT KICK IN THE JOHN THOMAS ONCE WE GET YOU BACK.
AIN'T HAPPENING, BUDDY. IT WAS A WASTE OF TIME, YOU FOLLOWING ME TO THIS HELLHOLE.
I TOLD YOU, I'M OUT. I'M DONE LETTING YOU PLAY DEVIL ON MY SHOULDER.
WHAT ABOUT YOUR BOYS? CROON... PIOUS... POM-POM--
KEEP THEIR NAMES OUT OF YOUR MOUTH, SUIT... OR I'LL RAM MY KNEE INTO IT A COUPLE OF TIMES, BLAST YOUR TEETH OUT THE BACK OF YOUR HEAD.
THERE IT IS... I WAS WORRIED ALL THIS DRAMA HAD KNOCKED THE PISS AND VINEGAR OUT OF YOU, BUT YOU'RE STILL ANGRY AS ALL GET OUT, AREN'T YOU?
GOOD... I CAN USE THAT.

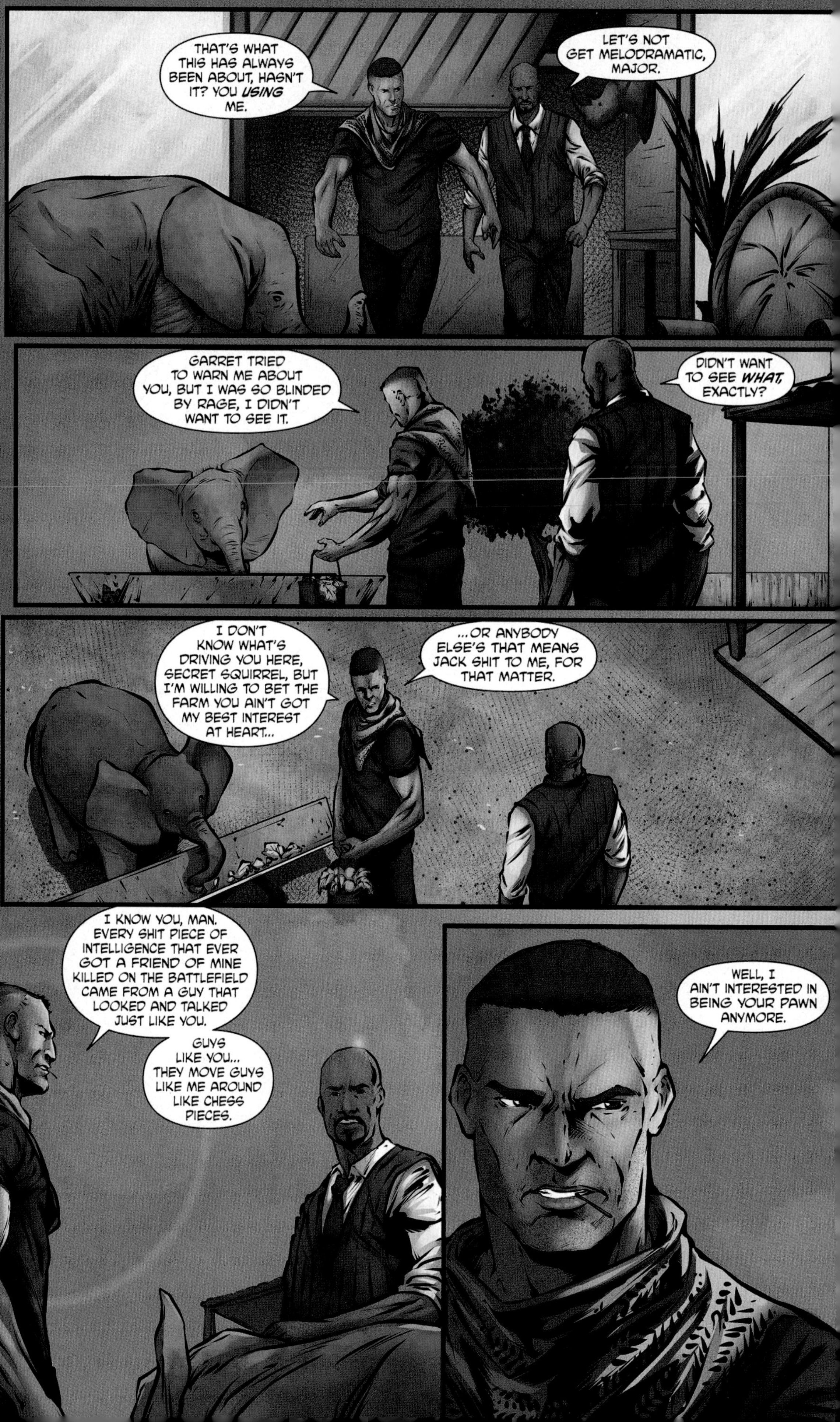
THAT'S WHAT THIS HAS ALWAYS BEEN ABOUT, HASN'T IT? YOU USING ME.
LET'S NOT GET MELODRAMATIC, MAJOR.
GARRET TRIED TO WARN ME ABOUT YOU, BUT I WAS SO BLINDED BY RAGE, I DIDN'T WANT TO SEE IT.
DIDN'T WANT TO SEE WHAT, EXACTLY?
I DON'T KNOW WHAT'S DRIVING YOU HERE, SECRET SQUIRREL, BUT I'M WILLING TO BET THE FARM YOU AIN'T GOT MY BEST INTEREST AT HEART...
...OR ANYBODY ELSE'S THAT MEANS JACK SHIT TO ME, FOR THAT MATTER.
I KNOW YOU, MAN. EVERY SHIT PIECE OF INTELLIGENCE THAT EVER GOT A FRIEND OF MINE KILLED ON THE BATTLEFIELD CAME FROM A GUY THAT LOOKED AND TALKED JUST LIKE YOU.
GUYS LIKE YOU... THEY MOVE GUYS LIKE ME AROUND LIKE CHESS PIECES.
WELL, I AIN'T INTERESTED IN BEING YOUR PAWN ANYMORE.

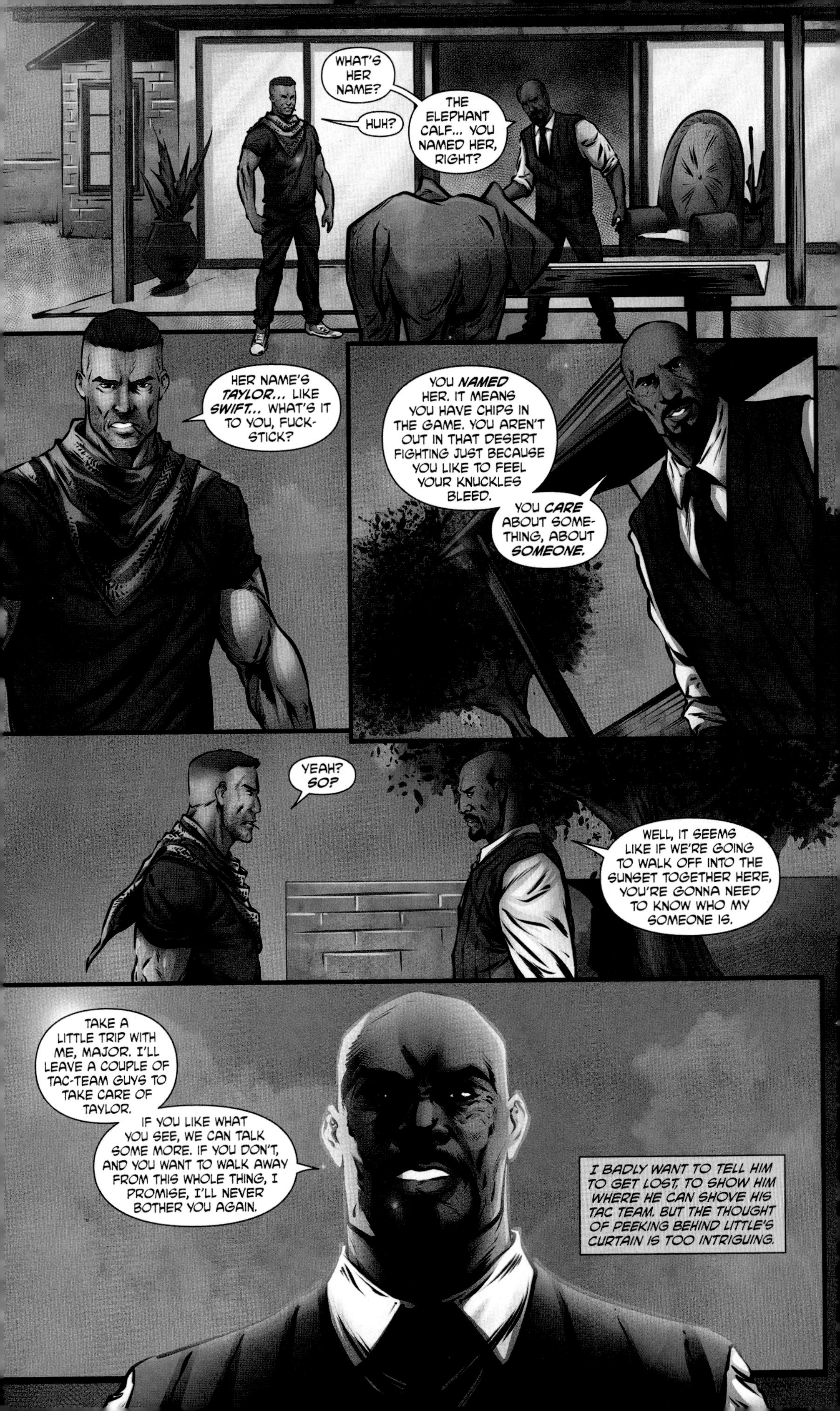
WHAT'S HER NAME?
HUH?
THE ELEPHANT CALF... YOU NAMED HER, RIGHT?
HER NAME'S TAYLOR... LIKE SWIFT... WHAT'S IT TO YOU, FUCK-STICK?
YOU NAMED HER. IT MEANS YOU HAVE CHIPS IN THE GAME. YOU AREN'T OUT IN THAT DESERT FIGHTING JUST BECAUSE YOU LIKE TO FEEL YOUR KNUCKLES BLEED.
YOU CARE ABOUT SOME-THING, ABOUT SOMEONE.
YEAH? SO?
WELL, IT SEEMS LIKE IF WE'RE GOING TO WALK OFF INTO THE SUNSET TOGETHER HERE, YOU'RE GONNA NEED TO KNOW WHO MY SOMEONE IS.
TAKE A LITTLE TRIP WITH ME, MAJOR. I'LL LEAVE A COUPLE OF TAC-TEAM GUYS TO TAKE CARE OF TAYLOR.
IF YOU LIKE WHAT YOU SEE, WE CAN TALK SOME MORE. IF YOU DON'T, AND YOU WANT TO WALK AWAY FROM THIS WHOLE THING, I PROMISE, I'LL NEVER BOTHER YOU AGAIN.
I BADLY WANT TO TELL HIM TO GET LOST, TO SHOW HIM WHERE HE CAN SHOVE HIS TAC TEAM. BUT THE THOUGHT OF PEEKING BEHIND LITTLE'S CURTAIN IS TOO INTRIGUING.

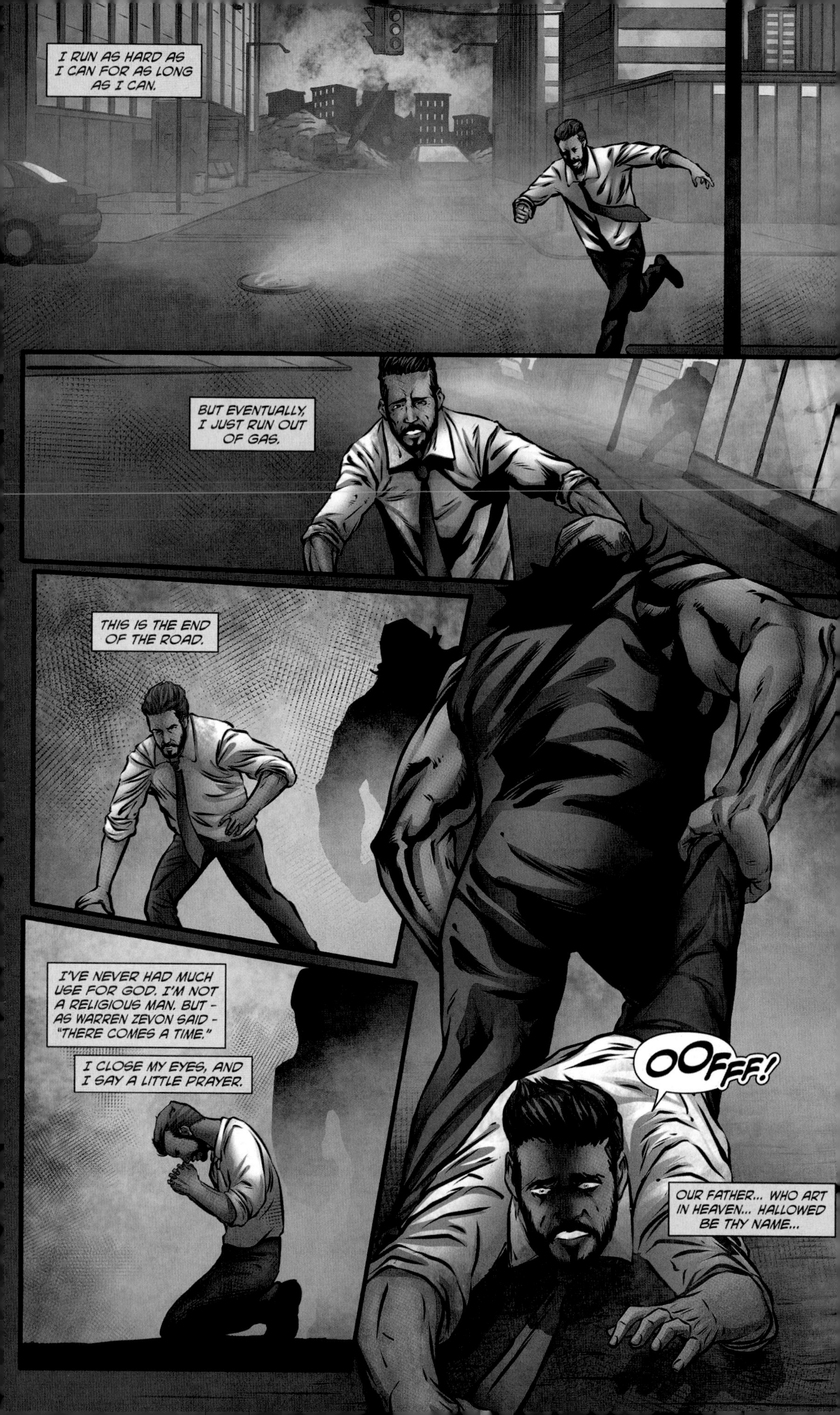
I RUN AS HARD AS I CAN FOR AS LONG AS I CAN.
BUT EVENTUALLY, I JUST RUN OUT OF GAS.
THIS IS THE END OF THE ROAD.
I'VE NEVER HAD MUCH USE FOR GOD. I'M NOT A RELIGIOUS MAN. BUT - AS WARREN ZEVON SAID - "THERE COMES A TIME."
I CLOSE MY EYES, AND I SAY A LITTLE PRAYER.
OOFFF!
OUR FATHER... WHO ART IN HEAVEN... HALLOWED BE THY NAME...

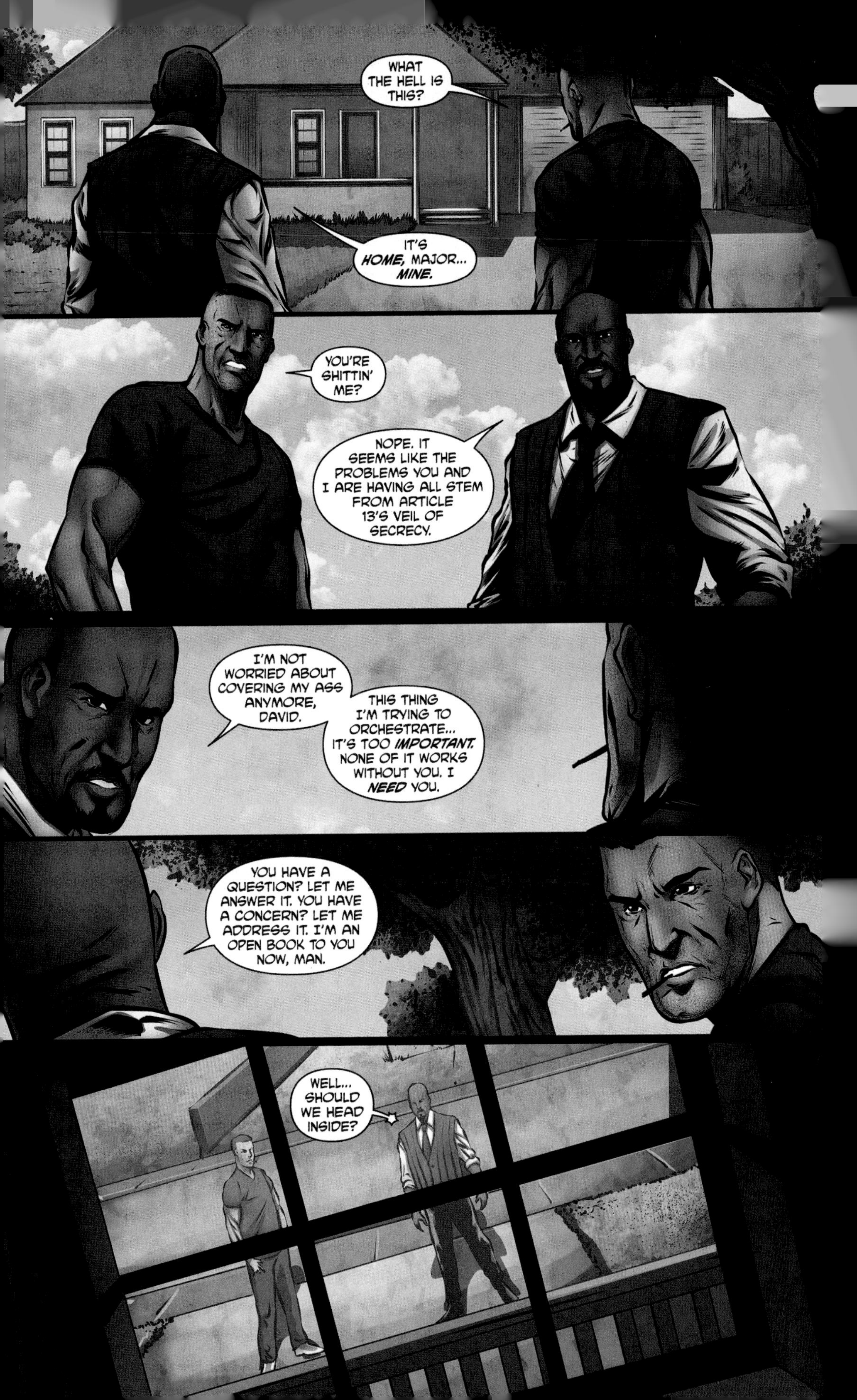

WHAT THE HELL IS THIS?
IT'S *HOME*, MAJOR... *MINE.*
YOU'RE SHITTIN' ME?
NOPE. IT SEEMS LIKE THE PROBLEMS YOU AND I ARE HAVING ALL STEM FROM ARTICLE 13'S VEIL OF SECRECY.
I'M NOT WORRIED ABOUT COVERING MY ASS ANYMORE, DAVID.
THIS THING I'M TRYING TO ORCHESTRATE... IT'S TOO *IMPORTANT.* NONE OF IT WORKS WITHOUT YOU. I *NEED* YOU.
YOU HAVE A QUESTION? LET ME ANSWER IT. YOU HAVE A CONCERN? LET ME ADDRESS IT. I'M AN OPEN BOOK TO YOU NOW, MAN.
WELL... SHOULD WE HEAD INSIDE?

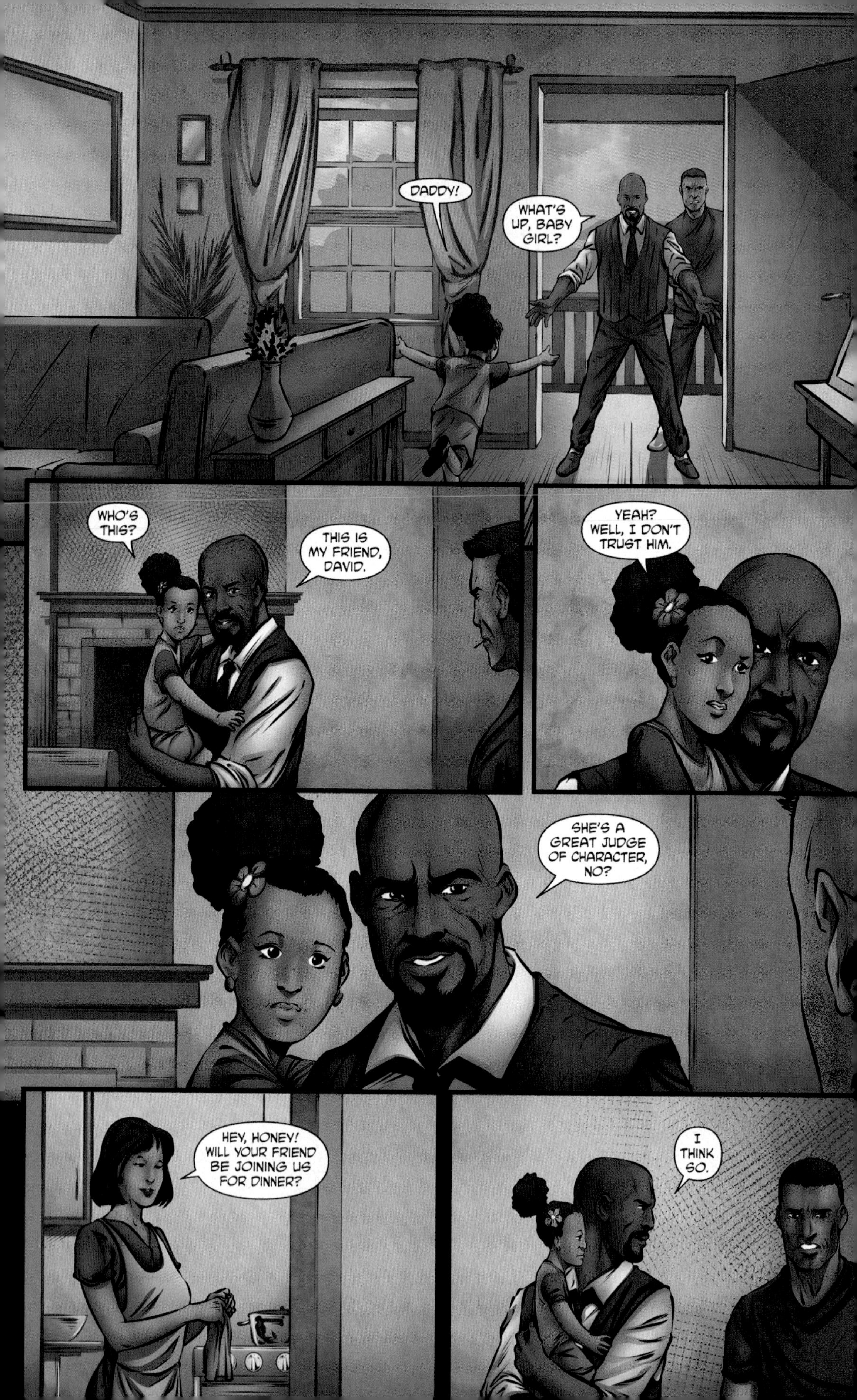
DADDY!
WHAT'S UP, BABY GIRL?
WHO'S THIS?
THIS IS MY FRIEND, DAVID.
YEAH? WELL, I DON'T TRUST HIM.
SHE'S A GREAT JUDGE OF CHARACTER, NO?
HEY, HONEY! WILL YOUR FRIEND BE JOINING US FOR DINNER?
I THINK SO.

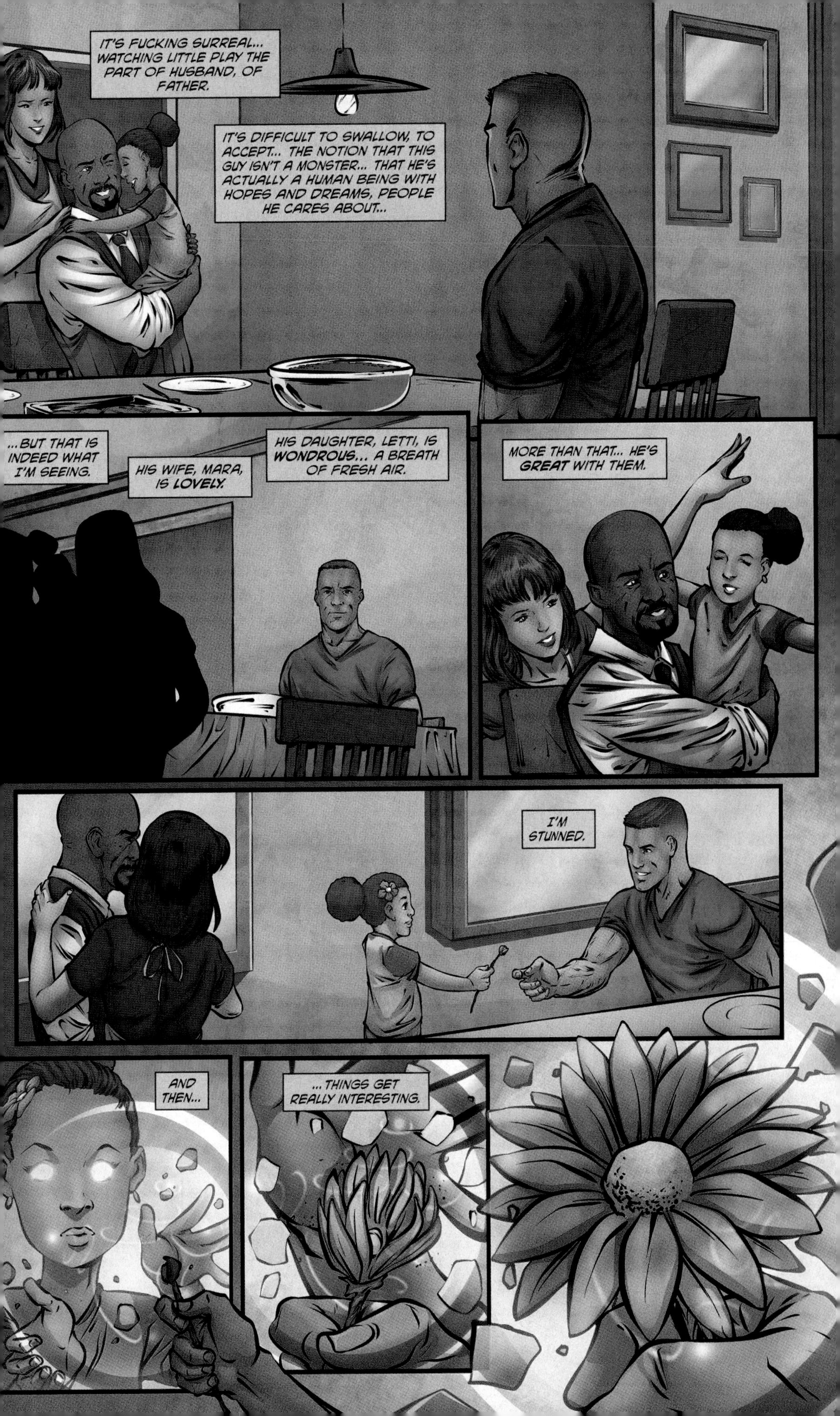
IT'S FUCKING SURREAL... WATCHING LITTLE PLAY THE PART OF HUSBAND, OF FATHER.
IT'S DIFFICULT TO SWALLOW, TO ACCEPT... THE NOTION THAT THIS GUY ISN'T A MONSTER... THAT HE'S ACTUALLY A HUMAN BEING WITH HOPES AND DREAMS, PEOPLE HE CARES ABOUT...
...BUT THAT IS INDEED WHAT I'M SEEING.
HIS WIFE, MARA, IS LOVELY.
HIS DAUGHTER, LETTI, IS WONDROUS... A BREATH OF FRESH AIR.
MORE THAN THAT... HE'S GREAT WITH THEM.
I'M STUNNED.
AND THEN...
...THINGS GET REALLY INTERESTING.

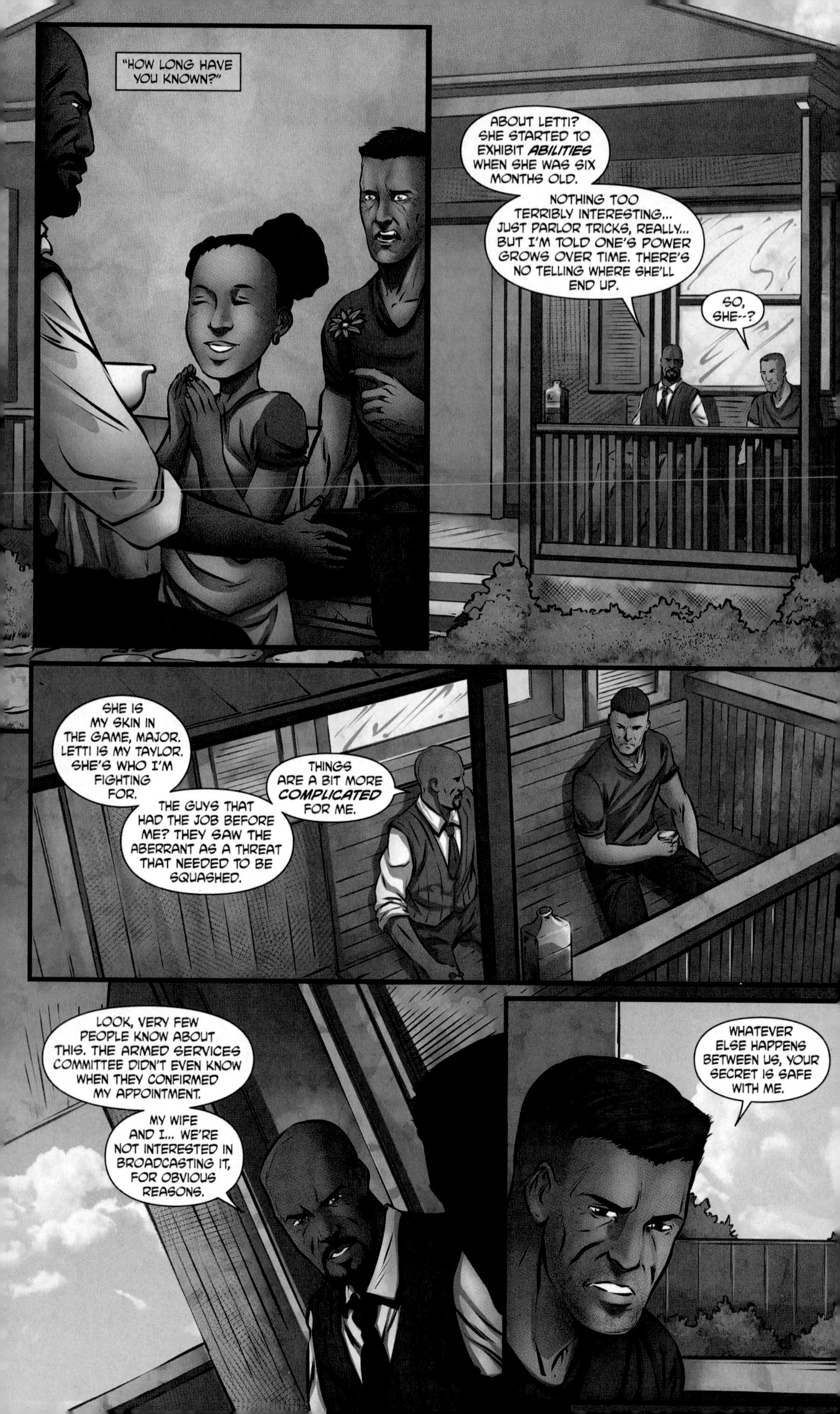
"HOW LONG HAVE YOU KNOWN?"
ABOUT LETTI? SHE STARTED TO EXHIBIT ABILITIES WHEN SHE WAS SIX MONTHS OLD.
NOTHING TOO TERRIBLY INTERESTING... JUST PARLOR TRICKS, REALLY... BUT I'M TOLD ONE'S POWER GROWS OVER TIME. THERE'S NO TELLING WHERE SHE'LL END UP.
SO, SHE--?
SHE IS MY SKIN IN THE GAME, MAJOR. LETTI IS MY TAYLOR. SHE'S WHO I'M FIGHTING FOR.
THINGS ARE A BIT MORE COMPLICATED FOR ME.
THE GUYS THAT HAD THE JOB BEFORE ME? THEY SAW THE ABERRANT AS A THREAT THAT NEEDED TO BE SQUASHED.
LOOK, VERY FEW PEOPLE KNOW ABOUT THIS. THE ARMED SERVICES COMMITTEE DIDN'T EVEN KNOW WHEN THEY CONFIRMED MY APPOINTMENT.
MY WIFE AND I... WE'RE NOT INTERESTED IN BROADCASTING IT, FOR OBVIOUS REASONS.
WHATEVER ELSE HAPPENS BETWEEN US, YOUR SECRET IS SAFE WITH ME.

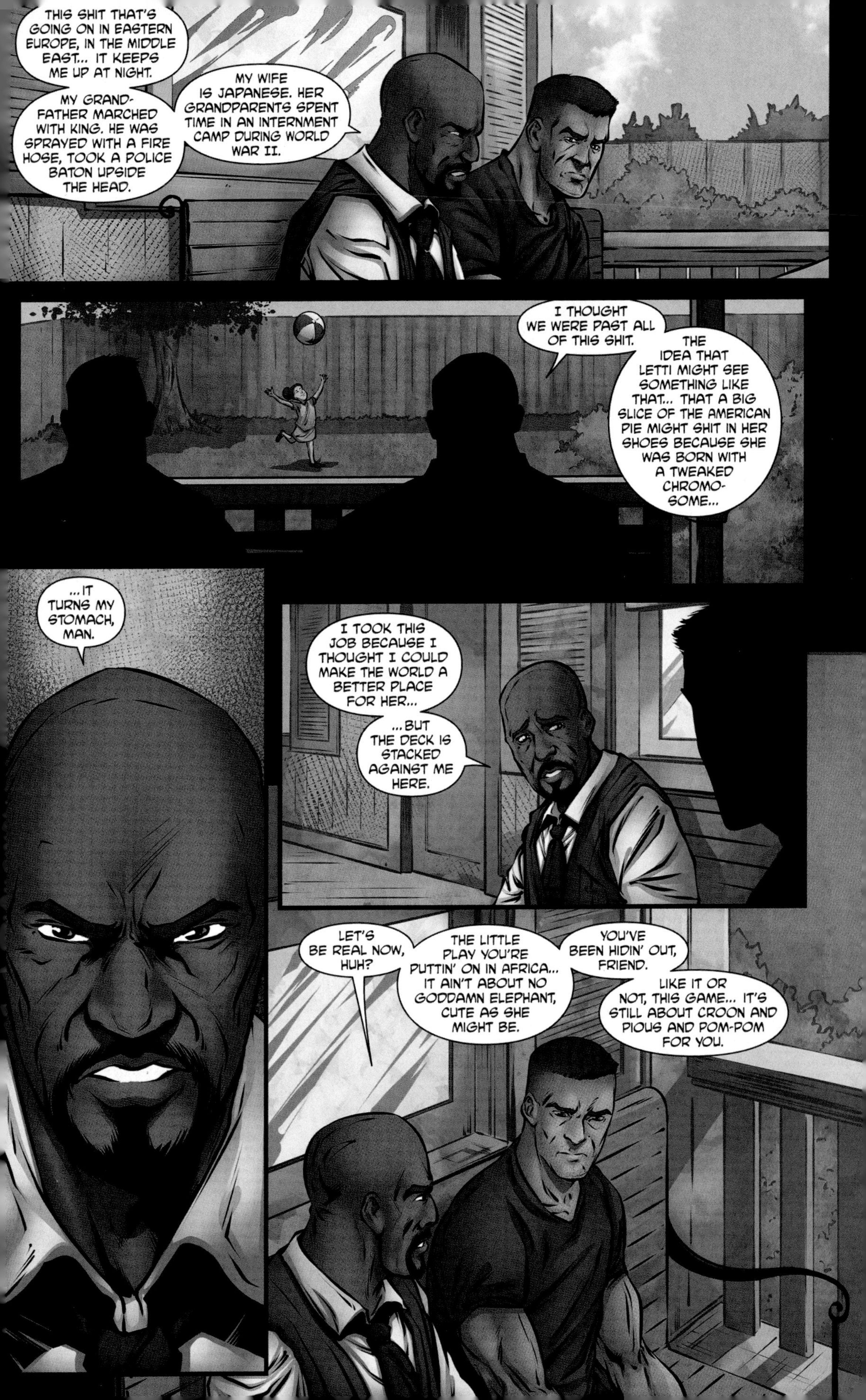
THIS SHIT THAT'S GOING ON IN EASTERN EUROPE, IN THE MIDDLE EAST... IT KEEPS ME UP AT NIGHT.
MY GRAND-FATHER MARCHED WITH KING. HE WAS SPRAYED WITH A FIRE HOSE, TOOK A POLICE BATON UPSIDE THE HEAD.
MY WIFE IS JAPANESE. HER GRANDPARENTS SPENT TIME IN AN INTERNMENT CAMP DURING WORLD WAR II.
I THOUGHT WE WERE PAST ALL OF THIS SHIT.
THE IDEA THAT LETTI MIGHT SEE SOMETHING LIKE THAT... THAT A BIG SLICE OF THE AMERICAN PIE MIGHT SHIT IN HER SHOES BECAUSE SHE WAS BORN WITH A TWEAKED CHROMO-SOME...
...IT TURNS MY STOMACH, MAN.
I TOOK THIS JOB BECAUSE I THOUGHT I COULD MAKE THE WORLD A BETTER PLACE FOR HER...
...BUT THE DECK IS STACKED AGAINST ME HERE.
LET'S BE REAL NOW, HUH?
THE LITTLE PLAY YOU'RE PUTTIN' ON IN AFRICA... IT AIN'T ABOUT NO GODDAMN ELEPHANT, CUTE AS SHE MIGHT BE.
YOU'VE BEEN HIDIN' OUT, FRIEND.
LIKE IT OR NOT, THIS GAME... IT'S STILL ABOUT CROON AND PIOUS AND POM-POM FOR YOU.

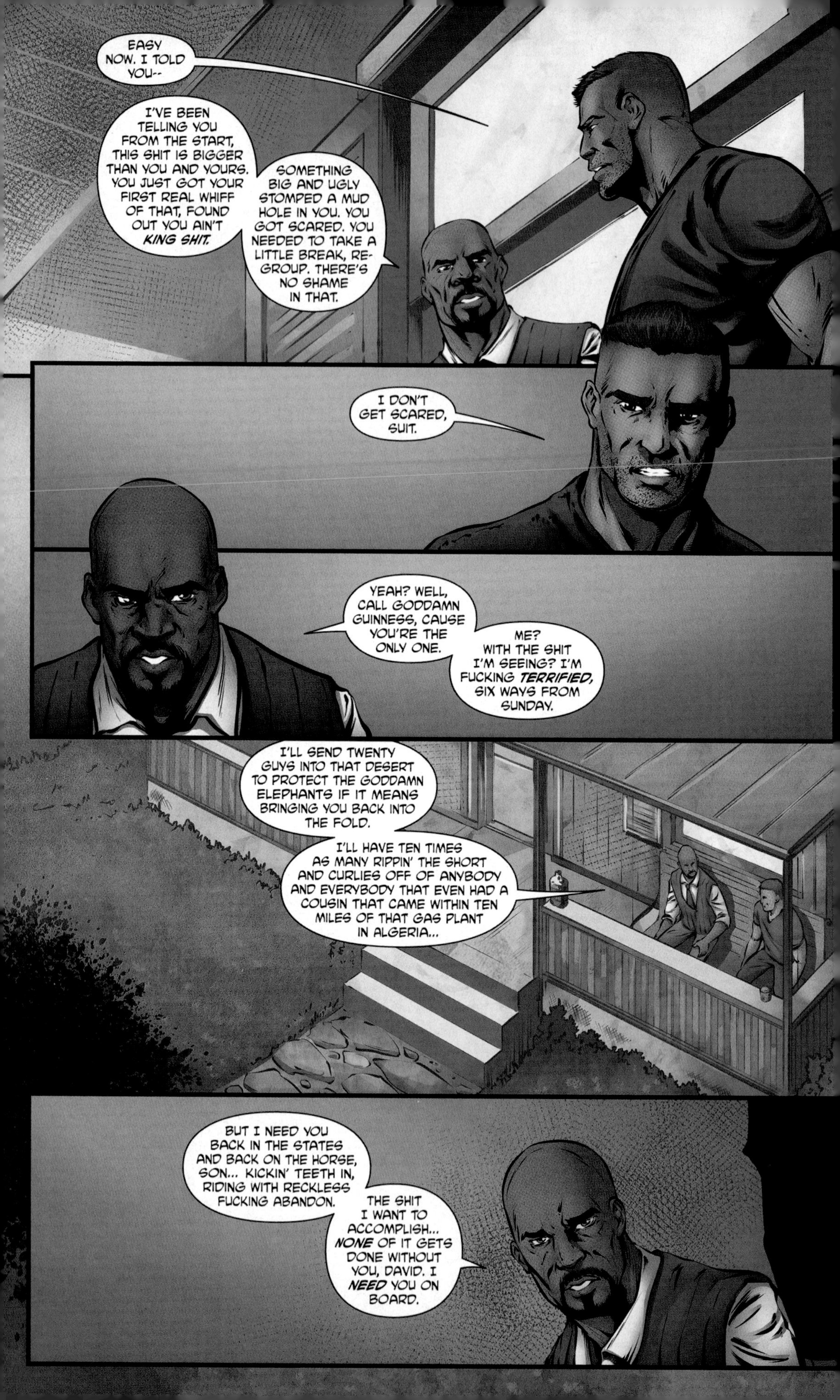
EASY NOW. I TOLD YOU--
I'VE BEEN TELLING YOU FROM THE START, THIS SHIT IS BIGGER THAN YOU AND YOURS. YOU JUST GOT YOUR FIRST REAL WHIFF OF THAT, FOUND OUT YOU AIN'T ***KING SHIT.***
SOMETHING BIG AND UGLY STOMPED A MUD HOLE IN YOU. YOU GOT SCARED. YOU NEEDED TO TAKE A LITTLE BREAK, RE-GROUP. THERE'S NO SHAME IN THAT.
I DON'T GET SCARED, SUIT.
YEAH? WELL, CALL GODDAMN GUINNESS, CAUSE YOU'RE THE ONLY ONE.
ME? WITH THE SHIT I'M SEEING? I'M FUCKING ***TERRIFIED,*** SIX WAYS FROM SUNDAY.
I'LL SEND TWENTY GUYS INTO THAT DESERT TO PROTECT THE GODDAMN ELEPHANTS IF IT MEANS BRINGING YOU BACK INTO THE FOLD.
I'LL HAVE TEN TIMES AS MANY RIPPIN' THE SHORT AND CURLIES OFF OF ANYBODY AND EVERYBODY THAT EVEN HAD A COUSIN THAT CAME WITHIN TEN MILES OF THAT GAS PLANT IN ALGERIA...
BUT I NEED YOU BACK IN THE STATES AND BACK ON THE HORSE, SON... KICKIN' TEETH IN, RIDING WITH RECKLESS FUCKING ABANDON.
THE SHIT I WANT TO ACCOMPLISH... ***NONE*** OF IT GETS DONE WITHOUT YOU, DAVID. I ***NEED*** YOU ON BOARD.

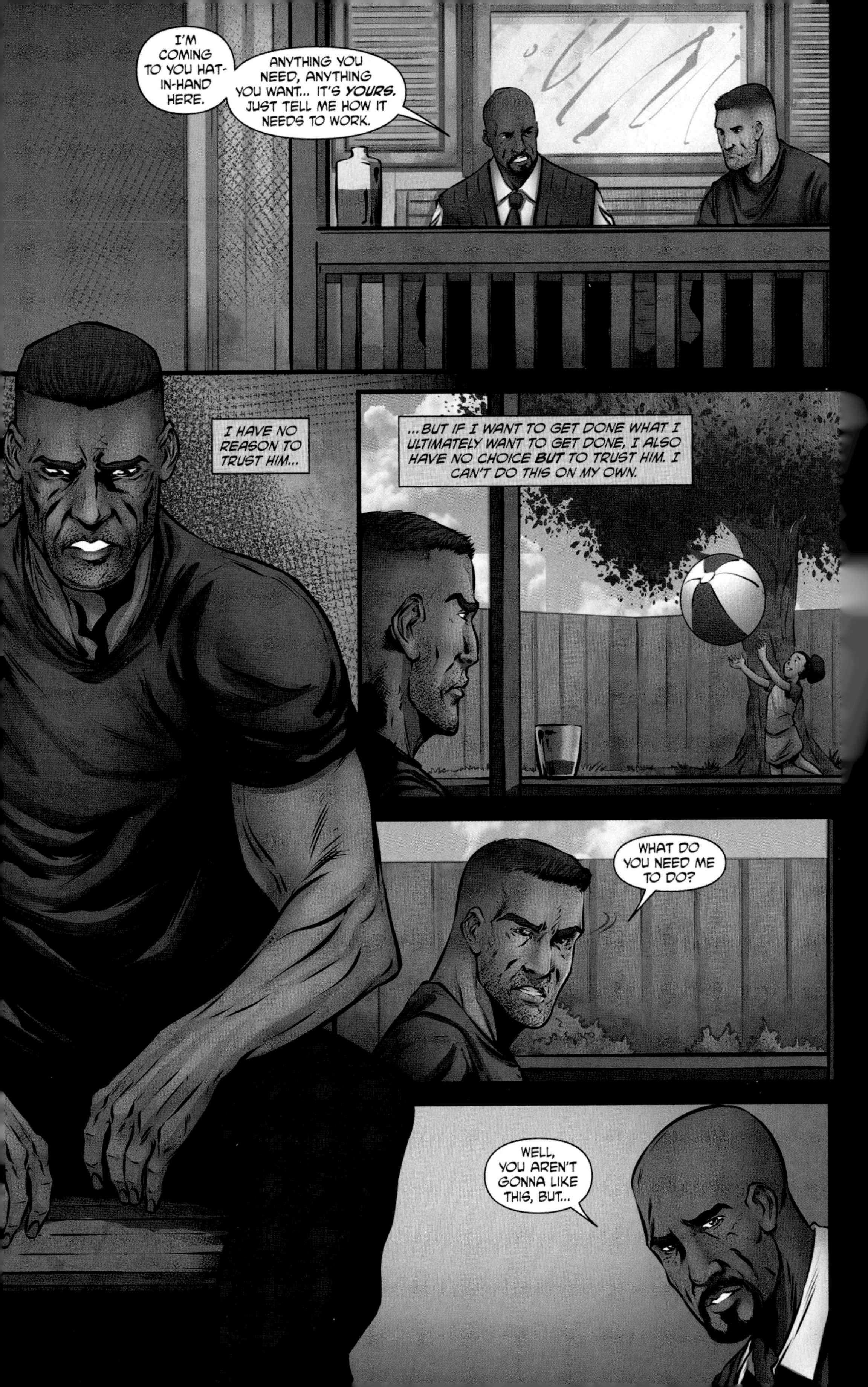
I'M COMING TO YOU HAT-IN-HAND HERE.
ANYTHING YOU NEED, ANYTHING YOU WANT... IT'S *YOURS.* JUST TELL ME HOW IT NEEDS TO WORK.
I HAVE NO REASON TO TRUST HIM...
...BUT IF I WANT TO GET DONE WHAT I ULTIMATELY WANT TO GET DONE, I ALSO HAVE NO CHOICE *BUT* TO TRUST HIM. I CAN'T DO THIS ON MY OWN.
WHAT DO YOU NEED ME TO DO?
WELL, YOU AREN'T GONNA LIKE THIS, BUT...

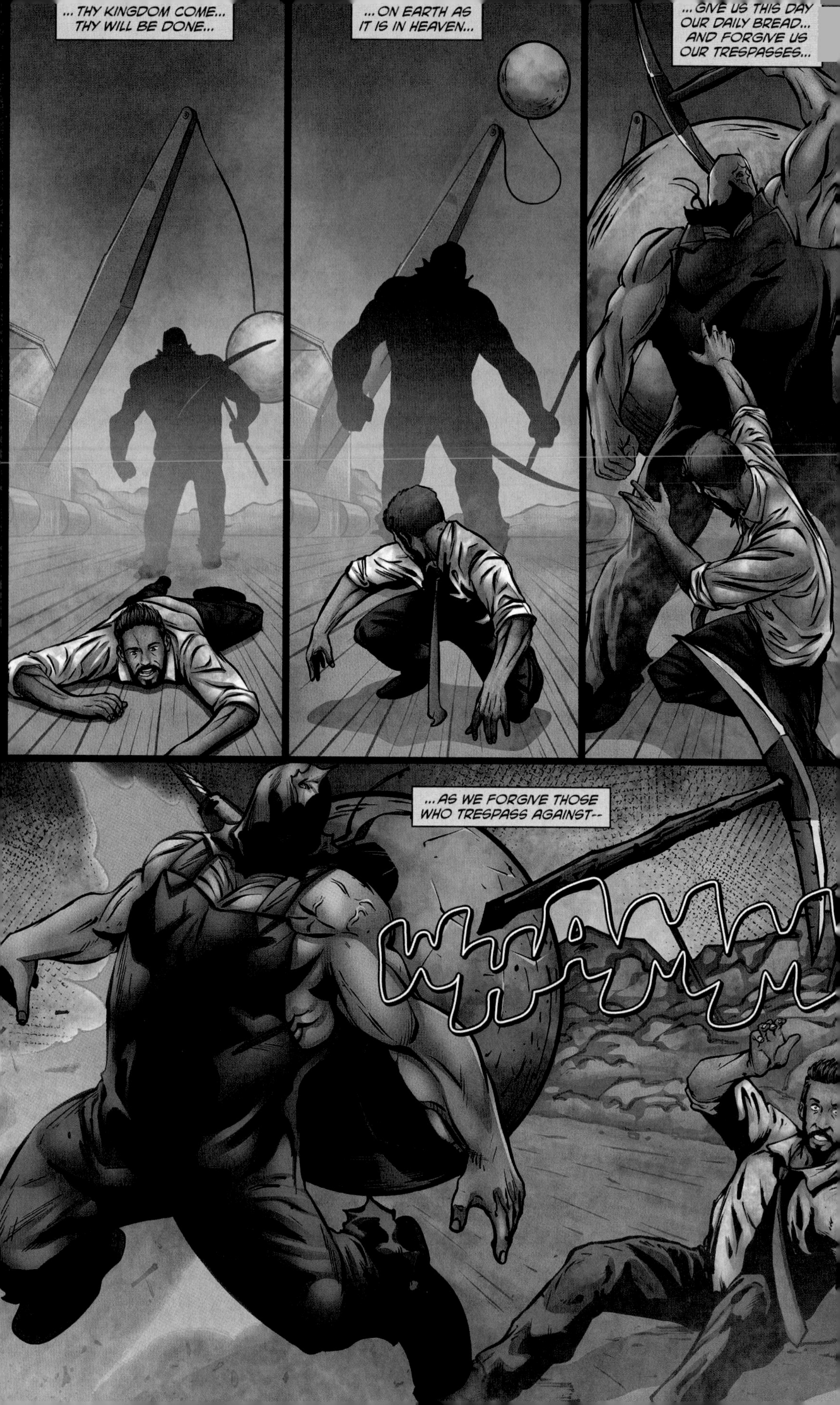
...THY KINGDOM COME... THY WILL BE DONE...
...ON EARTH AS IT IS IN HEAVEN...
...GIVE US THIS DAY OUR DAILY BREAD... AND FORGIVE US OUR TRESPASSES...
...AS WE FORGIVE THOSE WHO TRESPASS AGAINST--

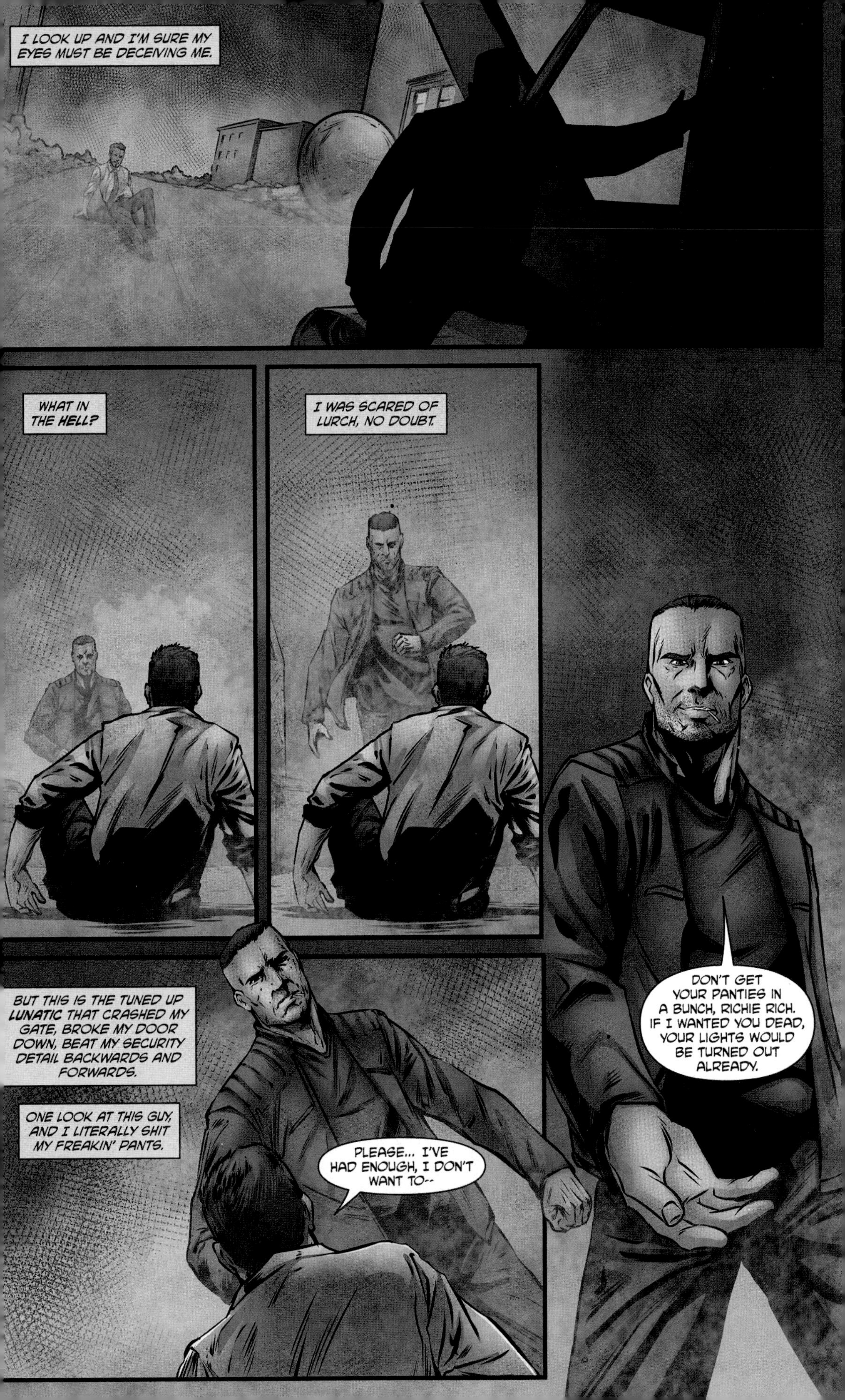
I LOOK UP AND I'M SURE MY EYES MUST BE DECEIVING ME.
WHAT IN THE HELL?
I WAS SCARED OF LURCH, NO DOUBT.
BUT THIS IS THE TUNED UP LUNATIC THAT CRASHED MY GATE, BROKE MY DOOR DOWN, BEAT MY SECURITY DETAIL BACKWARDS AND FORWARDS.
ONE LOOK AT THIS GUY, AND I LITERALLY SHIT MY FREAKIN' PANTS.
PLEASE... I'VE HAD ENOUGH, I DON'T WANT TO--
DON'T GET YOUR PANTIES IN A BUNCH, RICHIE RICH. IF I WANTED YOU DEAD, YOUR LIGHTS WOULD BE TURNED OUT ALREADY.

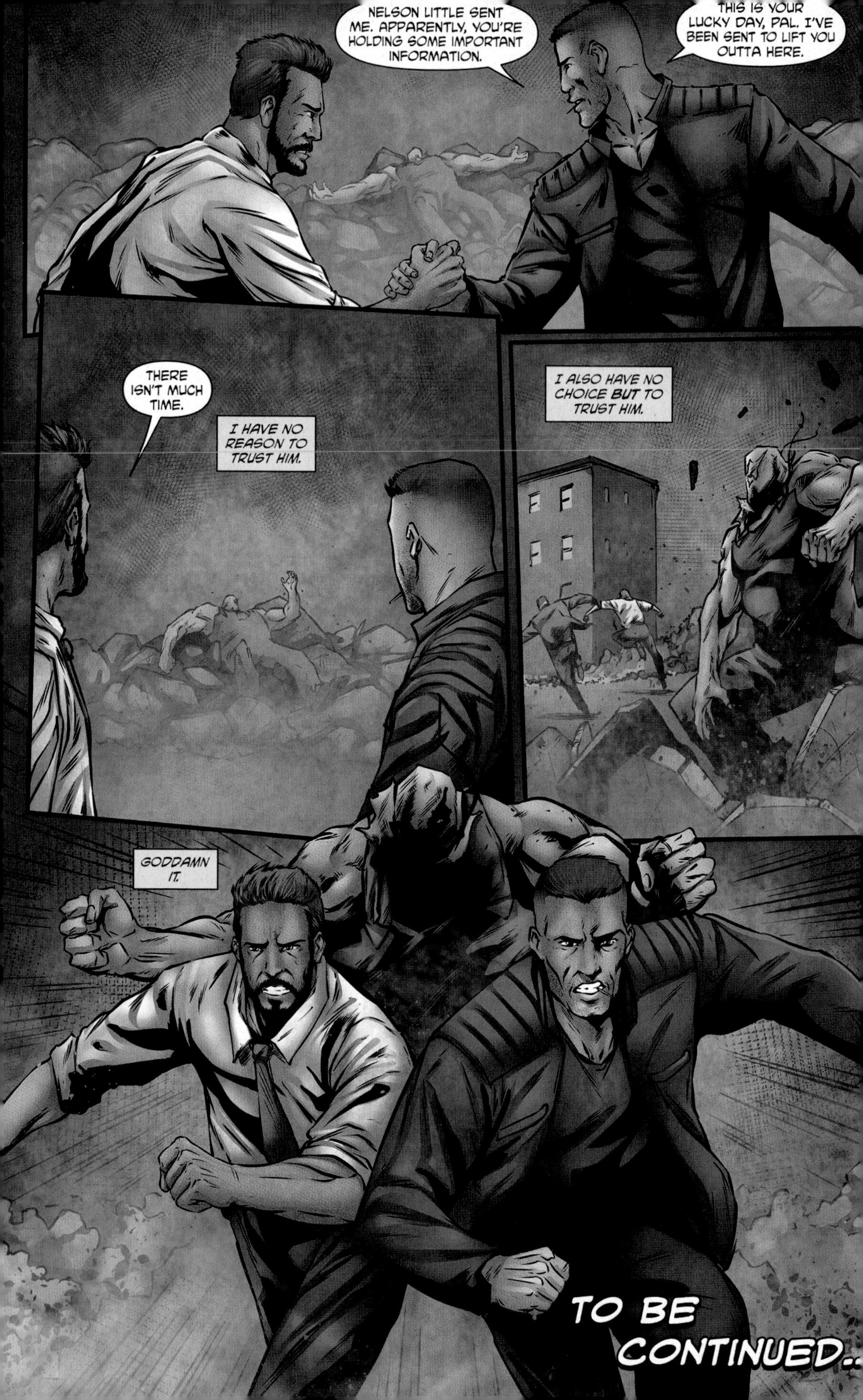
NELSON LITTLE SENT ME. APPARENTLY, YOU'RE HOLDING SOME IMPORTANT INFORMATION.
THIS IS YOUR LUCKY DAY, PAL. I'VE BEEN SENT TO LIFT YOU OUTTA HERE.
THERE ISN'T MUCH TIME.
I HAVE NO REASON TO TRUST HIM.
I ALSO HAVE NO CHOICE BUT TO TRUST HIM.
GODDAMN IT.
TO BE CONTINUED...

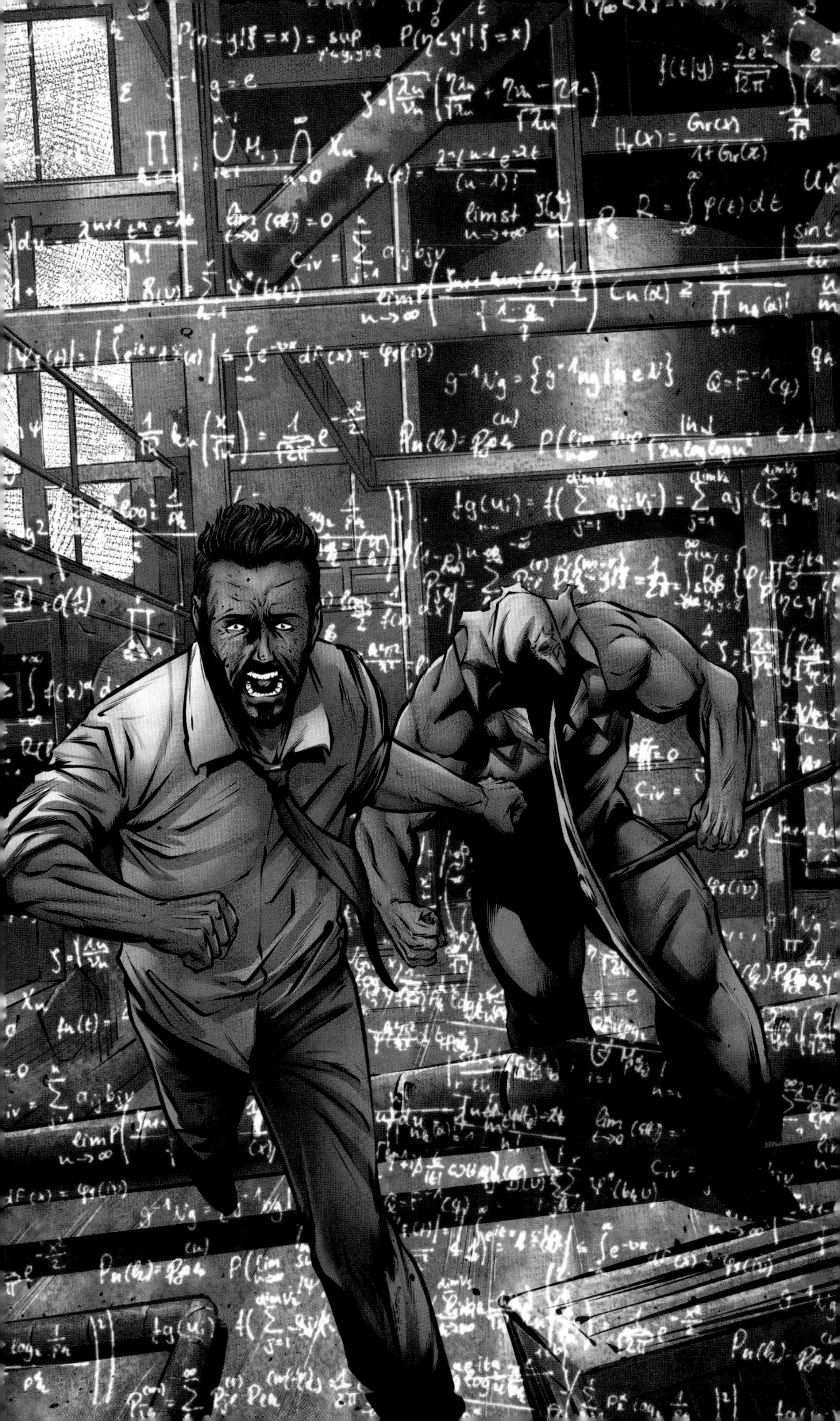

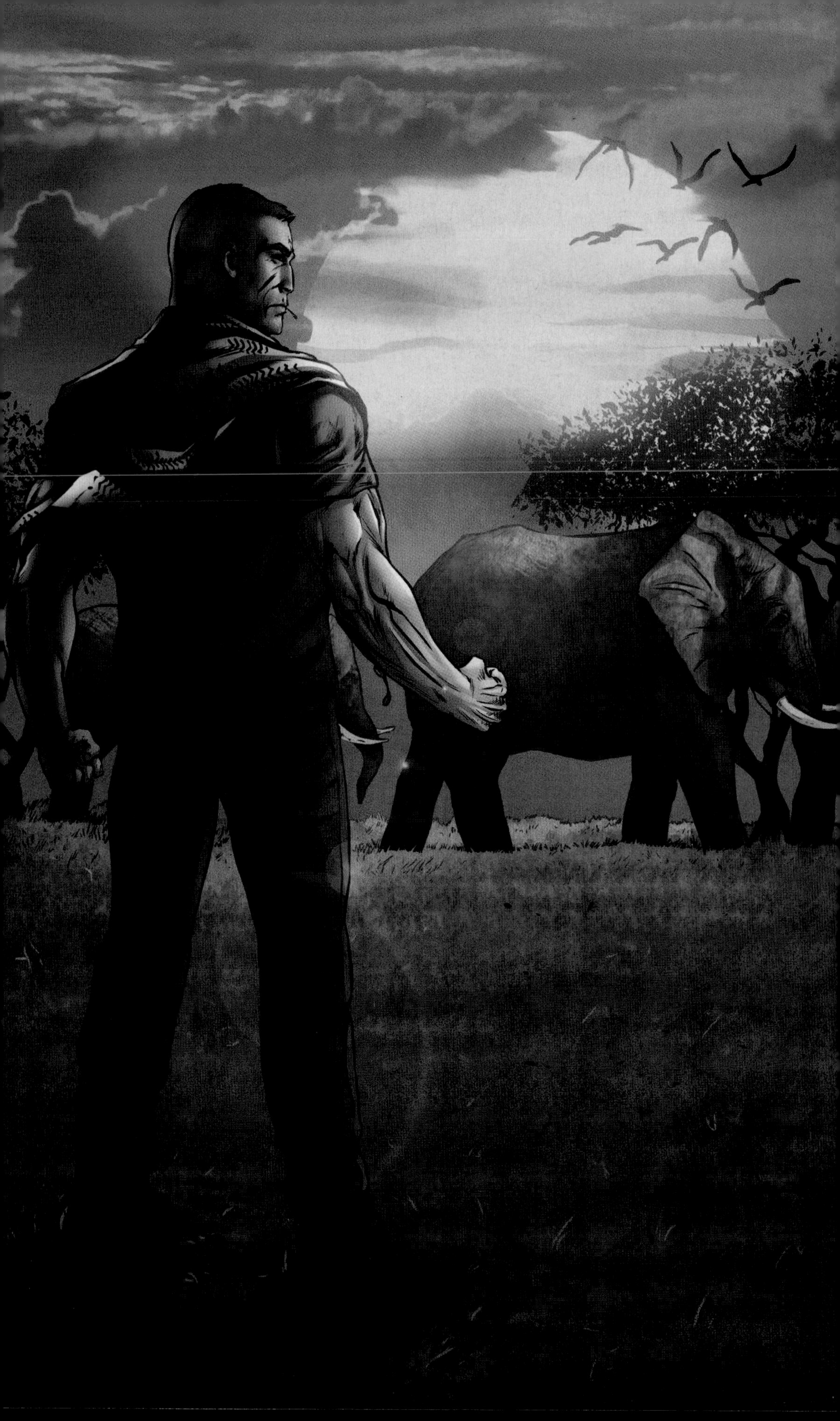

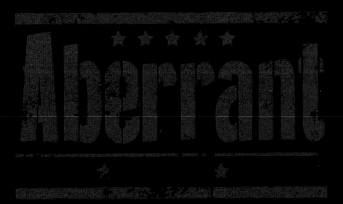

Aberrant

GOT ABERRANT-RELATED RANTS, RAVES, FULMINATIONS, VOCIFERATIONS, INVECTIVES, OR OBLOQUIES? GOT FAN ART? HELP! I'M CHAINED TO A DESK IN THE BASEMENT OF THE ACTION LAB OFFICES! THEY FORCE US TO DO TERRIBLE THINGS DOWN HERE. I'M SERIOUS! WE NEED--

SOUND OFF LIKE YOU GOT A PAIR!

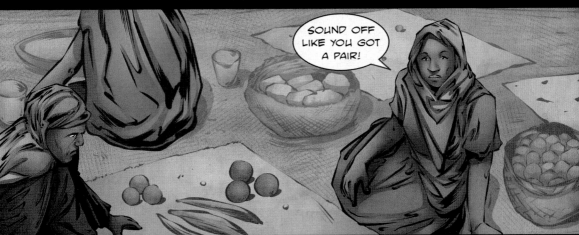

SEND ALL BUSINESS FIT TO PRINT TO: HALFEVILCOMICS@GMAIL.COM

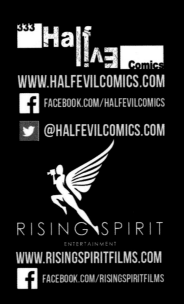

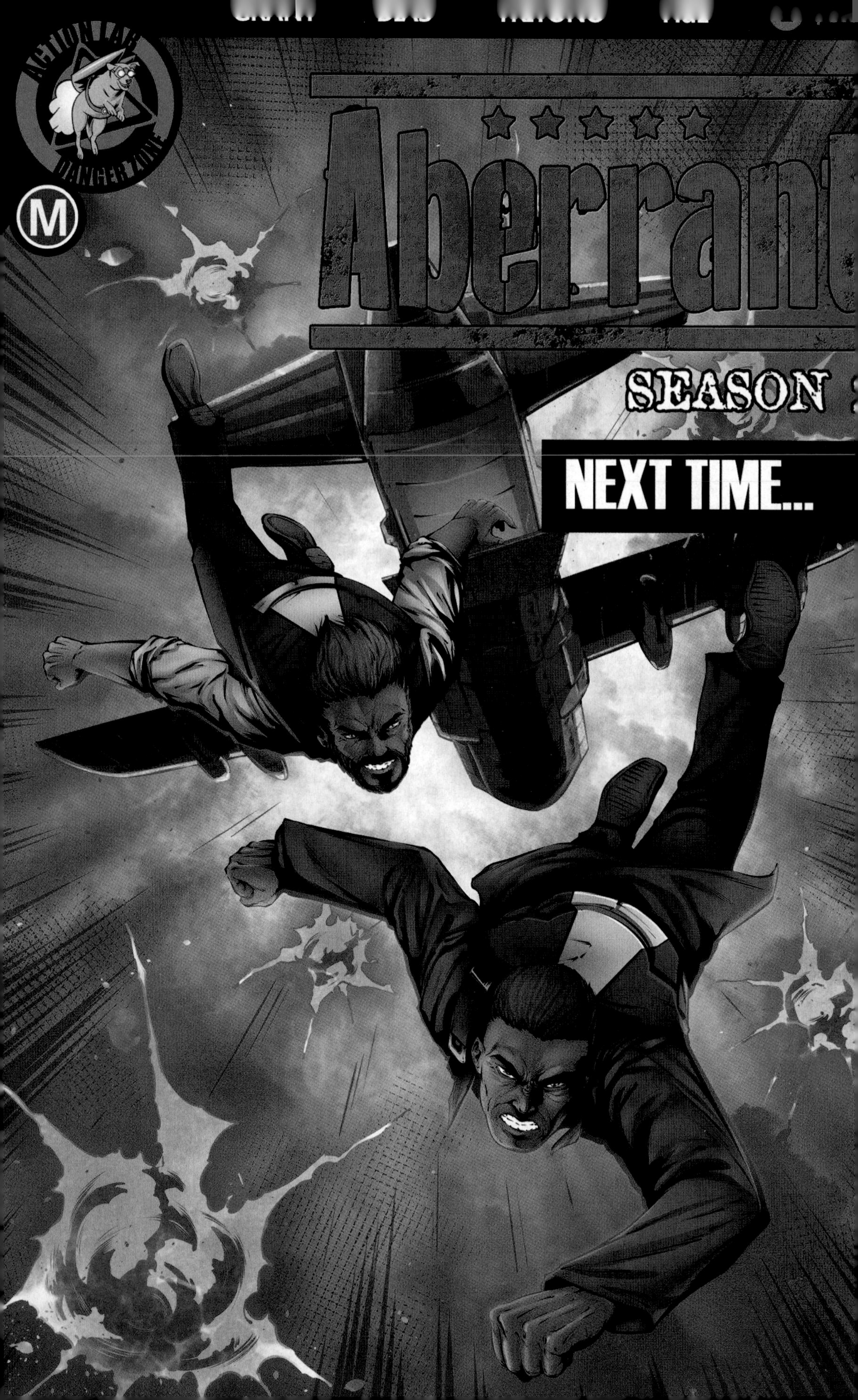
ACTION LAB
DANGER ZONE
M
Aberrant
SEASON
NEXT TIME...